"Maria's book will be useful to any cc
understand how to leverage their alumr
and career growth, and equally to high
charged with deepening alumni an
**Jay Le Roux Dillon, Executive Director, Alumni Relations,
University of California Berkeley**

"This book demonstrates how everyone can leverage one of their
most important connections – their alma mater – to fulfil multiple
objectives and goals. The interactive activities use the power of
reflection to make for a meaningful reading journey."
**Candy Ho, Inaugural Assistant Professor, Integrative Career
and Capstone Learning, University of the Fraser Valley**

"A terrific read! Next to Dr Seuss's *Oh, The Places You'll Go!*, Dr
Gallo's *The Alumni Way* deserves strong consideration as THE
perfect graduation gift."
**Tom Vosper, Associate Director Development and Alumni
Engagement: Toronto Region, University of
British Columbia**

"Maria's book is a practical guide for those of us invested in
developing and leading vibrant alumni networks."
Jihad Hajjouji, African Leadership Academy

"With engaging writing, Maria shares her research and practice
knowledge on alumni and drives you to unlock the power of the
alumni capital. An essential book to maximise your relationship
with alumni."
**Diana Aguiar Vieira, ICARe Founder and Associate
Professor, Porto Accounting and Business School**

"This readable book shows how to reach out to institutional
networks that are waiting hopefully for you to engage – diverse
ecosystems in which you can both give and receive lasting value."
**Keith Harrison-Broninski, author of *Supercommunities:
A Handbook for the 21st Century***

THE ALUMNI WAY
Building Lifelong Value from Your University Investment

Maria L. Gallo

First published in Great Britain in 2021 by

Policy Press, an imprint of
Bristol University Press
University of Bristol
1–9 Old Park Hill
Bristol
BS2 8BB
UK
t: +44 (0)117 954 5940
e: bup-info@bristol.ac.uk

Details of international sales and distribution partners are available at
policy.bristoluniversitypress.co.uk

Cover designer: Liam Roberts
Image credit: iStock/filo
Bristol University Press and Policy Press use environmentally responsible
print partners.
Printed and bound in Great Britain by CMP, Poole

For Morgan, Luca, and Tara
with all my love

Dedicated to alumni far and wide –
may you thrive

Contents

Acknowledgements ix

Foreword by J. Kelly Hoey xi

Introduction: We are all alumni 1

PART I Charting the course of the Alumni Way **9**
1 Starting at the finish line 11
2 The compass: Introducing alumni capital 15
3 Summary: Stepping forward by stepping back on 25
campus

PART II The Alumni Way trait: Reflection **29**
4 Reflecting on the 'keep in touch' call 31
5 Reflection signpost: Recognize the university is a city 35
6 Reflection signpost: Advance ourselves as alumni 45
citizens
7 Reflection trait summary: Alum from Day One, 59
revisited

PART III The Alumni Way trait: Curiosity **63**
8 Our career, our alumni capital, and our curiosity 65
9 Curiosity signpost: Build our alumni hypernetwork 69
10 Curiosity signpost: Leverage alumni capital for business 89
11 Curiosity trait summary: Shining a light 97

PART IV The Alumni Way trait: Passion **103**
12 Immersing in our passions: The alumni dimension 105
13 Passion signpost: Nourish our wellness through 109
our alumni capital

14	Passion signpost: Watch our alumni-self flourish	119
15	Passion trait summary: Our lives, our alma mater	131

PART V The Alumni Way trait: Generosity **135**

16	When giving back has new meaning	137
17	Generosity signpost: Recognize we are all philanthropists	139
18	Generosity signpost: Understand the power of giving	151
19	Generosity trait summary: Our generosity as service	169

PART VI Alumni: Bringing it into our lives **173**

20	Our potential: Building our Alumni Way	175
21	Our alumni call to action	185

Notes	191
References	217
About the author	245
Index	247

Acknowledgements

The journey of writing this book began over 15 years ago. I am indebted to the hundreds of people over this time who have listened to my ideas while I was on my alumni soapbox. In response, I listened to quirky, heartfelt, even harrowing alumni stories. I am glad, nay, excited, when I get a barrage of messages of any article, post, or public mention of the word alumni. I embrace it all and it has shaped my thinking on alumni citizenship – keep them coming!

I am continually grateful to my own alumni capital network, who have helped map out the direction of this book with constructive, critical support: Patrizia Albanese, Beth Breeze, Victoria Bruce, Richéal Burns, Elizabeth Clydesdale, Kelly Coate, Barbara Dick, Leah Fairman, Kevin Fleming, Melissa Gallo, Patti Gouthro, Candy Ho, Melissa Johnson, Karen Kelly, Seán Kelly, Silviu Kondan, Kym Madden, Connor McDonough, Paul Nazareth, Abi Nokes, Doireann O'Connor, Sandra Rincón, Jillian Ruggiere, Martin Russell, Teo Salgado, Amanda Scott, Simon Warren, and Anna Wilson. Many of our discussions were emotional, spirited, always lengthy, alumni-infused meanderings. I devoured every minute, thank you.

To the early reviewers, along with Laura Vickers-Rendall, my editor, and the BUP Policy Press team. Please accept my gratitude for your constructive feedback that positively shaped this final publication. An excited, honoured thank you to J. Kelly Hoey for writing the foreword to this book, and to Mary McKenna for the introduction – masterful networking in action! I am grateful to Lizane Tan for her creativity in bringing *The Alumni Way* to life in the diagrams throughout this book. To my Alumni Way Advisory Group, drawn from my own alumni capital – thank you!

This book also benefits immensely from the interviews and conversations with alumni, students, scholars, and advancement professionals. I also appreciate the stories proudly shared by universities, alumni, and advancement professionals worldwide. The alumni experience is such a personal one. I found the feedback and stories to be candid and illuminating, with only a fraction of them shared in the book.

I have drawn liberally on my own alumni experiences and I wish to acknowledge my own alma mater relationships, as they offer me constant creative inspiration. My connection with my extended Loretto 9T8 alumni community has had a particularly formative impression on the powerful potential of alumni capital.

I owe a tremendous debt to my family through my inevitable preoccupations of writing this book. My Donegal support system, especially Pierce and Angela, for their kindness and thoughtfulness. To my parents: thank you for the fundamental lessons about reflection, curiosity, passion, and generosity embedded in love and joy. I am thankful to Marco, Ruth, and Giacomo for your understanding and genuine interest in my work, not to mention bringing fun and relaxation to restore the balance in my life.

I am so thankful especially to my husband Morgan for his patience, faith in my work, continuous motivation, and love. To my children Luca and Tara, for your fun, energy, and love; you both enthuse me greatly. I am excited to see how you will embrace your future alumni identities. For now, we can celebrate!

Foreword

J. Kelly Hoey

Author of *Build Your Dream Network: Forging Powerful Relationships in a Hyper-Connected World*

I remember the email exchange with crystal clarity. Was I planning to attend my 35th high school reunion? That so many years had passed since I'd walked across a stage in a sea foam green dress, borrowed from my mother's closet, was rather a blow. Were the early 80s really 35 years behind me? How many years had I frittered away in a career I was OK at (but heck, it sounded darn impressive on my CV!)? Once I'd mildly recovered from the shock, I emailed the sender back with a short 'never heard a thing about it', to receive a rapid fire 'maybe they couldn't find you', response. OK. Or maybe the real answer to being left off the reunion guest list was karma: that is, my desire to never attend an alumni reunion was honoured.

Confession time! I have actively avoided alumni events (that is, even when I do make it onto the guest list).

Oh, the irony is not lost on me. I, a networking expert, avoid alumni gatherings. Perhaps it's the impending imposter syndrome that sneaks up as I imagine polite small talk about my life (two divorces you say?) and why yes, I'm a writer and speaker living in New York City (maybe drop the NYC mention, as I wouldn't want to come across as uppity when inevitably asked, 'what are you doing these days?'). All the while, during this imaginary alum exchange, I'm rapidly popping machine-cubed Swiss cheese into my mouth, gulping wine from a plastic cup, and wondering if I can discretely make a flash exit before someone from the alumni relations office approaches, seeking a donation.

Have you imagined similar alumni reception scenarios?

Thankfully for you (and me), Maria L. Gallo has written *The Alumni Way: Building Lifelong Value from Your University Investment*, banishing all the outdated notions of what is possible when it comes to engaging and contributing to alumni communities. And, preferably for both institutions and individuals, engagement should be approached as a lifelong, rather than a periodic, exchange, especially during those pendulous phases (between class reunions and/or capital campaigns) when our hopes, dreams, and ambitions could truly benefit from a boost of real support – the sort of support which only comes from being part of a familiar, trusted network.

Alumni is a bridge, not simply a destination. It spans our past and present. It's a bridge that does not need to be crossed once upon graduating or intermittently (say, when a direct mailing seeking a financial contribution or invitation to attend a 'class of' social gathering arrives). Rather, the alumni bridge should be traversed regularly, as it holds the potential to connect our dreams to vaster horizons. After majoring in political science, I pursued a law degree – 'cause what else was there to do with my degree! It didn't cross my well-educated mind to ask another poli-sci graduate if they had done something a wee bit more imaginative with their degree.

Networks matter more today than ever before – not simply because of the COVID pandemic (social isolation, and loneliness were well on the rise before 2020), or technology disrupting every aspect of our lives from the kinds of careers we'll pursue to the numbers of jobs we'll hold, plus the ways we'll communicate all these life transitions to our 'friends'. When everything around us is being up-ended, alumni is a reprieve from the chaos. It is a constant in our lives – a solid footing, a base to stay moored to, or as it happens, reconnect with to get a wobbly career or business venture back on course. It is a source of ideas and inspiration. It is comfort. Being an alum confirms that we belong.

Alumni is a network to contribute to, value, and leverage for life.

Coincidently, there is an actual alumni connection behind Maria, *The Alumni Way*, and me. While we met through a warm introduction, it was an alumni bond (shout-out to the University of Victoria!), which prompted me to immediately agree to write the foreword to this insightful book – and to reveal my alumni engagement transgressions. That we both share a strong commitment to providing people with the critical networking tools they need to maximize professional pursuits and strengthen human connections, has cemented our connection.

Two university degrees did not dissuade me to abandon my long-held scepticism towards alumni social events, however, Maria's *The Alumni Way: Building Lifelong Value from Your University Investment* has. I implore you: don't simply grab your degree and run! Dismiss the egregious notion that your alums are the equivalent of ATMs – open 24/7 for funding requests (only). Embrace the learnings in *The Alumni Way* to reorient the how's and why's of alumni engagement and start building better alumni connections.

Introduction:
We are all alumni

We are all alumni. Although we attended different schools, colleges, and universities, we share the same alumni status. By choosing this book, I hope this means you are curious to learn about the potential of your alumni network across your professional and personal life.

Initially, I planned to write this book for final year students, recent graduates, and alumni. *The Alumni Way* is still primarily for you and your supporters – parents, guidance counsellors, and career advisers. However, as I began writing this book, I realized *all alumni*, even ones *inside* the institutions themselves – faculty, university administrators, senior managers, and even advancement professionals – could also benefit from 'reimagining alumnihood'.[1] By learning more about alumni engagement, we can all *support* and *be* savvy alumni. What would it be like if *all* alumni recognized the value of staying connected to their alma mater? This is my ambitious aim for this book. Let's embark on this alumni journey together.

Alumni connection is more than a stroll down memory lane. Instead, the Alumni Way is a multi-lane highway, dotted with off ramps of creative possibilities along the route. By mapping our alumni potential, we open ourselves to a new way of thinking about life after graduation. I hope this book will give you renewed faith in the power of alumni connection in our highly networked world.

It's never too early (or too late!) to be informed about the perks of our alumni status. Even students can benefit from the

Alumni Way. The earlier we understand our lifelong alumni connections, the better. Whether our student experience is, or was, memorable, miserable, or forgettable, as alumni, we can start this relationship afresh. Our alumni network and our university can play a key part in our lives, *for life*.

It's easy to be cynical. Our university experience belongs firmly in the past, doesn't it? The call to keep in touch is vague: the alumni magazine and reunion invitations seem to hold little relevance to daily life. Drawing on the thinking from the Alumni Way, it may be worth considering or even embracing these invitations. And then there's the common complaint: the university only contacts me when they are looking for money. The alumni–university relationship doesn't begin or end with the fundraising ask; it is far more nuanced and complex. Viewing alumni solely as an income stream robs the university – and alumni – of the potential of a deep, enriching relationship.

I also want to debunk the myth that our alumni status is a ticket to an exclusive club. Instead, our alumni connection invites us to be a part of an *inclusive* community on and off campus. There is a place for this universal perspective because of our starting point: *we are all alumni*. Collectively, by following the Alumni Way, we can also address local community needs, tackle global problems, and transform society. These are colossal claims to the power of alumni potential. I hope this has piqued your interest to read on.

The four traits of the Alumni Way

Drawing on more than a decade of my research on alumni relationships, I have identified four key traits of the Alumni Way: reflection, curiosity, passion, and generosity. The Alumni Way challenges us to view the world through this alumni lens in all that we do. By doing this, we can reap immense personal, professional, and even societal benefit. This might seem like an incredible overstatement: can keeping 'alumni' in our minds *really* be so crucial to everyday life? I believe so and I invite you to join me to learn more.

Imagine our university relationship is an hourglass (Figure 0.1). At the top of the hourglass is our student life. How quickly the

Figure 0.1: Our lifelong university relationship as an hourglass

1 **Student life**
Time passes like grains of sand filtering through as our student experience.

2 **Graduation**
Grains of sand are still; this is a time for reflection.

3 **The Alumni Way**
Turning over the hourglass.

4 **Our alumni potential**
Filtering our university experience through each Alumni Way trait.

sand filters through the narrow neck of the glass bulb! This sand represents our memories and our affiliations – our discipline of study, our extra-curricular activities – gathered during our time at university. When the last grains filter through the narrow neck, this is graduation. As a contained vessel, once the sand reaches the bottom, nothing changes, our degree status remains with the stillness of the sand. It's easy to keep the hourglass still, a symbol of our university past. Ask any child what they would do with an hourglass. Exactly. Turn it over. This is our chance to turn the hourglass over and over as alumni. This time, and each time, viewing the sifting grains of sand of our alumni connections through the narrow neck of an Alumni Way trait. Part I maps these traits as we begin our journey.

3

The first trait: Reflection

In Part II, the trait of **becoming and being reflective**, begins with a familiar phrase heard at graduation ceremonies worldwide: keep in touch. We are introduced to alumni capital, a special form of social capital, to help us achieve the life we want. We view the university as a microcosm of wider society, with the amenities of a town or city. By keeping in touch, even passively, in the institution's activities, we become conscious of the opportunities available to us: online courses, events from farmers' markets to business strategy seminars, facilities like theatres, fitness clubs, conference centres, or cafés – the list is endless!

This section concludes by dispelling some myths about keeping in touch and the institution's alumni relations function. We also reflect on our own past university story. As the sands of the hourglass sift through the reflection trait of the Alumni Way, we are challenged to consider our own reasons, interests, and goals for an ongoing connection with our alma mater. The key question is:

> How can we reflect on the value of our alma mater as a partner for life?

The second trait: Curiosity

There is intense debate on whether a university degree contributes to a successful career path. By **becoming and being curious**, in Part III we consider the common degree-to-career coupling from an alternative perspective. What if the career game changer isn't our *degree* but our *alumni status*? Like detectives, we hone our curiosity. We ask astute, poignant questions to solve those career conundrums that may otherwise lay hidden in the ivory towers or with fellow alumni. Is the campus calling us back for a career? Don't discount the wide range of university jobs alongside the traditional academic track.

Universities also support start-ups and help businesses thrive. Look no further than campus to find industry-facing research. Or, an ideal place to bring products and services to market.

Through our playful curiosity, we can forge strategic business partnerships with universities or with fellow alumni throughout our lives and across the world. At the slenderest part of the hourglass, our curiosity is filtering through these ideas for professional advancement. The key question is:

> *How can we become curious about the work of our fellow alumni and our university to advance our professional life?*

The third trait: Passion

Part IV challenges us to see an alumni dimension to fostering our mind, body, heart, and soul. Alumni-curated examples are presented to showcase the next key Alumni Way trait, **becoming and being passionate**. By engaging with our alumni capital, we can unlock the values, communities, and passions we hold dear. The sands filter through the passion trait from the top to the bottom of the hourglass. We can also join fellow alumni with collective passion to address some of the world's greatest challenges too. The key question is:

> *How can our relationship with our university and fellow alumni fuel our life passions?*

The fourth trait: Generosity

The Alumni Way is not a finite stretch of road. In Part V, by **becoming and being generous**, we construct new laneways, avenues, and superhighways for others to build their own alumni capital. We are all alumni *and* philanthropists. This draws on the true power of philanthropy: the giving of time, talent, treasure, and ties. As alumni, we can share our expertise and resources to transform the institution, the lives of students and alumni, or even have an imprint on the wider world. As the sand filters through the hourglass through the trait of generosity, we can consider how we can make the Alumni Way a little less bumpy for others. This section also demystifies the financial component of giving – donations and university campaigns – arming us with knowledge to be discerning, informed alumni. The key question is:

How can we show generosity giving our time, talent, treasure, and ties in our relationship with our university for mutual and wider societal benefit?

By following the Alumni Way, the hourglass is constantly in motion. Our university experience is no longer the static, single focus of completing a degree. To maximize our university investment, we must apply the traits of **reflection**, **curiosity**, **passion**, and **generosity** throughout our lives, to this narrowest point of the hourglass. The Alumni Way is a multidimensional, strategic approach to building our opportunities, our networks, and ourselves. Part VI presents the ultimate Alumni Way test:

How can we extend our identity as alumni beyond the university to all our shared experiences?

Imagine the possibilities! This book challenges each one of us to spread our Alumni Way mindset across our shared life experiences. From former employers and conferences to summer camps and sports clubs. We can create networks *from* life *for* life.

Is the Alumni Way the solution to the malaise from a disappointing university experience? I am not so naïve. However, I hope to show you that by adopting the Alumni Way traits, we can start along a path of renewal with our alma mater. All is not lost; in fact, we have much to gain.

We might all be alumni, but each of us has a unique alumni experience. This is a chance to shine. Throughout this book, I have identified 23 alumni action points along the Alumni Way. Each of these action points includes practical activities to help us to:

- build a strategic, lifelong relationship with our university;
- create connections to build the ideal career through our alumni and university network;
- foster our life passions drawing on our alumni status;

- advance our leadership skills through giving and service involving our alma mater relationship;
- extend our networks and opportunities involving all our shared experiences from life.

This is a lofty value proposition for a small book. The Alumni Way is a manageable trek when we are open to the process. At the end of each section, there is a summary of the key messages and a checklist of practical activities. A set of reflective questions helps us to consider the Alumni Way thinking for our primary identity as a student, recent graduate, alum, parent, career adviser, university faculty, or administrator.

What would it be like if we all leveraged our alumni potential? Imagine the spill over impact of this Alumni Way thinking into greater society! Imagine people considering their alumni status throughout their lives – their employers, clubs, awards, sports teams – a widening alumni movement beyond education. I believe that as alumni, we are ready to be leaders of this movement. I believe universities are ready to foster this leadership for greater societal impact. Are you ready? Let's begin our alumni journey together!

The Alumni Way Workbook is also available. To access your free copy of the workbook visit https://www.thealumniway.com/

PART I

Charting the course of the Alumni Way

1	Starting at the finish line	11
	• How were you feeling the day after graduation?	12
	• Ordinary advice to graduates	14
2	The compass: Introducing alumni capital	15
	• Alumni Action 1: Claiming our alumni identity	17
	• Alumni Action 2: Reclaiming our university investment	19
	• Alumni Action 3: Opening to the growth mindset	23
3	Summary: Stepping forward by stepping back on campus	25
	• Key message from Part I	26
	• Checklist for Part I	27
	• Building the Alumni Way: Questions following Part I	27

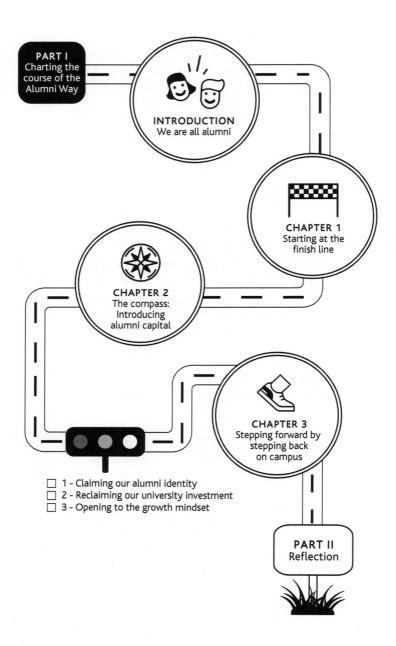

PART I
Charting the course of the Alumni Way

INTRODUCTION
We are all alumni

CHAPTER 1
Starting at the finish line

CHAPTER 2
The compass: Introducing alumni capital

CHAPTER 3
Stepping forward by stepping back on campus

☐ 1 - Claiming our alumni identity
☐ 2 - Reclaiming our university investment
☐ 3 - Opening to the growth mindset

PART II
Reflection

1

Starting at the finish line

At one stage in our lives, we were all there, stepping up to the podium to receive our diploma. Recent graduates only imagined this rite of passage, replaced with a virtual or physically distanced event. For still others, including myself, I crossed the stage and graduated with my undergraduate degree in the 1990s. This was a time when the internet was in its infancy, and social media non-existent. Times have certainly changed.

What hasn't changed is that the university wants us. As alumni, they appeal to us to keep in touch, get involved, and give back. They seek our alumni leadership. They describe ways we can contribute to the institution, fostering a place of learning and discovery for future students. Do *we* want the university? I believe the answer should be yes. Yes, to new and radical ways of thinking about our alumni network and our university. This book aims to support our journey as alumni and as leaders.

Our journey *begins* with graduation. Graduation changes our relationship with the university from a state of *doing*, to a state of *being*. As a student, this active state of *doing* was likely at a feverish pace: attending classes, writing exams, completing assignments, studying, reading, writing, thinking, researching (and of course socializing!). We met the academic requirements, performed impressive intellectual feats, and endured personal sacrifice. It ended with a single piece of paper: the degree. Graduation celebrates this impressive act of doing, allowing us to be swept up in the moment. Whether it was a massive formal gathering on campus, a virtual celebration, or a quiet parchment reveal at home, it remains the grand finale of our momentous achievement, closing our educational chapter.

Today, and over the days, months, or years following our success, we have a new static identity: we *are* alumni. Unlike our student identity that required energy and action, as alumni we are not required to *do* anything. Active or not, our alumni status doesn't change. We are alumni, no matter what. We are forever a member of our graduating class and the alumni community. This is our transition from *doing* to *being*. This book would end here if the state of being an alum were enough. The Alumni Way encourages us to transition from *being* an alum to *becoming* an active member of our alumni community with an ecosystem of networks for discovery. It begins at this finish line, the day after graduation. The day after graduation is the beginning of the rest of our lives.

How were you feeling the day after graduation?

'Your mountain is waiting, so ... get on your way!'[1] exclaims the conclusion to the Dr Seuss book *Oh the Places You'll Go!* Readers are treated to wacky illustrations and a quirky allegory navigating the unpredictable ups and downs of life. It's no wonder it remains a popular graduation gift. With his story, Seuss condenses the immensity of feelings of the day *after* graduation. Life as an alum can be an overwhelming prospect. There is a combination of elation and unease. Relief and melancholy. Sadness of what is left behind, and excitement for the future.

Our graduation – whether it was yesterday, virtual, or decades ago – marked our entry into the real world, while simultaneously closing the university door. 'You're on your own,' Seuss reminds us, 'And you know what you know. And YOU are the guy [sic] who'll decide where to go.'[2] The day after graduation, reality sets in. It's a mountain alright, and it can be a daunting one.

Graduation statistics only tell us part of the story. A 2019 Organisation for Economic Co-operation and Development (OECD) study forecasted that by 2030, there would be 300 million young people with a tertiary education worldwide.[3] These statistics don't account for graduates with associate degrees, college diplomas, or further education qualifications.

The statistics are also missing the diversity across our education system, including people returning to education who are not included in the 'young people' category. That's a lot of graduates climbing to the summit.

On one hand, we can think of ourselves as one of a rabble of graduates struggling to find a way to stand out among the thousands (even millions!) of others. Or, on the other hand, we can consider that, as graduates, we are part of a community of alumni who have shared the same experience. This book offers new ideas and enlightening strategies for whatever path we choose in life. We might have a map and a planned route. We may already have an established career on or off campus. This book is the flashlight, the torch, to illuminate our path to becoming a savvy, informed alum.

Our degree is the permanent marker on our CV or résumé. The purpose of this book is simple: we invested significant time and resources to get a degree. Now for the rest of our lives as a 'university graduate' we have a resource to draw on: our alma mater. The key question to keep in mind throughout this book is:

Alongside the lifelong value of my education, what is the value of my university over my lifetime?

I describe this book as an alumni manifesto. A call to arms for all of us to interact and engage with our alma mater. It's this alma mater that holds the potential for our aspirations and the communities we serve (or hope to serve) throughout our lives. By learning about the Alumni Way, we may also be able to support others to take a leap and embrace this mindset.

First, let's start with the basics. 'Why you'll never be an alumni.' This is a statement from Todd Pettigrew's article in *Maclean's* magazine where the professor responds: 'Because *alumni* is plural. You, an individual, can't be alumni any more than you can be a students.'[4] Pettigrew reminds us that a man is *alumnus*, a woman, *alumna*. A group of graduates, male and female, are *alumni*; a group of female graduates are *alumnae*. I use the dictionary-approved *alum* as a gender neutral and shorter alternative[5] in this book with the inclusive term *alumni* for a group.[6] Hopefully, with Pettigrew's blessing, we can all use these terms with more confidence. The term 'alumni' refers to our graduation from – or even attendance at – university, college, an institute, or school. I use university as the catch-all term for our alma mater throughout this book. Another Latin word, alma mater means nurturing or nourishing mother, referring to our institution of study. As alumni, we are the beneficiaries of this nourishment. Our alma mater is there to foster, cherish, develop, and cultivate our post-university life.

Ordinary advice to graduates

'Just because you've got a diploma in hand doesn't mean you know everything!'[7] reads the back cover of Alyssa Favreau's pocket-sized *New York Times* bestseller *Stuff Every Graduate Should Know: A Handbook for the Real World*. Giving graduates advice is a thriving industry. There are dozens of books to help navigate life after graduation. Perhaps we have given or received some of these books as graduation gifts. This is ordinary advice to graduates. They offer practical tips and promise answers to such questions as: How can you maximize your university experience? Gain post-degree success? Carve out a fruitful career path? These books treat graduation as the release date into the real world. Our alma mater plays a minor role in this process of life discovery. At best, alumni relations and career services may make a snowflake appearance in the blizzard of post-graduation advice.

Alumni are curiously absent from the many of the key books for university administrators too. If mentioned at all, alumni are referenced in two ways: as donors or as 'doers'.[8] The donor identity concentrates the value of alumni through their financial donations to the institution. The 'doer' identity recognizes the potential for alumni to act as mentors, student recruiters, or committee members among other acts of service. The relationship becomes one-sided, with alumni supporting the needs of the institution and its current students. There is limited discussion on how the university can support alumni in this relationship, creating mutually beneficial and authentic alumni capital. This is where the Alumni Way steps in.

2

The compass: Introducing alumni capital

Alumni capital is a powerful resource to help us achieve the life we want.
Set aside those graduation books: alumni capital is *extraordinary*
advice to graduates. Our alma mater is a hypernetwork at our
disposal: a multitude of connections. By following the Alumni
Way, these connections will emerge during the process, steering
us and acting as our compass.

We have excellent reasons to keep in touch with our alma
mater, for years and even decades after graduation. Alumni capital
is a form of social capital. We can profit from our alumni social
capital by connecting with the networks that share our values.
As with social capital, we can invest in our alumni capital and
expect a reasonable return on our investment.[1]

The bonding and bridging components of social capital are
also present in alumni capital. Robert Putnam, in his book
Bowling Alone, explains: 'Bonding social capital constitutes a
kind of sociological superglue, whereas bridging social capital
provides a sociological WD-40.'[2] In an alumni context, it's
easy to find a cohesive, bonding experience, say with a group
of former classmates at an alumni reunion. The diversity in
an alumni network can also be a flexible lubricant, a bridge,
such as an alumni mentorship programme for current students.
The bonding and bridging alumni capital is fluid, it happens
at the same time across a multitude of groups, even on an

intergenerational basis.[3] Our alumni community is an inclusive one: every graduate has alumni capital, as does every student, university administrator, professor, and career adviser.

This alumni capital also allows for the democratization of our networks, a linking capital.[4] These links help to extend the boundaries of our traditional network with alumni across the globe in different sectors and with different interests. History graduates are connected to engineers and business majors, who are connected to football players, debaters, and cooking enthusiasts, who are connected to alumni in Atlanta, Amsterdam, and Australia. This interconnectivity all by virtue of a shared alma mater.

The cynics in us might be thinking: I've connected with friends, former classmates, and acquaintances on social media. Why hasn't it had the transformational effect of alumni capital described here? Connecting with alumni is only the first, tiny step towards the Alumni Way. We might *know* there's an intrinsic value to getting a degree, but we can't put it into words. The research calls this degree premium.[5] This book takes this one step further, presenting *alumni premium*. This book doesn't dispute or negate degree value; we each have our own way to articulate the value our degree has had on our lives. The degree might open a door. Our alumni capital opens a *series of doors*. And we can't just stand at the threshold; connecting on social media as a passive actor, we need to step in and explore.

Alumni capital can be visualized by three key categories: the flow of **people, knowledge**, and **resources**. The **flows of people** include all our former classmates, university friends, students, and the wider alumni network. The research, courses and learning opportunities organized by the university create the **flows of knowledge**. Finally, the **flows of resources** include the amenities and places – virtual and campus-based – available to us. As outlined in Figure 2.1, at its core, the synergy of alumni capital is the overlap of these areas. The magic of this alumni bridging, bonding, and linking exists when we interact with it. We draw on the immense potential of what's available to us. We'll start at the beginning, at the base of the mountain.

Figure 2.1: Alumni capital – a visual representation

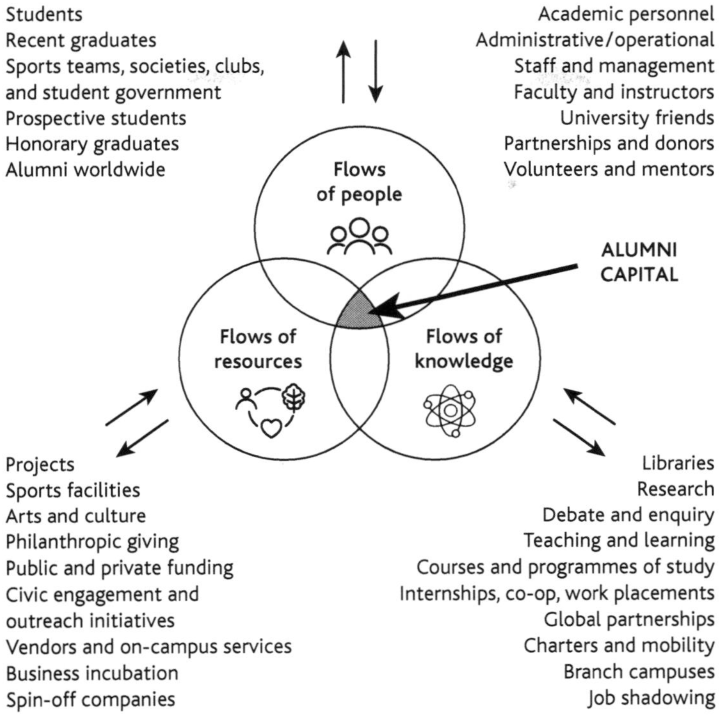

Students
Recent graduates
Sports teams, societies, clubs,
and student government
Prospective students
Honorary graduates
Alumni worldwide

Academic personnel
Administrative/operational
Staff and management
Faculty and instructors
University friends
Partnerships and donors
Volunteers and mentors

Flows
of people

ALUMNI
CAPITAL

Flows of
resources

Flows of
knowledge

Projects
Sports facilities
Arts and culture
Philanthropic giving
Public and private funding
Civic engagement and
outreach initiatives
Vendors and on-campus services
Business incubation
Spin-off companies

Libraries
Research
Debate and enquiry
Teaching and learning
Courses and programmes of study
Internships, co-op, work placements
Global partnerships
Charters and mobility
Branch campuses
Job shadowing

Alumni Action 1: Claiming our alumni identity

When discussing alumni identity, first we must *identify* as alumni. All former students – not just graduates – are alumni. Some people with the deepest affinity to the institution may not hold a degree to show it. Alumni identity is distinct – it's not about showing an alumni membership card for a discount or buying university branded clothing, *it's a feeling*.

We occupy many identities in our lives – sibling, parent, cousin, athlete, volunteer, musician, and many, many more.[6] Our profession or job title can also be part of our identity – administrator, writer, events coordinator, account manager, professor. As a new graduate, we may have grieved leaving behind the easy student identity and all it entails – member of a club, athlete, residence hall social director. Graduation wipes the slate clean of these identities, replaced with the catch-all alumni identity. Do we consider ourselves *alumni* in our multitude of other identities?

Our life identities and our alumni identity are not something we should take for granted. It requires our thoughtful reflection. Quoting pioneering educationalist John Dewey, reflective thought should be done with 'active, persistent and careful consideration'.[7] This reflection allows us to internalize our alumni identity. It helps us to maximize the opportunities it offers us throughout our lives. This epic trek of life begins with our reflection.

I recently attended a seminar on storytelling. The facilitator began by telling her own story. She started her story by mentioning that she graduated from a prestigious university. Her next slide showed her many life identities, including mother, sister, dog owner, and entrepreneur. After the seminar, I asked her, "Why is your degree a factor in your story, but alum wasn't part of your identity?" She confessed that it hadn't occurred to her that her alumni status should be part of her current suite of identities. While her education told an important part of her story, she didn't identify herself as an alum. The core purpose of this book is for all of us to consider our alumni identity as an essential constant in our lives. Our alumni identity is part of our present and our future. It opens networks and ideas. We need to shift our 'education-as-degree' linear thinking. We need to replace it with strategic, multidimensional thinking that considers the lifelong impact of our alumni identity.

Activity 1: Introducing alumni capital by claiming our alumni identity

To claim your alumni identity and begin to invest in your alumni capital, you need to advertise. Add 'alum of' or 'graduate of' to the bio section of your social media profiles. Fill in the education section.

Next, list your life identities and rank their importance in your life right now. Alum may or may not rank high on the list. Hopefully, after reading this book, I will convince you that alum is a lifelong identity that can shape your other life identities in so many positive ways!

Alumni Action 2: Reclaiming our university investment

Alumni play a key role in the current higher education landscape. Universities are competing in a race of international reputation, rankings, and financial viability. As alumni, we represent the institution's ideals through our success. Intentional or not, we are the university's informal ambassadors. Universities see alumni as the living embodiment of their values: excellence, diversity, integrity, and so on. Alumni are featured as global leaders and community change agents.[8] What does the university offer us in exchange for our lifelong modelling contract? For most of us, I argue that often the alumni-alma mater relationship remains unbalanced. Universities initiate the why, when, and how of alumni contact. As savvy alumni, we need to reset this balance and become proactive in seeking alumni value.

Never is the lifelong investment in a degree – and our alma mater – more important. Saddled with debt, years or even decades after graduation, graduates are questioning the value of their qualification. When universities closed their campuses en masse due to the COVID-19 pandemic, this intensified debates over the value of higher education. However, questioning higher education's worth remains persistent. Consider these provocative headlines:

'Is College Worth It?'[9]
'Americans Losing Faith in College Degrees, Poll Finds'[10]
'Are Graduates Good Value for Money?'[11]
'College May Not Be Worth It Anymore'[12]
'A College Degree Is No Guarantee of a Good Life'[13]
'My Students Have Paid £9,000 and Now They Think They Own Me.'[14]

These captions position higher education as a product. Professors and university administrators are under pressure to perform in their various roles as *producer* for the student *consumer*. We desperately need a repositioning of these university roles – including that of students and alumni. Despite all the concerns and pressures, there is evidence that a university degree remains a highly sought-after aspiration of young people and their families. It is described as a 'mission critical'[15] decision, something Anne Marie Bathmaker and her colleagues call 'the degree generation'.[16] Indeed, family pressure to complete a degree, and the increased cost of a university education has led to higher expectations by students. Faculty and university administrators are keenly aware of student demands, responding with key performance indicators related to student success and support.

Students are customers, aren't they? There is extensive literature that argues this point[17] and this idea has slowly seeped into our institutions. I wrote this book to disprove this student as customer myth. Scholar Malcolm Tight warns of the danger of the student as customer: 'It portrays the student as a relatively passive recipient of what the university has to offer,' he writes, 'Rather than the active, engaged, indeed self-directed, individual.'[18] Tight goes on to argue that the 'student as pawn' metaphor is more appropriate. Students (and by association, alumni), Tight contends, are leveraged in the higher education system towards certain ends: to contribute to the economy and achieve the university's key performance indicators. Before casting judgement or delving into debate, let's examine the student as customer concept further.

A customer relationship involves an exchange. In this case, a student fulfils the academic requirements and secures a qualification. With the exchange complete, theoretically, the new graduate severs this tie with the university, likening the process to a store purchase. However, the university-student relationship is far more complex. I argue students are not buying a product (or consuming one). Our education as a learning process includes, but is not exclusive to, completing a qualification. *A university degree is not shampoo.* We don't have a lifelong connection to our shampoo brand.

Instead of resisting this customer relationship with students and alumni, universities are often guilty of embracing it, focused on the need to satisfy student customers. This is not to discount some excellent examples of meaningful student and alumni engagement strategies within universities. In fact, the opposite, these loyalty-based programmes can be the foundation for deeper, authentic alumni–alma mater relationships.

As alumni, we need to reclaim our agency, our control, to becoming proactive in our alumni destiny. As with our student experience, as alumni, I argue we get out of our alma mater what we are willing to put in. The subtitle of this book 'Building Lifelong Value from Your University Investment' is certainly an attractive promise from the front cover. We can't just sit back. The focus in this subtitle is on the active verb – *building*. The Alumni Way gives us the tools to uncover a return on our investment – and our potential for so much more.

As alumni, we are also lifelong shareholders in our alma mater.[19] As an alumni shareholder, we have a vested interest in the reputation and advancement of our university. The investment pays us dividends, for our own personal and professional benefit. As alumni, we can become co-creators in the university. Overall, universities largely struggle to meaningfully engage alumni. The strategy, policy, and leadership – along with the will – need to be in place within the institution *and* among alumni. This creates the perfect alumni storm. What would it be like if we had heightened expectations of our alumni experience? Let's reimagine our relationship with our alma mater as this lifelong investment.

Alumni often go to great pains to distance themselves from their alma mater. We can be guilty of this estranged relationship by accident or by design. There is irony in this decision to become an *alum in absentia*. Think of the incredible investment of time, energy, and resources in higher education. Think back to the student recruitment strategies, wooing us with the glossy brochures, the slick websites, the student testimonials, and education fairs all orchestrated to give us a taste of university life. 'Invest now' flashes the key message, 'and the life you want is there for you'.

I argue there are three phases of investment in higher education. First, is the **foundation investment**. This is the preparation and financial investment in choosing an institution and subsequently meeting the entrance requirements. Securing a university place is, on its own, a monumental achievement.

The strategic personal and parental decisions begin as young as preschool. It can start with securing the best school, tutoring, and extra-curricular activities along with grades, finances, and scholarships. Securing a university place may follow a non-traditional path or involve overcoming immense adversity. This triumph reinforces the enormity of the feat.

Second, is the **focused investment**. This is the eye on the prize. Think back to the immense financial, intellectual, emotional, psychological, spiritual, and even physiological efforts of attaining a degree. This is focused investment and not degree investment because university learning goes beyond the classroom. Our focused investment includes the extra-curricular activities on one hand and the life lessons from navigating the university system on the other. Today, 'student success' and 'student experience' are common buzz words around campus. There is a support system in place to keep us in university and to help us to maximize the experience. With the diploma framed, the enormity of the investment seems over.

However, graduation is not the end of the investment. There is a third phase, the **strategic, lifelong investment in our education**. We hope to contribute meaningfully in the world. We want to build a satisfying career, to start life, or, to restart life on hold because of our studies. We hope to make money to begin paying off student loans. The university is a step in this direction. The university had – and continues to have – a role to help unlock our future. This alumni capital and the Alumni Way is our recalibration in this direction.

Activity 2: Introducing our alumni capital by reclaiming our university investment

To shift your mindset from one of 'customer' of higher education to 'investor' or 'shareholder', reflect on the following questions, focused on the foundation and focused phases of investment:

How did you (or your parents) invest in your university education *before* starting university? Think of the choices, sacrifices, or investment of time, money, and energy towards securing your university place.

Next, create a list with two columns. In the first column, list at least ten of your student identities. Be creative, think back to your student days! Student (ie studying your degree) can be one of your identities. Other academic student identities may include scholarship winner, researcher, work placement participant, class representative, teaching assistant. Be sure to include your student extra-curricular identities too, which may include team athlete, volunteer tutor, student union rep, club member, or residence hall occupant.

In the second column, consider how each of these student identities required financial, intellectual, emotional, psychological, spiritual, and even physiological effort. This gives you a snapshot of your past identities and your past investment in your university experience.

The rest of the book and activities will help you to shift your thinking and consider the strategic lifelong investment in your education and your life – read on!

Alumni Action 3: Opening to the growth mindset

The Alumni Way is inspired by the growth mindset, a concept developed in Carol Dweck's book *Mindset: Changing the Way You Think to Fulfil Your Potential.* Dweck, a Professor of Psychology at Stanford University, argues that with hard work and effort, we can achieve a growth mindset, the understanding that our abilities and intelligence grow throughout our lives.[20] The opposite is the fixed mindset, 'Believing that your qualities are carved in stone', Dweck explains, 'creates an urgency to prove yourself over and over. With the fixed mindset, you are of the belief that your intelligence stays the same. In the fixed mindset everything is about the outcome. If you fail – if you're not the best – it's all been wasted.'[21]

On the other hand, the growth mindset focuses on process, not outcome. 'The growth mindset allows people to value what they're doing *regardless of the outcome.*' Dweck says. 'They're tackling problems, charting new courses, working on important issues. Maybe they haven't found the cure for cancer, but the search was deeply meaningful.'[22] By investing in the right strategies and hard work, our alumni capital can be a platform for our own growth. The journey is as important as the destination. The Alumni Way reminds us of the infinite directions we can take our alumni network. At the same time, we can guide fellow alumni to forge their own path.

Other books use examples from celebrities, business moguls, or Fortune 500 companies. This book focuses on ordinary alumni and universities doing extraordinary things. Alumni is firmly an inclusive term. I chose examples that might resonate, spark ideas, and be inspirational. Through my research, I have gathered hundreds of examples of alumni connection. I share some of them here. If the only thing gained from this book is a heightened awareness and sharpened radar towards alumni and alma mater opportunities, this is worthwhile. Adding the Alumni Way to our arsenal, gives us a special lens to view other aspects of our lives. Key leadership advice and bestselling strategies also make a cameo appearance in this book. Imagine how powerful these techniques would be if we approach them drawing on our alumni capital!

Activity 3: Introducing our alumni capital by opening to the growth mindset

Take five minutes to complete a micro-reflection. Write down what you hope you will gain from this book, based on what you have read so far. Respond to the question: Where are you in your life right now?

If you are looking for a career change, or ways to gain value from your expensive education, write this down.

Review your answers and respond to the second question: Am I focused on journey or outcome? Consider whether you see yourself as open to growth that *enhances* the journey. Eventually, this learning may develop your direction or your outcomes in the long run.

3

Summary:
Stepping forward by
stepping back on campus

I am always surprised that a handshake and parchment satisfy most graduates who merrily start life in the real world. Why don't graduates ask, is that all? Here's a list of suggested questions to ask ourselves post-graduation:

- What does the university offer once we stop attending class?
- How can our student experience – good, bad, ambivalent – be turned into a positive, lifelong relationship with our alma mater?
- How does the university offer lifelong support for career, professional, and personal development?
- How can one graduate influence and seek advantages at their alma mater for mutual benefit?
- How can our collective alumni capital enable us to address some of the biggest challenges facing our communities and our planet?
- In what way does our alumni status span other shared experiences in our lives?

These are ambitious questions that require a fresh start to our alma mater relationship. We can forge a life as an engaged, invested alum regardless of how active we were in student clubs, sports teams, or campus parties. Each of us has a unique set of alumni opportunities to uncover. These opportunities are determined by certain practical logistics: the size of our university, the resources our university invests in alumni activities, and even how close we live to our alma mater. It is promising to see the increase in virtual initiatives organized by our alma mater and our alumni network. This gives us even more flexibility to participate. By drawing on our growth mindset, we can set ourselves to learning mode. We can forge new opportunities, knowledge, and skills that fit our circumstances.

Over time, our university experience may feel further and further away from our everyday life. This book shows that, even as the years go by, our relationship with our alma mater can hold relevance in our lives. These relationships are multi-layered, with the flows of people, knowledge, and resources. Drawing on our alumni capital, we might discover exciting opportunities or connections. They might come from an academic department, a groundbreaking research project, an inspiring professor, a new professional development course, student leadership activities, or energetic fellow alumni. It's always a good time to begin to develop a lifelong relationship with our university.

Key message from Part I

Be open to the value of our alumni status, alumni capital, and the university over our lifetime.

Disengaged alumni with a fixed mindset will:
- avoid new challenges presented in the Alumni Way;
- view graduation as the final chapter in the university journey;
- believe that if their relationship with their university is frayed, or so long ago, it cannot be restored.

Dynamic alumni with a growth mindset will:
- view graduation as the beginning not the end of the university journey;
- consider creative ways of developing their alumni capital;
- recognize that the university is a resource and investment for life;
- start their relationship with their alma mater fresh after graduation;
- relish the challenge and learning involved in acquiring the Alumni Way.

Checklist for Part I

To build your journey along the Alumni Way, don't forget to:

- ☐ add 'alum of' or 'graduate of' to your bio on your social media profiles (see Activity 1);
- ☐ create a list of your life identities (see Activity 1);
- ☐ consider your pre-university investment to date (see Activity 2);
- ☐ list your past student identities and university investment (see Activity 2);
- ☐ complete the growth mindset micro-reflection (see Activity 3).

Building the Alumni Way: Questions following Part I

- *Students, recent graduates, and alumni*: How has my view of alumni changed after reading this section?
- *University administrators*: How are alumni viewed across my institution? Donors or doers, or a combination of both?
- *Advancement professionals*: What is the first communication with the newest alumni after graduation? How does this set a tone for the university's lifelong relationship with its alumni?
- *Parents/career advisers*: How can I be supportive during this transition from student to alum?

PART II

The Alumni Way trait: Reflection

4	Reflecting on the 'keep in touch' call	31
5	Reflection signpost: Recognize the university is a city	35
	• Alumni Action 4: Engaging our alumni citizenship	36
	• Alumni Action 5: Reflecting on our university story	40
6	Reflection signpost: Advance ourselves as alumni citizens	45
	• Alumni Action 6: Creating our alumni services wish list	46
	• Alumni Action 7: Recognizing our global alumni passport	49
	• Alumni Action 8: Updating our alumni record	53
7	Reflection trait summary: Alum from Day One, revisited	59
	• Key messages from Part II	60
	• Checklist for Part II	61
	• Building the Alumni Way: Questions following Part II	62

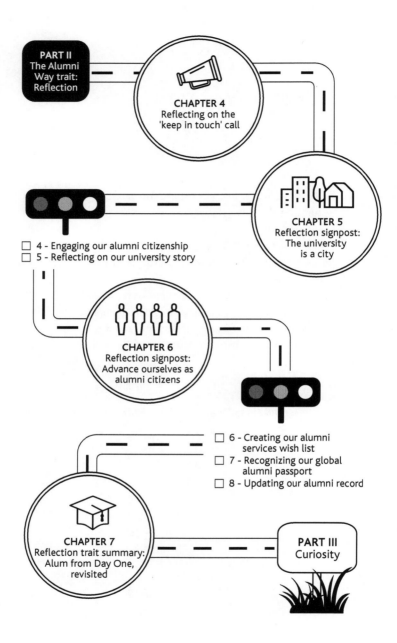

PART II
The Alumni
Way trait:
Reflection

CHAPTER 4
Reflecting on the
'keep in touch' call

CHAPTER 5
Reflection signpost:
The university
is a city

☐ 4 - Engaging our alumni citizenship
☐ 5 - Reflecting on our university story

CHAPTER 6
Reflection signpost:
Advance ourselves as
alumni citizens

☐ 6 - Creating our alumni
services wish list
☐ 7 - Recognizing our global
alumni passport
☐ 8 - Updating our alumni record

CHAPTER 7
Reflection trait summary:
Alum from Day One,
revisited

PART III
Curiosity

4

Reflecting on the 'keep in touch' call

As each person picked up their gown, the tent provided some relief from the September heat. There was a frisson of excitement for the occasion. The group shuffled in the long lines wondering what's happening next. This isn't graduation day, Julia Morrow assured me. Instead, Morrow was describing her first day at Georgetown University. The orientation programme included a special ceremony for new students. "They gave you a black gown as a symbol of your graduation in four years," Morrow remembers, "They said that forever when you graduate you will be part of the Georgetown community." With all the look and feel of commencement, the new students filed into the first few rows of seats for this event. They beamed from this initial accomplishment. "It's something you've been looking forward to for a long time and you are finally there," Morrow says. Julia Morrow is not the only one who noticed a special tone set from the moment she stepped onto campus. Universities across the globe are establishing an 'Alum from Day One' approach.

Universities often start the alumni education early. It is hoped that with these efforts, students will subconsciously develop an active student life to eventually translate to becoming an active alum. For Julia Morrow, life wasn't so linear. She came from a family of Georgetown graduates. This made Morrow's decision to transfer to another university after her first year even more difficult. Now a proud double Trinity College Dublin graduate, Morrow remains active with her alma mater. She attends campus events and volunteers as a student mentor. She attributes her understanding of keeping in touch from Georgetown. The ultimate beneficiary? Her current alma mater. Think back to the first day of university. Was there any subtle hints of an alumni presence? In my case, legendary author and alum Margaret Atwood spoke at orientation. This impressed even my teenage self, though I didn't grasp the magnitude of alumni connection at the time.

Fast forward to graduation day. Standing at a podium, or, as part of an online broadcast, a president, vice-chancellor, or rector reminds graduates to *keep in touch*. This is our invitation to remain connected to our alma mater. There *is* fullness in this seemingly empty sentiment. For many graduates, securing a degree signals a rite of passage. The closing of the university chapter of life. It's easy to slip out of touch with almost everything from the university days, forging ahead with the real world. For some, university offers many great memories. For others, it's the end of an unpleasant experience and the pressures of intense study. For still others, a traditional graduation ceremony was an aspiration unfulfilled replaced by a celebration at home.

Whether we attended a university known by one name – Oxford, Yale, McGill – or by an acronym – UCL, CEU, NUS – or our alma mater fits into a category – state school, red brick, sandstone, comprehensive, community college – the institution's desire to connect with us remains the same. These institutions educate, foster new research discovery, and serve the community. They also organize themselves with roughly the same systems and structures. Therefore, identifying alumni opportunities at our own alma mater follows a 'sea of sameness',[1] identical wherever we go. There are variations by region, by country, or in terms of breadth of services, programmes, or initiatives available to alumni.

Research shows what we already know: alumni experience feelings of uncertainty after graduation, especially if coupled by financial pressures or unrealistic career expectations.[2] Universities are responding with supportive transition programmes after graduation. There are final year capstone courses or an outduction, the opposite of the first-year induction. 'The university experience is not just about getting a student through their course and obtaining a qualification', explains student transition specialist Michelle Morgan, 'but a journey of learning, exploration and growth by the individual'.[3] This book is our outduction of sorts towards a smooth introduction into life after graduation, whether it was last week, or, like me, last century, we can discover our alumni potential.

In the first part of this book, we grabbed our compass – our alumni capital – to keep us on track. We had a brief introduction to the first Alumni Way trait: reflection. In this part of the book, we delve deeper into the reflection trait to view our university as an ecosystem and a thriving city. Let's consider how having a map to this city – through our alumni capital – helps our journey through life.

5

Reflection signpost: Recognize the university is a city

The university is a city *within* a city. Some small cities are even known as college towns. The population swells during the academic year, offering a boost to the local economy. The cafés, restaurants, shops, banks, theatres, sports facilities, and student accommodation all thrive during the academic year. On campus, there are libraries, parks, sometimes campus police, and hospitals. The campus is home to religious services and spaces, childcare facilities, pubs, community centres, even schools. Virtually all amenities found in a city are available on campus. If not, they have grown on the campus periphery. The university administration, the groundskeepers, the cleaners, and service staff keep the university operating as a smooth, well-oiled machine. There are also committees, volunteers, and even politicians (student politicians at least).

Recognizing the university as a microcosm of society means we can view the institution differently. It isn't just a place of learning, a place to grab a degree and go. These halls of learning form an economy. It is no wonder the university takes on several identities too: employer, carer, healthcare provider, wellness purveyor, educator, restaurateur, consumer, producer, landlord, and tenant. For instance, Simon Fraser University (SFU) was featured in an article for an initiative called UniverCity.[1] Working within a community trust, SFU aims to create sustainable neighbourhoods for better living on Burnaby Mountain.[2] This 'univer-city' idea aptly defines all universities; they are not just part of the city – they *are* the city, as outlined in Figure 5.1.

Consider how the university spills over into the local community. It draws on this diversity to become a place of learning and service. This is a democratization of the university-community relationship, breaking down the traditional university ivory tower.[3] Cities wishing to attract further inward economic investment tend to promote the excellence of their local higher education institutions. This fully maximizes the 'town and gown' relationship, supporting cities to become more globally competitive.[4] Meric Gertler, President of the University of Toronto and urban geographer, describes the university as a 'city-building organization'.[5]

The university also affects the local creative ecosystem. In his book *The Rise of the Creative Class*, author and urban studies theorist Richard Florida, describes universities as key enablers of creative places. People flock to live in places like San Francisco, Florida contends, because of the three 'Ts' of creative places – technology, talent, and tolerance. The university helps support these three 'Ts' especially as 'talent attractors'.[6] 'By attracting eminent researchers and scientists', Florida argues, 'universities in turn attract graduate students, generate spin-off companies and encourage other companies to locate nearby in a cycle of self-reinforcing growth'.[7] This is an interdependent, symbiotic relationship between university and city. This synergy also occurs between the university and its citizens: its wider alumni diaspora.

Alumni Action 4: Engaging our alumni citizenship

Cities like Copenhagen are reaching out to their diaspora – former citizens of the Danish city – to find economic, social, and cultural connections towards prosperity.[8] This diaspora model might look suspiciously familiar. This is like universities calling alumni to reconnect back to their alma mater. Alumni are the only permanent stakeholders of the university. We are the *citizens of* and *shareholders in* our alma mater.

Through our daily routine, wherever we are in the world, we represent our alma mater as informal alumni ambassadors. We have a stake in the reputation of our alma mater, if for no other

Figure 5.1: The university is a city – a visual representation

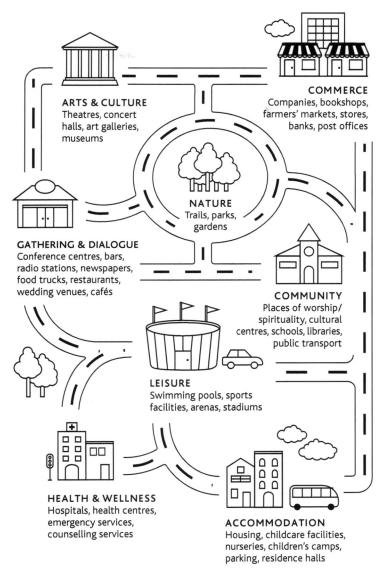

ARTS & CULTURE
Theatres, concert
halls, art galleries,
museums

COMMERCE
Companies, bookshops,
farmers' markets, stores,
banks, post offices

NATURE
Trails, parks,
gardens

GATHERING & DIALOGUE
Conference centres, bars,
radio stations, newspapers,
food trucks, restaurants,
wedding venues, cafés

COMMUNITY
Places of worship/
spirituality, cultural
centres, schools, libraries,
public transport

LEISURE
Swimming pools, sports
facilities, arenas, stadiums

HEALTH & WELLNESS
Hospitals, health centres,
emergency services,
counselling services

ACCOMMODATION
Housing, childcare facilities,
nurseries, children's camps,
parking, residence halls

reason than for its prominent place on our CV or résumé. Instead of members of a diaspora with an ancestral homeland, we are alumni of our alma mater. In the 1960s, communications scholar Marshall McLuhan coined the phrase 'global village' to describe the extent to which technology and communication would connect people worldwide. McLuhan hadn't envisaged the sheer scale of this idea over half a century later. No other entity embraces the global village ideal better than the university. The elements of the growth mindset permeate McLuhan's definition of a university as 'a community of continuous learning, a single campus in which everybody, irrespective of age, is involved in learning a living'.[9] Universities repackage the global village feeling with modern marketing taglines like 'global reach', 'centre of innovation' and 'supportive community'.

Choosing the city-citizenship metaphor is deliberate. For too long, alumni participation with their alma mater has been largely tokenistic, near the bottom rungs of Sherry Arnstein's citizen participation ladder.[10] As alumni, we are often on the passive, receiving end of information from the university. We have few opportunities to flex our life experience muscles, to participate or enact change in our university. The top rungs of the ladder are delegation and citizen control.[11] If enacted at a university, alumni citizens become equals in decision-making and steering the direction of alumni engagement. 'Alumni must made to feel like insiders and be assured they are important members of the community,' states advancement strategist Mark Jones, 'They must believe their opinions matter and they have a meaningful stake in sharing and advancing their alma mater.'[12] With alumni-led governance, alumni associations are at the forefront of this work. There needs to be a meaningful understanding of how alumni participation across the entire university is mutually beneficial. Genuine alumni involvement enables the university to be more inclusive and transformative places. Universities need to create the conditions for this alumni citizenship participation. We need to recognize and seize the opportunity to be active, lifelong alumni citizens.

The first step to securing alumni citizenship is to embrace it. Our challenge is to reflect on how to participate in this ecosystem. As with any ecosystem, without participation from one part – in this case alumni – it throws the entire system out of balance. Alumni are like bees to the university hive. We explore far away fields collecting pollen. We enable flowers and plants to pollinate, bloom, and thrive. As we return to the hive, we release our collective wisdom, to ensure the hive prospers, creating the nourishment for others – and for ourselves. Without the return of these alumni bees, the hive is merely a shell. As alumni, we are the key external connectors in the university biosphere.

Activity 4: Recognize the university is a city by engaging our alumni citizenship

Review your résumé or CV to ensure that you have fully embraced your alumni citizenship. Your university credentials are your passport to connect with others. Double check that the name of your university, college, department, and name of your degree are correct. Your alma mater may be your common connection with a prospective employer, an interviewer, or reviewer of postgraduate study applications.

If you kept a tally of your extra-curricular achievements as a student through a co-curricular record or transcript, well done. You can now draw from this list to provide concrete examples of your involvement on campus that form part of your experience. Using action verbs will allow you to specify and quantify your achievements. For example, coordinated ticket sales for three sold-out drama society productions. Be sure to add the details from any internships, job shadowing, or work placements along with any awards or scholarships.

Add a section for alma mater service to your résumé or CV, perhaps a sub-section of your community service. This will showcase your involvement as mentor, volunteer at student recruitment events, or member of a university committee. This shows prospective employers your commitment to an institution where you invested your time, energy, and resources. This service may also prove to be a talking point at an interview.

Alumni Action 5: Reflecting on our university story

Reflecting on our university story is the first step in adopting a growth mindset. It is a key component of learning and leadership. 'The hardest leaders to coach are those who won't reflect,' reports executive coach Jennifer Porter in the *Harvard Business Review*, 'particularly leaders who won't reflect on *themselves*'.[13] Each of us has our own unique university story. It's good to take time to process it, to reflect on what we learned, and to recapture our experience.[14] Our university story becomes a key learning signpost of our life journey. Reflection guru Donald Schön believes we should become the reflective practitioner of our own lives. To develop our future career, Schön argues that we need to reflect on our past and current position.[15] Applying Schön's reflection-on-action concept, we can explore questions like: What did I gain from my university experience? What would I do differently?[16] Our learning becomes central to our university story.

We are often telling and retelling our university story to others. We might adopt a cheerleading tone, excited to share the highlights. We might convey a bland, uninspiring story. Our university experience might conjure up feelings of sadness, bitterness, or anger. Reflection allows us to look deeper. We are central to our university story. We choose our reaction. Learning from experience is central to Dweck's growth mindset. We can take control of our own circumstances – our university experience – and own it. Since it's over now, we can decide how to extract learning from it too. Regardless of our university past, we can choose to maximize our alumni future.

This is also an opportunity to reflect on how we identify with our alma mater. Is it merely the school we attended? Did our time in university have a transformational effect on our lives? If so, it is worth thinking about *how* we changed following our university experience. Do you remember the idealism of applying to college or the nervousness of the first day at class? Reflection is a fundamental trait for life and leadership. It allows us to stop, take stock, and learn. The more we reflect, the more it becomes as a lifelong habit for all our life experiences. This is key for adopting a growth mindset, and for the Alumni Way journey. Here are some short reflections with the voices of alumni front and centre.

Laura Estrada Prada invited me to the American University of Rome (AUR) campus when she worked in alumni relations. An alum and her class valedictorian, Estrada Prada was passionate about her time studying fine arts in the eternal city. Originally from Colombia, Estrada Prada found the community feeling and warmth with an international group of people at AUR, which fostered her personal and professional growth. "As a student, as a staff member, as an alum, AUR's greatest gift to me was the people I met," she says. "The world *is* small when AUR is the common denominator." Years after my visit, Estrada Prada now has a role with the European Space Agency, as she explains: "Thanks to those relationships [at AUR] I found out about the job posting." She is grateful for the lessons in collaboration and connection she gained during her time at university that she takes with her throughout her life.

A double graduate from Monash University, Rufimy Khoo draws on her education in law and commerce for her career in the superannuation industry: 'Both degrees shaped me into an evidence-driven person with a curious mindset and helped me be an all-rounder. This has certainly helped me solve complex issues,' Khoo reflects. 'With my focus now on Responsible Investing and integration of ESG [Environment, Social, Governance], I am able to influence policy makers, companies and investors.'[17]

Following his elected positions on the students' council at the University of Toronto, Teo Salgado considered a role in government as a natural career progression. Salgado found himself searching for more from his career after graduation. He reflected on what he enjoyed about his university experience. 'Initially, I thought I enjoyed policymaking,' Salgado said when I interviewed him, "What I missed was connecting with students." Salgado spent more than a decade working for Canadian universities – including his alma mater – in strategic roles supporting students and alumni. When he founded VerveSmith Independent Education Consultants, this positioned him to draw on his interests and strengths that he first gained as a student. 'I enjoyed working with young people,' Salgado says,

'Now, I work with students with big aspirations to help them realize their goals. It's very rewarding work.'[18] There is more to learn about Salgado's story in the next section.

The energy from Maria Bonovich-Marvich's reflection of her time at Rhodes College leaps off the webpage. 'Rhodes was a bastion of opportunity for me,' Bonovich-Marvich explains. 'I joined the cross-country team, having never run on a cross-country team … It was a busy time but taught me that if I wanted to do it all, I needed to manage my time very efficiently.'[19] Now a patent analyst with the United States Patent and Trademark Office, Bonovich-Marvich shares her fondest memories of her time on campus. Along with remembering her favourite courses, Bonovich-Marvich attributes her passion for running and science-based research from her time at Rhodes. Alongside the qualities and skills she gained through her university experience, she reflects on the key life lesson she still draws on today: 'Anything and everything is possible if you put your mind to it!'[20]

'My two years as a student were enhanced by our cohort of students who became close, and in some cases, lifelong friends,' reflects Tabrina Clelland on her time studying public policy at Simon Fraser University. 'Now, years later,' she says, 'we've expanded into a fantastic network of supportive and well-connected policy professionals eager to see each other succeed.' Clelland also considered the way the skills she gained during her studies integrate into her daily practice: 'I learned how to approach, define, and deconstruct problems and action a rigorous process to make decisions, weigh trade-offs, and communicate recommendations. This skillset is tangible, actionable, and practical – and completely transferrable to a variety of career choices that require strategic thinking and decision making.'[21]

Shriharsh Chandak, an education graduate from Azim Premji University (APU), draws on his university experience in his current role working in the technology innovation software company Next Education: 'Looking back, I feel APU made me a more observant and reflective person,' Chandak explains. 'It built my mental stamina to take on complex situations or problems with an ease. It brought back compassion and sensitivity to me. Now, when I try to conceptualize or design any new products, these learnings help me to look things in much wider and holistic way.'[22]

Even in these short reflections, alumni present vivid stories. They highlight those small moments of inspiration that, to this day, have an impact on their lives. Those all-important work-ready and soft skills also appear in the reflections. Leadership, communication skills, and key attributes? These reflections are well seasoned with these qualities too. What links all these alumni voices together is the power of reflection. Taking the time to reflect is the growth mindset in action. These alumni connect their student learning to their lifelong story.

We can say the same about our own story. It can be a challenge to look back on university; it can feel like part of our distant past. What are those stand-out memories? Think of the inspiring lectures, a eureka moment in a lab, or even a marathon study session. How about the successful group project, a stellar presentation, or kind work placement mentor? Mapping out our alumni capital – those flows of people, knowledge, and resources from our student life might offer some insights too. Tune in to the qualities and attributes we gained outside the classroom. Think back to our volunteering, teams, sporting events, or activism. Our university learning included enquiry, experimentation, and exploration.

Activity 5: Recognize the university is a city by reflecting on our university story

Complete a short reflection by asking yourself the following question:

What did I learn about myself during my university journey?

Think of the qualities, lessons, skills, and knowledge you gained both inside and outside the classroom. This is a way to flex your growth mindset muscles. Ensure this reflection is both critical and constructive. The Alumni Capital diagram (Figure 2.1) from Chapter 2 might offer some inspiration. What did you love and what did you loathe about the experience? How does this contribute to learning more about yourself?

6

Reflection signpost: Advance ourselves as alumni citizens

We all want our career, our personal life, our wealth, and our health to improve, to *advance*. Yet the term advancement in a university setting has a different meaning. The university has internal structures responsible for promoting and enacting the strategic advancement of the institution, including alumni relations, communications, marketing, and development (fundraising).[1] These integrated functions create a comprehensive ecosystem to advance the mission and priorities of the university.[2] Advancement may extend to include the service by an alumni association or a philanthropic foundation.

After graduation, we are usually contacted first by an alumni or advancement office. Alumni relations happen in different ways in different institutions. It can be a sophisticated operation involving a suite of alumni relations staff and a robust database, or it may be a small staff team or alumni association of volunteers managing alumni contact. The common thread for all alumni relations is the desire to build, maintain, and support lifelong connections with us, as alumni. With thousands, or even hundreds of thousands of alumni, keeping in touch with each of us individually is a formidable task. Truthfully, it's an impossibility. With regular email updates, an alumni magazine, and event invitations, this tends to be a one-sided relationship. Our alma mater doing the work to keep *us* in touch.

Being a passive alumni citizen is comfortable. To advance ourselves, we need to become active. We need to become dynamic, alumni citizens. Sometimes, we position ourselves as the bystander of our lives. We watch things happen to us. We wait for opportunities to come to us. We respond to a university event or webinar invitation. Perhaps it's a reaction after years of our proactive position as a student. Pressure to step up and pass every exam or turn in assignments on time. It's easy now to sit back, diploma framed on the wall, and disengage. It's like watching television. This is a chance to shake out of the trance and explore advancement for ourselves and for the university too.

Alumni Action 6: Creating our alumni services wish list

In the past, connecting with fellow alumni was a cumbersome process. The university was the alumni gatekeeper. We needed to consult an alumni directory or request the university to send a postcard on our behalf to reconnect with a fellow alum. These methods of communications – not that long ago – seem like the ancient times now. 'Itching to get back in touch with your old flame from senior year?' asks Andrew Shaindlin now Vice-President of Alumni Relations at Brown University, 'A powerful online search means you'll scan Google, Facebook, and LinkedIn without wondering whether your alma mater will put you back in touch.'[3] This is a phenomenon called disintermediation.[4] The university is no longer the mediator between fellow alumni and us. Social media dominates, stripping the university of their gatekeeper status.

Cue the dramatic music. Don't worry, alumni relations is *not* in peril. The alumni relations sector continues to reinvent itself and remain relevant to us. Here lies our strategic opportunity. As one of the most crucial and strategic functions at the university, alumni relations has the potential to be a 'relationship broker',[5] Shaindlin argues. In this role as relationship broker, the university broadens our network. Alumni relations is the weaver of the university tapestry. We are the threads – alumni from different backgrounds, locations, and with different interests. Alumni engagement activities allow us to weave in our networks and relationships. This is alumni capital in action. Our challenge is to reconnect, as key university shareholders. We can become actively involved in shaping the alumni engagement, activities, and involvement of the future.

From the day after graduation, we have an array of alumni opportunities waiting for us. And what a buffet! For starters, there's the extended career services and the alumni publications. The main course consists of a delectable range of events: reunions and career-facing options. For dessert? We may find special retail discounts or preferential insurance rates as tasty options. The dessert cart might also include an affinity credit card, with a university photo or crest. These perks and much, much more are often available throughout our lives. Our alumni status provides us with many all-you-can-eat options. A quick visit to the alumni webpage allows us to discover these core alumni benefits for ourselves.

There is comfort in a tried and tested signature dish. The same is true for the traditional, annual alumni events: homecoming, sporting events, or reunions, even annual seminars. These events are popular, if not predictable. They play on our wistful longing for our past lives as students. At the same time, nostalgia is often not enough to compel us to attend an annual event. We tend to seek a purpose, a call to action, or even a sense of urgency.[6] 'If the event is exciting or inspiring enough, that may become part of a collective experience of repeat attendance,' says Jon Horowitz, a seasoned alumni professional and strategist, 'If the event is boring, uninspiring, or worse, that may also have a powerful impact on subsequent attendance decisions.'[7] Giving our time to an alumni event is our investment to ourselves and for the university. It's the 'what's in it for me' factor. We consider the cost-benefit of attending alumni events. We scan the online RSVPs, or check the bios of the key speakers, to see if the event will be insightful and strategic (and fun!).

Tempted to go off-menu? Universities are always coming up with innovative, new programming and initiatives to involve its wider community, including alumni. In the advent of social media, we have educated our palettes for more online and virtual connection. Our universities are responding too, with webinars, virtual lectures, and even online alumni communities. These online communities are open to all alumni (and usually students too). It's easy to register, we can migrate our current social media profile onto these university-curated alumni platforms. Voila! An enriching alumni directory at our fingertips. We can often filter the list of fellow alumni by location, employment sector, year of graduation, even job title. In the next section we discuss the massive potential of these networks, suffice to say here, by registering, we are signalling our interest in learning more and staying connected.

An online format eliminates so many of the social conventions of exchanging business cards or bumping into someone at the buffet. However, there are immense advantages to an online model of alumni events. Online connection has become more intimate in its approach with breakout rooms and chats. Most importantly, it has levelled the playing field for alumni event participation. Now alumni from around the world can participate from their device – the flexibility to engage with or without caring responsibilities or free from a commute to campus.

We certainly aren't going to eat the same dish day in, day out. The same goes for our choices in alumni activities year after year. While our identities shift throughout our lives, so does the alumni programming that appeals to us. As a new graduate, for instance, the career-focused networking mixers or mentorship programmes might be our priority. As a parent, I find the online baking demonstrations and virtual family scavenger hunts are getting my registrations first. Menus change, as do our tastes, so keep checking – the perfect event could be around the corner!

Activity 6: Advance ourselves as alumni citizens by creating our alumni services wish list

Take a piece of paper and draw a line down the middle, creating two columns. Think back to what you learned earlier in the section about the university as a city. Think of all the services, programmes, and initiatives you feel the university might have that are of interest to you based on your current circumstances. Consult the University is a City diagram (Figure 5.1) and the Alumni Capital diagram (Figure 2.1) for some more ideas. Devise an ideal wish list – be creative!

Next, on the right side, take a few minutes to visit your alma mater's alumni website. Make a list of some of the current services available to alumni. It might be an exhaustive list or a paltry one, depending on the institution. Compare the two lists and make a tick beside the services that match. Put a star against the key service you *hoped* was available from the left side of your list. Contact the alumni office to see if this benefit or service might be available to you through a referral to another university office. Begin the process of signing up or registering for the services, programmes, or events that interest you the most. Put a double star on the services on the right side of the list that you didn't think of, but now will keep an eye on for future engagement.

Be realistic and flexible. Some of these ideal alumni services might not be available because of the limits to university resources or wider appeal to the alumni community. You might consider getting involved, to start the work on some of these 'wish list' initiatives yourself. Be an alumni trailblazer!

Alumni Action 7: Recognizing our global alumni passport

I live over 3,000 kilometres away from my original alma mater – eight time zones away from another. My closest alma mater is a three-hour drive from my home. We might have this in common. For others, the university might be on the doorstep. Proximity to campus gives the Alumni Way a different perspective. It's easy to pop over to campus for a farmers' market, exercise class, or concert. If we are at a distance from our alma mater, perhaps there is another institution offering interesting services near to home? Virtual campus activities and events have certainly made the campuses closer for all of us. As alumni, we are a global community with a shared place in common – a special diaspora connection.

When we spend time somewhere, we leave our imprint on that place. We become a member of a city, country, or regional diaspora. We are a member of the diaspora from our original place of origin and our place of birth too. I use the term diaspora with some hesitation, as I am aware of the contentious nature of stretching its definition. Traditionally, diaspora refers to 'the dispersal of a people from its original homeland'.[8] Permit me some latitude in the boundaries of the term diaspora,[9] when describing affinity diaspora like alumni. In this book, I apply the use of alumni as diaspora as an anchor for our multitude of communities. By virtue of our alumni status, we are also connected to the countries, cities, states, or regions where we spent time during our studies.

A university is a diaspora haven. We bring our diaspora spirit with us from other places to the university. This creates the diverse learning environment so many universities promote in their marketing materials. Most importantly, universities are the hubs of diaspora activity, from language learning to cultural student societies. As students, we shared our diaspora connections and our identities. After leaving university, we are dispersed again, often scattered across a city, region, and beyond.

The life that lies ahead post-university might include our move to a new city, region, country, or even continent. When we head to New York, or Beijing, or Buenos Aires, our alma mater may already be there. Universities operate international branch campuses and global centres in strategic locations around the world. This is a local connection for us to match our alma mater's global ambition. The university might have an alumni representative to give us one more person to meet in our city or country too. A person who, at least, has had a shared experience to us. There might be an alumni chapter or branch group to join in the area. 'One of the first things I looked up when I got to Paris was if the city had a University of Edinburgh alumni group – it did,' explains Business School graduate Orestis Brentas, 'The alumni network made me feel part of a special group, in a place where I knew nobody.'[10] Brentas attended nights out and golfing outings, which helped solidify his network. Even if we aren't a business graduate or golf enthusiast, we can seek out fellow alumni in places we visit and places we live. This expands our networks locally and globally.

Don't underestimate that sense of identity from a semester abroad or an exchange programme. Our time away can be a fundamental part of our learning experience. This is the expansive nature of our alumni status: we may feel as much affinity for the university where we spent four months on exchange, as the one that gave us our degree. If so, reconnect with this exchange university too. Going on exchange tends to be an immersive experience with special memories.

Earlier in the book, we met Julia Morrow, who left the United States to study in Ireland. She describes her experience as an international graduate moving back home: "When I moved back to DC after my undergraduate studies", Morrow says, "I reached out to the alumni chapter of Trinity in DC." Morrow established a monthly happy hour for alumni: "These are people who I have something in common with, they are a way for me to keep up my Irish connection for networking, jobs and just general social life. I wanted to do something, and I saw this as a group of people I could reach out to." Although Morrow only stayed in DC a short time, her energy for organizing events created the momentum to sustain this alumni community. These regional chapters and branches at our universities offer us a group to join, events to attend, and instant network at our fingertips. In big cities like New York, Shanghai, or London, meeting new people can be a challenge. Alumni WeChat or WhatsApp messaging groups abound in alumni circles. These message groups share career information and arrange social events for alumni in the area.

North Carolina-based Campbell University introduced the 'Welcome to the City' initiative, based in six cities across the south-eastern United States. As Campbell young alumni and recent graduates settle in a new place, they have a conduit to reconnect with former classmates or expand their Campbell network.[11] 'I didn't realize how many connections I had with alumni I hadn't met before, whether it was working for the same company or sharing mutual friends,' explains Katherine Fullwood a recent Campbell graduate. 'Welcome to the City allowed me to rekindle friendships, make new connections, and share stories of my time at Campbell with those who love Campbell just as much.'[12] Even without a formal programme, a quick search might unearth some fellow alumni to contact in your new hometown. The search might take five minutes on the alumni webpage, the university's online alumni community platform or even on LinkedIn. Take another five minutes to reach out with a personal message and watch the alumni magic unfold!

If we're going global, we might as well go big. 'All-alumni' events in large cities are common, such as the 'all-Canadian' alumni events in London open to alumni from any university in Canada. Online global alumni networks, coordinated by national governments, also entice us to reconnect. This just adds more people to our broad alumni capital network. For instance, the Netherlands (NL) Alumni Network links people from around the world who studied in the Netherlands. With over 70,000 alumni signed up to their online community, the NL Alumni Network organizes events worldwide. One of the most popular is the pre-departure events for new international students about to travel to the Netherlands to study. These new students receive advice and information from alumni on their experience, as they were once in their shoes.[13] Coordinated by Nuffic, the Dutch organization for internationalization in education, the NL Alumni Network promotes the value of a Dutch education to the next generation of students about study in the Netherlands. The NL alumni are the ambassadors of the power of their Dutch qualification around the world. Australia, France, Hungary, Germany, and other countries have similar national alumni initiatives to coordinate international efforts – open to our connection.[14]

Where can international graduates turn for career advice if they decide to stay to work in their country of study? This is the question Sandra Rincón, a global alumni specialist, asked herself when she reflected on the support offered to international graduates in the Netherlands. She approached Nuffic with her idea, to mirror the NL Alumni Network on home soil. 'Our research identified international graduates' top resources requests,' Rincón explains, 'career advice; job and internship opportunities; and information on Dutch taxes, and business culture'.[15] The NL Alumni Network-The Netherlands (NLAn-NL) was established shortly after to offer an alumni volunteer-led network to support these international graduates. 'Alumni expressed interest in offering professional knowledge, giving guidance on study and working in the Netherlands and organizing network and career events,'[16] says Sandra Rincón, now the president of NLAn-NL. Even if we didn't study or stay in the Netherlands, we can draw from this example our own ambitions to connect with others who had a shared experience. With macro-networks, all-alumni events, even scholarship programme alumni networks are potential avenues to meet new people. They expand our professional development and networking acumen too.

Activity 7: Advance ourselves as active alumni citizens by recognizing our global alumni passport

Visit the alumni website to identify the alumni chapters in your region and around the world. Make a special note if a location is somewhere you plan to visit or a place you hope to move to in the future. If you went on a study abroad or exchange programme, reconnect with this host university too. This reminds you of the breadth of your connections worldwide. Be sure to look for any 'all-country alumni' groups or national networks to join too.

Share this tip with your former classmates and friends looking to expand their own global networks.

Alumni Action 8: Updating our alumni record

Let's face it. We've all been tainted by the alumni grinch. It's our unconscious bias telling us to slip away from university life without a trace. 'They only want your money,' our inner voice tells us. We forgo all the possibilities and opportunities for fear of a fundraising ask. Following extravagant buffets and our jet-setting lifestyle, this alumni action returns to the basics. Reflecting on our university experience first implies that the university can reach *us* and we can reach *them*. We need this basic conduit for our alma mater relationship.

It starts with the tale of two databases: the student and alumni systems. Our student record includes our contact details, degree studied, and extra-curricular involvement. In North American institutions, our individual alumni record is often a transfer of our basic student record. In other places, we may need to opt-in to the alumni database, providing our contact and degree details.

Here's some of the fine print up front. These databases adhere to the local data protection laws and university data policies. Universities do not sell or share their lists to third parties. These university databases are very secure, sophisticated customer relationship management systems (CRMs) with limited access to designated university personnel.

What does our individual alumni record say about each of us? We have the right, in most universities, to view our full alumni record and all the information stored about us. The general rule of thumb is that information on our record includes the things that the university would be happy to let us read. The Principles of Practice for Alumni Relations Professionals at Educational Institutions governed by the international association for advancement professionals CASE (Council for Advancement and Support of Education) states as one of its principles: 'Ensure information provided by alumni is always handled in a professional and confidential manner.'[17] We can rest assured our institutions abide by these principles.

Now here are some of the fascinating mechanics (at least fascinating to me!). When we receive an alumni magazine or attend an event, these are tagged on our record. These tags begin to create a profile of our engagement with the university. If our parents or children also graduated from the same institution, sometimes these connections feature on our record too. Our social media activities connected to university content – our likes and shares – might also be noted on our record. Our giving patterns to the university – giving to a fundraising appeal or acting as a mentor – form part of our record. Our profile clearly shows our deep affinity for the institution or a fuzzier picture of a passive alumni recipient of university content. The segmentation possibilities of the database are endless – by graduation year, degree, location, donor status – slicing and dicing the information into digestible strategic pieces.

We have immense power over the type of contact we can receive from the university, too. We can go all-in and receive everything: mailings, magazines, event invitations, and solicitations. Not interested in getting a fundraising ask at the moment? Request a 'do not solicit' code on your record. Rather not get snail mail? Opt-in to receive only electronic contact from the university by email.

In Europe, the General Data Protection Regulation (GDPR) means we need to opt-in to receive alumni information from the university. Universities attempt to sign us up right before or at graduation. Even if you sidestepped this sign-up at graduation, it's not too late. The university *wants* to keep in contact with us. Without this basic connection, we sever a strategic tie in our life. If the university can help *us* enhance our lives and support our communities – we miss out by not opting in. Information gives us choice. We decide what information is valuable for our purposes. Many of us become lost: alumni citizens-at-large.

As we move through life, it's easy to slip into the 'lost alumni' group: the university has no contact details, no address, no number, no email. A disconnection. When we haven't heard from our alma mater – no magazine, no emails, no event invitations – this might be us. Or we could be an alum I call 'lost in time'. The university can still contact us, but it's at our family address, not our everyday home. When we visit every so often, a neat stack of alumni magazines and letters wait for us in our old room.

The university spends a great deal of creativity to minimize the lost alumni effect. I have visited many an alumni office with stacks of alumni magazines in the corner. Marked 'return to sender', these magazines destined for alumni now lost. Bounce back emails are the online equivalent. Universities are trying cost-effective ways to combat this returned magazine tower. Columbia University circulates their magazine via email only.[18] *The Irish Times* national newspaper distributed alumni magazines for University College Dublin.[19] University of Limerick offers a comprehensive online edition of their magazine.[20] Other universities have resorted to creative means to track down lost alumni. For the University of New Brunswick, it was a social media campaign featuring Freddy John. This quirky cartoon UNB alumni ambassador travelled the world searching for lost alumni. Through fun messaging and cash prizes, UNB re-engaged with over 6,000 alumni from 90 countries in less than a year.[21]

Putting in even the minimal effort – updating our contact details – puts us in the driver's seat. We have all the university opportunities and ideas, for our discerning review. When we follow the university's social media channels, we can scroll through the daily insights, too. This preparation allows us to see new possibilities. Dweck reminds us how even small, growth-minded activities lead to mastery: 'Effort is what ignites that ability and turns it into accomplishment.'[22]

When we make a conscious effort to keep the communication with our university open, this creates a two-way sharing of information, too. We can use our university's hashtag to share our good news: a promotion, or new start-up business. Don't discount the power of class notes either. Even with social media, class notes remain a popular feature in alumni publications and in online alumni communities. Bestselling author Dorie Clark, a self-invention strategist, agrees on the importance of alumni class notes. She advocates for once in a while including our own update: 'It provides an easy opportunity for existing contacts with whom you've fallen out of touch – so-called "dormant ties" – to reach out again.' Clark says. 'These connections can be quite powerful, because you have the sense of familiarity and trust born of a long history, but your careers may have taken unexpected directions that have suddenly become relevant.'[23] This brings alumni identity to the front and centre again: the more we review and share, the more we can find the people and opportunities relevant to our circumstances *right now*.

There's the alumni network too. 'You're now part of a proud community of alumni who dream big,' states the *University of Waterloo Handbook for New Graduates*, 'Chart unconventional paths, embrace innovation, and inspire others through their actions. Welcome to the Alumni Club. We're glad you joined us!'[24] Universities, like Waterloo, make special efforts to inform their newest alumni, described as GOLDs (Graduates of the Last Decade), of the benefits of the lifelong connection. Joining means our connection. We certainly don't know all our fellow year graduates or fellow GOLDs. Most of our fellow alumni are weak ties. In the 1970s, Mark Granovetter never imagined the relevance of his article 'The Strength of Weak Ties' to the world of alumni. He described how our acquaintances, or those with a weak connection to us, are often our gateway to enhancing our social networks.[25] Weak ties are the game changers. Our alma mater offers us endless potential for connection to weak ties. The magic begins when we share our updates, join our alma mater's online community, or update our contact details for our alumni record.

Activity 8: Advance ourselves as active alumni citizens by updating our alumni record

Time to update! Does your alma mater have your most up-to-date contact details? Find the address update section of the alumni webpage or email your alumni office. Be sure your message includes your full name, year of graduation and degree (so they can find you on the database). An alumni update form might ask for a lot of information, such as your current employment details. You can decide how much or how little information you wish to provide to the university. Include your social media handles if prompted too. You can also select your preference for contact by the university – by post/mail, by email, or both. Don't forget to update your contact information when you move or change your email address.

7

Reflection trait summary: Alum from Day One, revisited

An 'Alum from Day One' strategy permeates across the University of New South Wales Business School in Australia. The school constantly reminds its 80,000-plus alumni that they are part of a cohesive network. 'By participating in student and academic life you are actively shaping the culture, values and traditions of the Business School,' explains the webpage dedicated to Alum from Day One. 'This makes you an integral part of the UNSW Business School and alumni communities. Your involvement, engagement, and commitment are the hallmarks of being an alum from day one.'[1] The school's programming for students and alumni reinforce the reflective, supportive culture. Structured mentorship, alumni-led business case studies, and industry-focused networking events are available in Sydney and across the globe. What makes this case unique? The school coordinates its programming from this core belief of Alum from Day One. We can all create our own Alum from Day One thinking, as new or seasoned alumni. *This* is our Day One. We can start over. We can reflect on our past and how our evolving alumni capital can affect our future.

Reflection is a continuous process of self-awareness and personal alignment. While both time-consuming and challenging, reflection leads to immense returns. 'The process of personal alignment may begin with the commencement speaker who urges you to reflect on the advantages you've been given and how you will apply them in the years ahead,' explains Jay Lorsch and Thomas Tierney in their book *Aligning the Stars*. 'But if it stops there, you're in trouble because the challenge of leading a fulfilling life lies in consistent attention to your own priorities.'[2] Hyperawareness of alumni opportunities allows us to keep an eye on the prize – our key priorities – and view the university in a more strategic way. This book challenges us to reinvent our relationship with our alma mater from strangers to life partners.[3]

An alumni speaker in class, a welcome BBQ organized by the alumni association, 'Class of' paraphernalia – not all 'Alum from Day One' strategies are obvious. The sentiment is the same: our *alma mater* wishes to keep in touch from the moment we step onto campus until well after our graduation day. From day one, we hold multiple identities *with* the university. We are informal ambassadors, mentors, recruiters, critics, governors, innovators, learners, even teachers. We can enrich the campus and ourselves. We can graduate from our alma mater with our alumni citizenship.

Key messages from Part II

- We are an Alum from Day One. We have a stake in the reputation of our alma mater for life.
- Universities have all the amenities and opportunities of a city. We are lifelong alumni citizens of the campus and the worldwide university network.
- Learning percolates to the surface when we reflect on our university experience and our alumni potential.
- Be found: keep contact details up to date with the university.
- Become a savvy, informed alum, who views the university as a lifelong investment. This is not a passive activity; to make a return on our investment, filter the noise. Focus on the opportunities that match current life identities (eg parent, career novice, volunteer).

Disengaged alumni with the fixed mindset will:

- close themselves off from learning about the university as a lifelong resource;
- reflect on their university experiences in a negative way, laying blame on others or the university for the experience;
- gain limited learning in the process of reflecting on their university experience;
- not identify themselves as an alum or see value in holding this lifelong identity;
- remain lost and choose not to update their contact information with the university;
- view their university experience as something in the past, not the future.

Dynamic alumni with the growth mindset will:

- consider themselves alumni from the moment they start studying, through graduation and beyond;
- reflect on their university experience – positive and negative – as a learning experience;
- identify all their current life identities, including as an alum; be open to how the university can support their most important identities today;
- reframe their thinking to consider the university as a lifelong resource;
- see the value in keeping contact details up to date with their alma mater;
- be open to receiving university information that may be insightful and useful.

Checklist for Part II

To build your Alumni Way, especially your ability for reflection, don't forget to:

- ☐ check your CV/résumé for the correct alma mater details. (see Activity 4);

☐ add your university experiences to your CV/résumé using action verbs (see Activity 4);

☐ start building your own university story with a short reflection (see Activity 5);

☐ become familiar with the alumni services at your alma mater (see Activity 6);

☐ locate the worldwide alumni chapters or branches that might be of interest to you (see Activity 7);

☐ update your contact details with your alma mater (see Activity 8).

Building the Alumni Way: Questions following Part II

- *Recent graduates and alumni*: What are my key identities from my time at university? What are my current life identities as an alum?
- *Students*: How can I become more aware about alumni programming and think about being an Alum from Day One?
- *University administrators*: How can I create an Alum from Day One strategy across the institution that is mutually beneficial for the university and for alumni? Do we have alumni involved in meaningful governance and leadership activity in the institution?
- *Advancement Professionals*: How can I directly involve alumni in developing alumni services and programming to become co-creators in this work?
- *Parents/career advisers*: How can I communicate and encourage students and recent alumni to see the benefit of keeping in touch with their alma mater throughout their life?

PART III

The Alumni Way trait: Curiosity

8	Our career, our alumni capital, and our curiosity	65
9	Curiosity signpost: Build our alumni hypernetwork	69
	• Alumni Action 9: Mining our alumni capital	71
	• Alumni Action 10: Assembling career stories	75
	• Alumni Action 11: Learning about earning on campus	80
	• Alumni Action 12: Sharing our good news	84
10	Curiosity signpost: Leverage alumni capital for business	89
	• Alumni Action 13: Remembering the university is a city – and a potential client	90
11	Curiosity trait summary: Shining a light	97
	• Key messages from Part III	98
	• Checklist for Part III	100
	• Building the Alumni Way: Questions following Part III	100

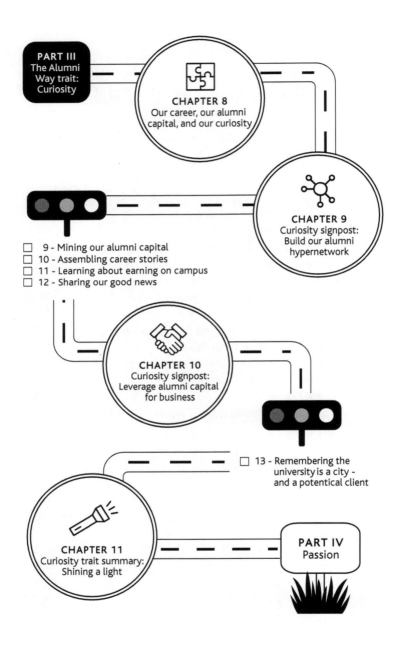

PART III
The Alumni Way trait:
Curiosity

CHAPTER 8
Our career, our alumni capital, and our curiosity

CHAPTER 9
Curiosity signpost:
Build our alumni hypernetwork

☐ 9 - Mining our alumni capital
☐ 10 - Assembling career stories
☐ 11 - Learning about earning on campus
☐ 12 - Sharing our good news

CHAPTER 10
Curiosity signpost:
Leverage alumni capital for business

☐ 13 - Remembering the university is a city - and a potential client

CHAPTER 11
Curiosity trait summary:
Shining a light

PART IV
Passion

8

Our career, our alumni capital, and our curiosity

We all have those moments of serendipity. An informal chat that leads to a job interview. A career mentor from a chance meeting in the corridor. My key moment of serendipity was my job-shadowing placement during spring break. When I opened the envelope to reveal my placement, my heart sank. My assignment: the university's public affairs department, not a big downtown corporate. As a student who was ultra-involved in the campus community, it was a logical match for me. The serendipity from week-long placement led to so many of my lifelong connections. It was also the catalyst for my career in higher education advancement.

Serendipity is not the work of fairies. The phenomenon is what researchers call *planned happenstance*. A theory developed by psychologist John Krumboltz, planned happenstance is orchestrating events and opportunities *for ourselves*. This is also our ability to take strategic action once we are there. 'Serendipity is not merely waiting for a fortuitous event to happen,' Krumboltz explains, 'Serendipity requires action on the part of the recipient – action to create favourable circumstances, action to recognize opportunities when they arise, and action to capitalize on unplanned events in a timely manner.'[1] This is more than being at the right place at the right time – or good luck. Planned happenstance is creating the conditions for serendipity. We put ourselves out there. We become visible. We are the conductors of our lives. We don't 'meander through experiences initiated by others while passively awaiting a "knock on the door"'.[2] This section examines how our alumni capital sparks our curiosity. A curiosity that allows us to create serendipitous moments in our professional lives.

To identify, build, and sustain our career, we need a curious mind. We recognize that healthy choices lead to peak physical fitness. For the mind, this exercise is curiosity. As educationalist John Dewey says of curiosity, we must be 'constantly alert and exploring, seeking material for thought'.[3] We can seek this nourishment through our alumni capital. 'The truly curious will be increasingly in demand,' says Ian Leslie, author of *Curious: The Desire to Know and Why Our Future Depends on It*. 'Employers are looking for people who can do more than follow procedures competently or respond to requests, who have a strong intrinsic desire to learn, solve problems and ask penetrating questions.'[4] Where is a natural place to start or practise curiosity? Our university. First, switch to constant learning mode, Carol Dweck reminds us, fostering our growth mindset.

What about the glimmer of hope that our degree is our all-access pass to a successful career? Don't be fooled, that's the fixed mindset creeping in. Resting on our degree laurels is a dangerous ticket to the game of comparing our success to others. A front row seat to a false sense of entitlement. A half-time show of sidestepping challenges. One diploma, representing our knowledge, skills, and competences, extends us only so far.

No longer the spectators of the game, we are the athletes. Our new exercise regime? Our ability to be suitable for paid employment after graduation. Employability is the new star coach of the degree game. Universities want to help us to become and be employable. They put us through our paces with career services, job shadowing, and work placements at play. The game requires our mental stamina too. This is our employability equipment including critical thinking, problem solving, and character-building experiences. The subject specific knowledge from our degree might get us on the field to certain career paths. Prospective employers are looking for more. We need to know how to play the game.

The wider university experience *is* a game. A place of wider discovery. As athletes, we didn't confine our learning to the basic rules and drills of the degree. For our game analogy, it's the finesse, the intuition, the drive to become the best players possible. In life, these skills include our flexibility, our adaptability, and our ability to take initiative. They involve our effective work within diverse teams and our leadership. This is the New Learning Paradigm. Charles Kivunja described this New Learning Paradigm as our wider career and life skills.[5] The university's challenge? Integrate this New Learning Paradigm into course curriculum and extra-curricular activities. It's a bigger challenge for us to then extract these qualities throughout our alumni lives. For the rest of our lives, it's game time. Our time to step up and score big. That's where curiosity comes in. Suffice to say, our curiosity helps us to build a career, start a business, follow a vocation, or forge a meaningful life path.

In his book *21 Lessons for the 21st Century*, Yuval Noah Harari presents a future focused on the growth mindset, including resilience. Harari argues to keep up with the rapid pace of change, we need to be open to learning new things and embrace the unfamiliar. 'You will need not merely invent new ideas and products,' he explained, 'you will above all need to reinvent yourself again and again.'[6] Harari views education as preparation for lifelong change in our lives. The change that comes from the world around us. The COVID-19 pandemic seismically altered the way we interacted with people, shifting almost exclusively online. We needed to adapt and become flexible. Most importantly, we begin to ask inquisitive questions. How is connecting online supporting the sustainability of our planet? Do we really need long commutes and frequent corporate travel?

Movements like #blacklivesmatter and #metoo, open the dialogue on systemic racism and sexual harassment. They call on us to be the change needed across our institutions, our workplaces, and our communities. On our Alumni Way journey, curiosity is our guide, fostering our global competences. The OECD presents a framework for global competence defined as:

- the capacity to examine local, global, and intercultural issues;
- to understand and appreciate the perspectives and world views of others;
- to engage in open, appropriate, and effective interactions with people from different cultures; and
- to act for collective well-being and sustainable development.[7]

Intercultural dialogue, sustainable development, equitable societies? This requires our deep learning to be the actors for change. This is not a tick box exercise demonstrating a competency achieved. As active alumni citizens with curious minds, we can build our knowledge arsenal, our humility, and our understanding. We can listen to how these critical issues impact our lives. This next part of the book focuses on activities for listening, a key component of the trait of curiosity.

9

Curiosity signpost: Build our alumni hypernetwork

From the moment we graduate, we begin a race. We scramble to get ahead, secure our first job, our first promotion. Training for this race begins earlier and earlier. Internships, work placements, job shadowing, and mentorship options abound, all before graduation. These options may have factored during our studies. Sociologist Phillip Brown describes this as the 'opportunity trap': 'Middle-class families are adopting more desperate measures to win a positional advantage,' Brown argues, 'They are having to run faster, for longer, just to stand still. Yet if all adopt the same tactics, nobody gets ahead. This is the *opportunity trap* as few can afford to opt out of the competition for a livelihood.'[1] Another sociologist, Pierre Bourdieu, calls this 'playing the game'.[2]

In the last chapter, I presented an extended game analogy. In this chapter, we take it one step further to include our alumni capital. Some of us didn't even get the chance to enter the competition. Many of us had work or family caring responsibilities during our studies. Ironically, this left less time to prepare for life after graduation. Maybe we were first in our family to go to university. Or the first person in our friend group to go abroad for university. Or even the first person we know in our community to study a subject. It's not only playing the game but also 'knowing the game to play'.[3] This book offers a clear response: our advantage is our alumni hypernetwork. This network is *hyper* as the breadth is so wide, the depth so deep. If, suddenly, all alumni discovered their alumni capital, there is plenty to go around. Our network of alumni opens our world to so many other networks too.

When we met, Jessie Cripton set a clear agenda. We connected on the University of Toronto's online community platform. Through sophisticated algorithms, the platform makes student-alumni or alumni-alumni matches. If the matches agree, they can arrange a short meet-up. Cripton recognized, even as a student, the value in connecting with as many alumni as possible. She was first in her family to attend university and wanted to broaden her network. As Bourdieu points out: 'Whoever wants to win this game, appropriate the stakes, catch the ball ... must have a feel for the game, that is, a feel for the necessity and the logic of the game.'[4] A lively discussion ensued between us over my first-ever cold brew. She talked about her university experience. I navigated her through my career path. I responded to her prepared, inquisitive questions. I was curious too. Cripton was candid about her juggling act. She wanted to maximize her university experience balanced with work and family life. In just 20 minutes, we had both learned more about the value of alumni citizenship.

Alumni should no longer be synonymous with elitism, an exclusive old boys' club. Alumni networks are *inclusive*; they involve everyone with the same shared experience. Alumni provide us with insider links to organizations, companies, expertise, professionals, and creatives in our community. Fellow alumni are everywhere. We can change the game played. We can decide *not* to compete in the race. We may have the same degree, but building our network gives us the edge. This alumni hypernetwork helps others to do the same too.

The hypernetwork idea challenges the comforts of our small circle of friends. This is *homophily*. A phenomenon best understood with the saying 'birds of a feather, flock together'. Homophily can occur across race, ethnicity, religion, gender, age, or even by occupation and location.[5] Engaging with our alumni network diversifies our perspectives and our ideas. All with a common link: our alma mater. Imagine the creativity unleashed with normally uncommon mashups. How about an alum with a tech background connects with a fine arts graduate? Or the lively debates when a millennial recent graduate meets a baby boomer alum to discuss online marketing strategies? This network adds richness to our lives. Our alumni citizenship links us to valuable contacts, referrals, and career advice.[6]

These are the weak or even dormant ties in our lives. Don't dismiss them; they can contribute to launching and developing our career. David Burkus, in his bestselling book *Friend of a Friend*, modernizes Marc Granovetter's research on 'the strength of weak ties'. Burkus calls this 'the forgotten network'.[7] He argues that acquaintances or distant connections can be very valuable – even more valuable than close friends – to support our career trajectory.[8] 'Weak ties are irregular contacts precisely because they tend to operate in different social circles,' Burkus argues. 'As a result, *weak ties become our best source for the new information that we need to resolve our dilemmas*.'[9] Our alumni capital is our bridge to this diversity. By extension, our alumni hypernetwork is the place to connect to this diversity and develop our curiosity.

Alumni Action 9: Mining our alumni capital

Imagine we are prospect miners, hopeful for the discovery of precious gems. The mine is our alumni capital. With time and gruelling hard work, we can extract those brilliant career nuggets. Surveying the surface of the mine will yield little treasure. This work requires our concentrated effort, building our growth mindset. Mining *is* networking. This is a sustainable form of mining too, one that can promote growth for you and for those in your network. These connections, especially in our hypernetworked world, never leave us. We need to become and remain curious to the potential of our alumni capital to enhance our career. Our degree doesn't prepare us for independence, but *interdependence*. We must embrace collaboration, partnerships, and teamwork, fostering our potential for effective leadership.[10]

Amassing followers on social media is a useful *first* step in developing our alumni network. A balance between 'High Tech, High Touch' is the ideal. Technology is only a *tool* to forge meaningful human relationships and genuine connection.[11]

Communications and career strategist Mac Prichard reminds us: 'If you are networking correctly, you are in the relationship business. Spend time sowing seeds of genuine connection, and you will ultimately reap the rewards of mutual assistance.'[12] The key is *mutual* benefits. We contact a seasoned alum to learn about their leadership success. At the same time, we mentor a current student as they complete their studies. This is the healthy equilibrium of paying it forward. This generosity with our time is another key trait of the Alumni Way discussed in Part V.

"My goal is to meet ten people I've never met before,"[13] explained Tina Gourley, Director of Volunteer Programs at Cornell University. This is a formidable but achievable challenge at the annual Cornell Alumni Leadership Conference. Alumni networking is central to the two-day event. Alongside leadership training and inspirational alumni speakers, alumni meet – serendipitously – over their shared affinity for their alma mater.[14] Networking opportunities like this are common at universities worldwide. Many traditional reunion events are now infused with career-facing elements. Some universities even offer the attendee list in advance. We can plan fellow alumni we would like to meet in advance. Our prospect mining for planned happenstance in action. Be warned; this approach may dash any excitement of meeting an excellent contact entirely by chance.

Our alumni relations or career services offices usually offer the first introduction to our alumni network. Alumni made an appearance at résumé or CV writing clinics, workshops on personal branding, and career case studies. Keep on the lookout for university emails and social media posts brimming with career-focused learning too. No longer should we scroll past these opportunities in our newsfeed.

'Alumni Networks Less Helpful Than Advertised,'[15] reads one provocative headline. *Forbes* online reports: 'Alumni Networks and the Job Market: Help or Hindrance?'[16] Are alumni networks *really* effective? My response is a resounding yes! To take advantage of our alumni network, we need to be proactive, *become curious*. This isn't an instant process. This could be why an alumni network doesn't *seem* worthwhile.

Does the alumni network still seem daunting? Where do we start? After our early mining on the dedicated alumni page of our alma mater, it's time to delve deeper. How are alumni organized? Some universities support online communities, a separate platform for alumni interactions. Others use existing social media sites like LinkedIn. Still others use integrated communications platforms like Slack, WeChat, or WhatsApp to connect alumni. The evolution of these social media and online platforms continues. Our curiosity should remain; sign up or follow these platforms. Filter the registered alumni by location, by career sector, even by employer.

Sometimes the university completes this filtering for us through professional networks, career communities, affinity groups, and identity groups. Colgate University offers a good overview of the potential of these segmented networks: 'Whether your goal is to expand your own professional network, hear from leaders in your field, explore new industries, engage in cutting-edge conversations, discover employment options, or seek expert opinions, Colgate faithful around the world are ready to connect with you.'[17]

We aren't all Colgate alumni. The sentiment still rings true. This pushes our thinking on the power of our networks. These groups – sometimes called career communities or affinity groups – can be as broad as a 'health and wellness network' or as narrow as an 'entertainment industry group'. Identity groups, such as alumni of colour, multicultural or LGBTQ+ groups are another avenue of connection. These specific networking groups are not available at every alma mater. We can take the lead to start a specialized network with the support from the alumni relations or career services office. Let our curiosity lead our network expansion!

So many places are vying for our attention. My favourite strategy to be intentional about alumni mining is to block out time for this important work. I call it Alumni Fridays. The last Friday of each month, I block out 30 minutes to an hour to be an alumni sleuth. I like to see what's new and available on my alumni website. I follow up with interesting fellow alumni I read about in the alumni magazine. I make notes on key alumni I would like to meet and reach out to on LinkedIn or online communities.

What could an Alumni Friday, an hour each month – or even each week – uncover in potential magic moments?

Imagine we approached all the communication from our alma mater with curiosity. The alumni magazine. The email invitation. The social media post. Think about its value for our lives. It might have little value to us, but we might share, tag, or forward the opportunity to someone else, who might benefit. The transactional passive nature of these communications become active and transformational. If we are reflective and curious about our alma mater, we can uncover a gem!

Activity 9: Build our alumni hypernetwork by mining our alumni capital

First, to mine your alumni capital, you need to excavate. Dig deep and create the conditions for effective mining. Connect or follow your alma mater through your favourite social media channels. Be sure to check for separate identities on social media such as career services, alumni, your college, departments, clubs, or sports. Follow these social media channels too.

Second, create a profile on your alumni online community or career community. To speed up the process, these sites often allow you to migrate your existing social media profile. Spend a few minutes navigating the site. Check for features that showcase the alumni in your city or country. Spend time filtering alumni profiles by degree, by graduating year or even by professional industry. These searches may yield some interesting alumni to contact (or old friends – weak ties!). Make a note, don't reach out yet. Finally, set your notifications. Ensure you receive alerts for the most relevant content for you. Be sure to opt-in for the regular daily or weekly digests of activity on the site too.

Next, join any university industry, affinity, or identity groups and networks that interest you – whether these are professional networks, young alumni, or multicultural groups. Check to see if your alma mater offers an alumni mentorship programme. If time permits, sign up as a mentee or mentor.

Finally, create your own Alumni Friday! Block out an hour a week or a month to rediscover the events, networks, opportunities, and follow-up with alumni towards building your network.

Share this discovery with your alumni friends, so they too can begin to mine their own alumni capital!

Alumni Action 10: Assembling career stories

Reflecting on our university experience helps to refine our own story. For this alumni action, we look outwards, to learn from the career and business stories of alumni. 'Instead of asking alumni or co-workers for routine career advice, ask them to tell you their stories,' Jeff Selingo recommends in his book *There is Life After College*. 'People love to talk about how they got to where they are today. In doing so, you will get the advice you were initially seeking but will also hear how they construct their narratives.'[18] As our own career story develops, it will be shaped by the structure and style we hear from others. The university is an ideal place for mentorship, informational interviews, and introductions. They can orchestrate our lifelong career curiosity.

Assembling other people's career stories is not their career history. This chronological heavy lifting is available on LinkedIn. Career stories give us a sense of the changes and challenges a person overcame to get to the current point in their career. 'A story has details, emotions, change, tension, time, and action,'[19] explains career strategist Kerri Twigg, author of *The Career Stories Method*. Twigg describes an effective story as one we can learn from because it captures our senses. This is different to a static, factual example.[20] A story can also focus on those elements that led to a career, such as postgraduate or professional study. These are the pieces in a person's wider career puzzle. This fosters our growth mindset too. We listen to how fellow alumni manage setbacks and failures. We draw inspiration from their resilience and success.

This work *is* putting ourselves out there. It's *networking*. Don't let the word scare you, this is an important step of the Alumni

Way. Kingsley Aikins, Founder of the Networking Institute, believes effective networking is synonymous with listening. 'Being a world-class listener may be the best skill you can develop,' Aikins says, 'We all like to think we're good listeners, don't we? But think how often you're in a conversation with someone and, after you talk for ten seconds, they jump in to wow you with information about themselves.'[21] Listening to career stories takes our concentration. We need to hold back on the ping-pong nature of conversation. Instead, we immerse ourselves in the story and ask questions from a place of curiosity.

Sometimes a mentor rises from our alumni capital ranks to help us to assemble career stories. This mentor may pop up organically, through informal conversations, or a formal mentorship programme. Varying in size and scope, mentorship programmes involve exchanges between mentees and mentor. So many mentorship programmes shifted online, allowing for flexibility for participation. I have mentored students and recent alumni all over the world from the comforts of my home. Other face-to-face meetings, like York University's TASTE (Take a Student to Eat) mentoring lunches, offers a 'bite-sized mentoring opportunity' for students to meet with York alumni over lunch.[22] Micro-mentorship opportunities like TASTE are common (and not time-consuming!), offering valuable feathers in our career curiosity cap.

Mentorship also offers advantages for both mentee *and* mentor. When a mentor approaches the experience with a growth mindset, it's a learning experience for them too. A mentor reflects on their own experiences along with gaining insights from mentees and even fellow mentors. There is an element of gravitas in taking on a formal role as an alumni mentor. It's an endorsement from our alma mater.[23] Learning how to be an effective mentor also builds our leadership and self-awareness skill set.

We can't sit around and expect serendipitous moments – including our careers – to land on our laps. They won't appear in our inboxes or as a direct message either. We need to become active players in the game. When I spoke to Ryan Catherwood, then Assistant Vice-President of Alumni and Career Services at Longwood University, he described the importance of what he called "connection-ready students and activated alumni". He sees immense potential synergies between students, recent graduates, and alumni. Why? He pointed me to the Hiring Manager's Story, a narrative constructed and promoted at Longwood.

The story begins with a twist on the common saying 'It's not about who you know. *It's about who knows you.*'[24] Let's take things from the perspective of a hiring manager. They want to find the best possible candidate for an advertised job. They also want to minimize the risk of hiring the wrong person. They often cast out the net with a job description to current employees (and former employees – corporate alumni!). They encourage internal staff to suggest or support potential applicants. This is where referrals come in. We want to be on the radar of people who make referrals: this is the *who knows you*. How can we become connection-ready and activated? Among the strategies, Catherwood suggests, is the informational interview.

The informational interview is another easy way to learn from the career stories of fellow alumni. Warning – this is more than a cup of coffee and a chat. An informational interview is a proactive career exploration. It offers learning for both people involved in the process. Catherwood reminds us that the information interview is not about us: "It's about the person you're interviewing. If at the end of it you do a good job, the person will say: 'How can I help you?'" Our response? Catherwood suggests, "Keep me in mind when opportunities arise".

These strategies allow us to enlarge our circle. We also start to emerge on the radar of others. This is a form of wayfinding – the idea of finding our way – by making decisions based on knowledge and experiences we gather.[25] In this case, we gather information from alumni with interesting career paths. Informational interviews are useful whether we are growing our career or finding our first job. They are a springboard to building our alumni capital while learning about a sector, an occupation, or a company. This is a low stakes way to explore certain careers too. If the response from an informational interview isn't what we expected, we can shift our career direction. This is a form of 'rapid prototype testing'[26] in a career sense.

Asking someone for 20 minutes of their time requires our advanced preparation. Be clear to the alumni interviewee on the purpose of the informational interview. An introduction email or message like 'I am curious to learn more about what you do and how you got there', is an honest way to open the conversation. As people have so many demands on their time, be flexible and request a meeting either in person or by online video platform. Researching our interviewee in advance is essential. It might seem like spying, but the trusty internet allows us to look up the interviewee's LinkedIn profile, staff webpage, or media features. What questions came to mind reading over these sources? For every 20-minute informational interview, set aside at least the same time again for this preparation. Informational interviews are beneficial for the interviewee too. *When* we are called on to be an interviewee (this isn't an if!) we can take time to reflect on our own careers. Both the interviewer and interviewee get to flex their Alumni Way muscles!

How do we find an alumni mentor or informational interviewee? We can start in our comfort zone: a family member, neighbour, a fellow alum, a colleague from a volunteer or work placement. When we get more confident, we can cast our own nets to include our wider alumni capital. We can invite inspiring faculty members, residence hall advisers, former alumni guest lecturers, friends of alumni friends. Peruse the alumni profiles with career services. Filter alumni on a university-supported alumni online community platform. Social media platforms like LinkedIn also provide a good place to identify alumni with interesting career stories to tell.

In their book *The Slow Professor*, Maggie Berg and Barbara Seeber argue that academics need time for thinking and reflection. This allows faculty to let ideas marinate in our frenetic world.[27] What if professors viewed their relationship with former students as an opportunity for such an exploration? Inviting a professor for an informational interview allows everyone involved to draw breath and let the conversation unfold. Don't underestimate the value of these conversations. Fellow graduates have found that their professors provide some of the best career advice.[28]

Then there is the introduction. Often a family member, friend, or fellow alum may think there is someone worthwhile for us to meet. Taking the form of a simple email, an introduction is from someone who wants to connect two people – in this case alumni – with shared interests. The email usually includes a few sentences on both people. It also outlines why the introduction would be fruitful to both alumni. The follow-up from an introduction might be a short video chat to see how the new connection can be mutually beneficial. An introduction may lead to an informational interview. If both alumni are growth minded, both parties can learn from the new connection. When I wanted to ask J. Kelly Hoey to write the foreword to this book, I went to a generous mutual connection and asked for an introduction. I outlined my purpose for seeking the introduction. I also outlined my alumni connection to Hoey, to show a shared connection (we both graduated from the University of Victoria). When Hoey agreed to the introduction (it is always courteous to ask if someone *wants* to be introduced, to ensure timing and purpose are right), an email introduction popped into my inbox. The rest is history!

Alumni have intriguing career stories, so we can relish in the listening. Ask questions from the point of curiosity and learning. Don't be judgemental or too personal. Be sure not to ask for something in return, especially not a job. Approach the relationship with curiosity, kindness, and gratitude. Through alumni mentorship, informational interviews, or even introductions, opportunities may arise. By making a good impression, establishing a rapport, sustaining the relationship, this planned happenstance – this serendipity – may emerge too.

Activity 10: Build our alumni hypernetwork by assembling career stories

Invite a fellow alum with an interesting career path to an informational interview. This isn't a casual cup of coffee. Be professional, prepared, and thoughtful to maximize the experience for you and the invited alum. Be sure you are clear about the purpose of the 20-minute chat. Be curious in your questioning (and prepare questions in advance!), focusing on their career story. Stick to the agreed time and choose a location that is convenient for your alum interviewee (or set up a meeting on an agreed web-based platform like Zoom). Send a thank you note or email afterwards to acknowledge the alum's time.

After the first informational interview, they become easier. Make a commitment to yourself to conduct at least one alumni informational interview per month (or set another realistic target). Jot down the key points from the meeting. These ideas, actions, and follow-up can help to assemble your own career stories.

Take the extra challenge!

During the information interview, ask for an introduction (or offer one!) to a fellow alum. An introduction might be the response to asking the question 'Who else should I speak to?' Follow up by email to thank your interviewee and briefly outline what you gained from the meeting in one or two sentences. Add to the email a gentle reminder for the introduction. If you offered an introduction, be sure to ask your contact first if they are happy for an introduction, before sending an email to both people. This could be your next informational interview!

Alumni Action 11: Learning about earning on campus

Scientist. Police officer. Construction worker. Nurse. Lifeguard. Teacher. Musician. Window cleaner. This is part of the list compiled by my young children and nephew. I asked them to create a list of jobs. This full list[29] reinforces my argument that the university *is* a city. Every job imaginable is available on campus. There are enough cranes on campus to sustain many roles in the construction industry. The emergency services liaise regularly with the university. Some campuses have their own police services. Universities foster sports, the arts, and transportation services on campus. Academics chart the history of many occupations. Many other jobs are visible on campus: scientists, doctors, nurses, teachers, shop workers. They keep the university ecosystem in check. Interested in event management? The university coordinates graduation ceremonies, reunions, open days, conferences, and online events. Want to be a musician? There are nightspots for rock and jazz gigs. Classical concerts abound. Duets, quartets, and choirs offer ambience for campus events. We can open our eyes to the breadth of careers on campus. Take a quick campus stroll or visit the university webpage.

Did you know the university is the largest employer in Rochester, New York?[30] Universities are some of the main employers in towns and cities worldwide. They are often rated as some of the best employers too. With hundreds to tens of thousands of employees, universities *are* cities. Confession time: I started working at my alma mater immediately after graduation. It allowed me to extend my cosy campus lifestyle I enjoyed as a student and be paid – the best of both worlds.

The benefits, job security, and career promotion vary from institution to institution. So do the perks: some institutions offer discounted tuition for families or comprehensive health benefits. There might be special recreation centre rates or professional development opportunities. This is not only a rose-tinted view of campus employment. Recent zero-hour contracts for academics and casualization of the sector abound. There can be job insecurity coupled with enormous workloads.[31] The COVID-19 pandemic led to a sharp decrease in university income and widespread job losses.[32] Despite this, the university remains a sought-after employment choice.

One reason the university remains attractive is the inclusive, open environment. It swirls with innovative ideas and passion underpinned by academic freedom. Universities strive for and align to ambitious values. Environmental protection and sustainability. Human rights and social justice. Diversity and community outreach. They focus on advancing knowledge, education, and research. The public hold the university to a high standard. With my soapbox firmly in place, I believe the university is a wonderful place to work. I have done so for over 15 years.

I suspect Sinéad MacBride would agree. MacBride forged an excellent career plan. She had an undergraduate and master's degree from a prestigious university. A recognized student leader, she excelled in student government roles and extra-curricular activities. Shortly after graduation, she began a promising law career at a firm near her hometown. "The economic downturn led to a last one in, first one out scenario," MacBride explained to me in our interview. She found herself unemployed for the first time. She didn't focus on her shock and sadness for long. With some persuading, MacBride applied for a job that led to a complete career pivot. Sinéad MacBride found herself back on a university campus.

MacBride secured a key role in the Secretary's Office at Trinity College Dublin. As the corporate, legal, and governance epicentre of the university, MacBride found a niche to reinvent her legal career. "No two days are the same," she remarks, describing the work that crosses her desk. She regaled me with stories of overseeing art acquisitions and reviewing research contracts. She discussed the meticulous documentation for the university's governing body. She even arranged support to students with legal matters. When I interviewed MacBride, it was obvious she enjoyed the challenge of her varied role. Her story is extraordinary, and, at the same time, not that unusual. Our university, or other institutions like it, can offer us fulfilling, lifelong careers.

My own story follows a similar path. Within months of starting my career at the University of Toronto, my own alma mater, I heard the following: "Congratulations for choosing a career in advancement. You will never be out of a job again." This proclamation opened the newcomers' conference organized by the Canadian Council for Advancement of Education (CCAE). Even two decades on, the advice holds true. Educational institutions and charities seek professionals with fundraising, alumni relations, and communications experience. My advancement experience proved to be an asset as I moved to Ireland too. Advancement is often the ultimate in planned happenstance for keen student leaders. Savvy relationship building skills? Visionary leadership? Passionate changemaker? Advancement might be a potential career option too. To give a sense of scale, there are over 80,000 advancement professionals worldwide.[33] Other strategic roles on campus might also offer a satisfying career path. There are professionals in student life, career services, and international education among others.

There are critics to the growing emphasis on 'student experience' in the academy. The belief is that university should focus on its core work: education.[34] I don't view this as an either/or prospect. There is a place for creating an environment conducive to learning *and* creating active citizens. Love it or loathe it, university administration is a professional business. What would it be like if every university administrator attended their professional association conference at the same time? A mass exodus! If you added all the professors attending their academic discipline conferences into the mix, campus would be empty. Imagine the intricate web of intra-university networks that involve our alma mater and institutions worldwide. Consider the multi or interdisciplinary academic collaborations and partnerships. Our alumni capital can introduce us to relevant institutional contacts not only at our own alma mater but also to this extended network. We need to know who and what to ask.

Professors and academics are the anchor of the university. The challenges of working in academic roles are well documented. It often combines the pressures of significant workloads, publication outputs, and demanding students. It's not surprising when reports show PhD graduates choosing industry over academia.[35] Enter Alexander Clark and Bailey Sousa, authors of *How to Be a Happy Academic*. They offer advice to be effective (and happy!) in the teaching, research and administrative expectations of an academic career.[36] Clark and Sousa advocate for academics sharing both their successes *and failures* with their students. This sets a tone for continuous learning, instead of the pursuit of perfection. This vulnerability might also go some way in rekindling interest in pursuing an academic career. 'Your biggest asset for academic career success?' Clark and Sousa ask rhetorically, 'A growth mindset.'[37] This mantra rings true for any career on campus.

Activity 11: Build our alumni hypernetwork by learning about earning on campus

Identify and invite a faculty member or university administrator to an informational interview. Treat this as any other informational interview and be well prepared with questions. Be sure to make the purpose of the interview clear. First, you hope to understand their career story. Next, ask some questions about their professional or academic association connections or networks outside the university. Finally, discuss how their work involves (or could involve) alumni. During the 20-minute meeting, ask about any learning opportunities, seminars, or events open to alumni.

After the interview, complete a short reflection. Ask yourself the following questions:

- What were the three top learning points from the meeting?
- What professional associations, academic societies, or alumni-focused events are interesting and require follow-up?
- Would I want to work on campus? If yes, what types of roles interest you? If not, why not? This might help in choosing future alumni capital-inspired informational interviews.

Alumni Action 12: Sharing our good news

Our alma mater – this nurturing parent – is proud of our achievements. University social media posts tease us with phenomenal alumni achievements. Alumni magazine articles offer the unabridged version of the accolades of fellow alumni. A friend once told me she stopped reading the alumni magazine. She couldn't identify with the world leaders and CEOs featured in the publication. With the growth mindset, we can learn from these tremendous stories of success. This is another exercise in analysing the career stories of others. It also gives us an opportunity to delve deeper, to review and focus on our own personal and professional goals. We can also share *our story*. Shouting it from the rooftops might not be a glossy cover story or trending tweet. But we can *be* inspirational. There is space to celebrate the extraordinary that arises from the ordinary.

After graduating from Brown University, friends Rachel Kapelke-Dale and Jessica Pan made a pact. They promised to email each other faithfully as their lives took them around the world. The correspondence formed the basis for their post-graduation memoir, aptly titled *Graduates in Wonderland: The International Misadventures of Two (Almost) Adults*.[38] Once published, Kapelke-Dale wrote a nostalgic piece to promote the book in *Brown*

Alumni Magazine. In an article entitled 'The Odd Couple', Kapelke-Dale detailed how she met co-author Pan in the first year.[39] As if on cue, the top right-hand corner of the article was the advertisement: 'Calling all Brown Authors!'[40]

Pan followed with a solo book offering, *Sorry I'm Late, I Didn't Want to Come: One Introvert's Year of Saying Yes* also featured in *Brown Alumni Magazine.*[41] Many other universities promote books published by alumni. The University of Sheffield hosts a dedicated webpage for alumni authors with direct book links.[42] Other universities host books fairs. Still others feature alumni authored books as part of an online alumni book club. Whether promoting our new book, product, or accomplishment, let's share our good news with the affiliations *within* our alma mater too. Student clubs, academic departments, even sports teams might be our niche target audience.

Here's the second call for aspiring writers. University publications have a broad international readership and circulation in the thousands. These magazines, newsletters, and blogs are an excellent addition to our writing portfolio. Universities often seek out alumni or students to write for their publications. Alumni often serve as volunteers on editorial boards for an alumni magazine. These editorial boards help to identify publication themes and review content. We can pitch our own personal story, write a feature on a fellow alum, or highlight the institution's response to current hot topic.

Sharing our good news doesn't always need to include the flashing lights of the media. As growth-minded alumni, we can share our story to let others learn from our stumbling and our success. We can be a guest speaker in the classroom to bring a concept to life. We can write a case study based on our career or business experience. As students, sometimes the imprint of alumni support is invisible. Alumni may have co-designed a market research project or authored industry reference materials. Through service learning, many universities also like to work with alumni working in non-profit organizations to co-create projects that solve a problem in the community. We can begin this process of sharing our professional selves by connecting with an old professor or with career services. We enhance our own leadership skills while boosting the experiential learning opportunities for the next generation of students.

We gravitate to stories that resonate with us. When we share our good news with our alma mater, we allow them to share this – or invite us back – to begin a ripple effect. 'I have learned that first-generation college students tend to learn best when they hear lessons reinforced by alumni who were once in their position as students,'[43] explains George Sanchez, who delivers a programme at the University of Southern California for first-generation students. Alumni contributions within the classroom are crucial. It enables students to identify with and be inspired by people they relate to. Maybe we saw this inspiring alum at the lectern – or wish we did. This is our chance, today or tomorrow, to be that motivating voice in the classroom.

I have a friend who is a tireless advocate for the transformational effect of education on her life. As a mature student and single parent, she successfully completed an access to higher education programme. After finishing her studies to postgraduate level, she remains a regular guest speaker and mentor to current access students. A celebration of our career triumph, however minor we may feel it is, may be an inspiration to others. Alumni in the classroom can be a student's first introduction to alumni capital. The university's career services office undertakes a mammoth task to support students and recent graduates towards professional success. A bespoke, individualized career service is almost an impossibility. To put it in context, across surveyed institutions in the United States, the median ratio is one career services staff to more than 1,500 students.[44] We can take positive action. As a member of a robust alumni network, we can share or acquire career stories. We can also encourage fellow alumni with exciting news to share to contact their alma mater. Suddenly more and more extraordinary ordinary stories of alumni will appear in the next magazine or in the classroom.

There are regular calls for universities to build the work readiness of their graduates.[45] Career fairs and seminars, online or in person, are another way for us to re-engage with our alma mater. There is the bonus too: we might identify prospective employees or internship opportunities. Open days, once recruitment focused events, are now often family friendly, community events. Our employer or business might benefit from securing an exhibitor's booth or acting as an event sponsor. Work readiness is not just a strategy or programme, it's individual. We can't dismiss our ability to support the student–alumni transition. Recent graduates are gold dust. We don't need to be a senior executive to share our good news. Want to see a flock of final year students? Volunteer to run a session titled: How I secured my first full-time job after graduation. We can celebrate our achievements and let some future graduates in on our secrets of career resilience.

We are the university's success story, even if we don't establish our own fashion label or lead a Fortune 500 company. Constructing our own career stories is crucial. Career strategist Kerri Twigg warns us without a compelling career story, our CV or résumé has the danger of 'blanding in', she says, 'where you blend in so well you become bland'.[46] As someone who has read hundreds of CVs and résumés, I can attest that this dullness *is* possible! To practise celebrating our career success and thinking about our career stories, we should take advantage of the university tools available. We can complete a profile for the career services office. We can offer a testimonial for our programme of study. This becomes the counterbalance to the superstar narrative often featured in our university publications. We have our own extraordinary stories. At the University of Greenwich, they took this extraordinary ordinary into overdrive. The Greenwich Snapshots series features the alumni stories of teachers, legal administrators, marketing officers, business owners, and cyber security analysts as a start.[47] It is the voice of alumni loud and clear. The webpage offers alumni the platform to tell their life after Greenwich story in their own words. How can we formulate our own career story and celebrate our own career success?

Activity 12: Build our alumni hypernetwork by sharing our good news

Formulate a short paragraph to begin your career story. This can be a simple document or an online e-portfolio you return to every so often. When you achieve a major milestone in your career or business, take five minutes to add it to your story. Potentially, alert your alumni office too. Tag your alma mater in your social media post, marking your achievement. Use a university hashtag. Your university might share or retweet your good news. Your achievement might turn into a feature for the alumni magazine, blog, or class notes.

Next, it's time to hone that curiosity trait. Visit the career services webpage and look for alumni profiles. If your university doesn't have these available for public view to alumni, see if you can find other examples online. You're reading for content but also for structure and style. Think about what makes the story engaging and exciting. Does it tell a good story? Jot down the phrases or the ideas from these career profiles. Keep a bank of these ideas to help construct your own career story.

Finally, see if your career services or alumni office accept alumni profiles. Download the form or copy the questions and section of the profile sheet. Use these questions as prompts for your own story and as a way to practise writing about your achievements. No pressure to publish your profile immediately!

Return to your career story and career profile every so often to reread, edit, and add your accomplishments.

When you're ready, fill out the live alumni profile sheet and send it to your alma mater!

10

Curiosity signpost: Leverage alumni capital for business

Kevin Boylan slowly pours water onto the fire. Flames rise high in the sky. The audience gasps. Boylan reminds families at the fire station open day of the dangers of a grease fire. As with many firefighters, Boylan's role affords him time for another venture, in his case, as co-founder of Firecloud365. A cloud-based fire safety software company, Firecloud365 targets public sector and hotel industry clients with large-scale building works. As a start-up, Boylan and co-founder Ryan Bradley participated in New Frontiers, an entrepreneurship acceleration programme. The co-founders received mentorship support, funding, and incubation space in the CoLab on the Letterkenny Institute of Technology campus, Boylan's alma mater. The Institute was among the company's first clients, offering Firecloud 365 credibility in the marketplace. In return, the Institute secured a fire safety system to align with its risk management portfolio. Stories like Firecloud365 show the immense potential of our alumni capital for start-up business success. The alumni–alma mater as a symbiotic relationship in action.

Symbiotic indeed. A recent University of Toronto Instagram post included this attention-grabbing caption: 'Did you know #UofT has helped over 350 start-ups scale and bring their ideas to market?' When I fact checked this post two years later, this number had jumped to 500.[1] Other universities can also boast this claim. The scale might be different, but the sentiment is the same: universities support business. Our alma mater provides the tools, knowledge, and support for us to allow our business acumen to shine. While entrepreneurial universities are not new,[2] an emerging trend is the key role of the university in the local economy to foster business growth. As part of the entrepreneurial ecosystem,[3] universities offer start-up incubation space, research support, technology transfer offices, and technology parks. They support spin-off companies and acceleration programmes, even academic courses designed specifically to meet industry requirements.

Alumni Action 13: Remembering the university is a city – and a potential client

Let's cast our mind back to the 'university *is* a city' concept. Companies permeate the campus: stores, cafés, restaurants, banks. Look closer. The university also has virtual subscriptions from computer software to online publications. The university community cares for and nurtures trendy, ecologically minded, and social inclusion focused businesses too. Students seek part-time or casual work on campus. The work rosters ebb and flow with class schedules and campus closures. It is easy to imagine that alumni with businesses on or near campus can draw on their alumni status. They can promote their business through university and alumni communication channels. The captive audience is front and centre: students, staff, and faculty on campus daily. Relationships run deep; it is less like a city and more like a village. What if we channelled our past student involvement for our business? We could offer sponsorship, discounts, or venue space to our beloved sports team or student club.

Many years ago, in my secret life as a student, I sampled new fruit drinks, face creams, and music singles. I minored in focus groups and free merchandise of any kind. I earned what seemed like a second degree in market research. Even decades later, universities remain a clear route to the key 18–25-year-old demographic through events like orientation or homecoming. Students *still* love free stuff. The university and student government are a way to access this market. Students themselves recognize the value of this market. Harvard Student

Agencies recently acquired Campus Insights, an alumni-run market research start-up. Campus Insights, describing the company as 'fluent in Gen Z and Millennial speak',[4] offers UX (user experience) for the student demographic.[5] Students are a discerning client base too. Prepare to respond to queries about product ethical practices, sustainable packaging, and diversity business practices. Clever, inclusive advertising also helps us convert students into a loyal customer base.

Apart from the youth market, universities employ hundreds (or thousands!) of faculty and staff. These employees are usually an educated, open-minded bunch. They are often urban/suburban dwellers. Our product or service pitch? It could be as broad as children's books, massage therapy, outdoor adventures, or interior design. It might take our curiosity to find the exact niche. Our megaphone might become online staff newsletters, campus lounges, or faculty events.

Let's not discount alumni in this equation. Our fellow graduates span from their 20s to centenarians. They live all over the region and around the world. They represent broad diversity too: young alumni, ethnic and racial communities, and LGBTQ+ groups. The alumni demographic can span wide or narrow. When I met Roy Moëd, he recognized the benefit of reaching alumni. LifeBook, Moëd's company offers a ghostwriting service for our own written and bound autobiography.[6] He viewed alumni as an accomplished group of people interested in leaving a special legacy of family story. Moëd's tenacity to get into the alumni sector paid off. Lifebook is now an affinity partner with my alma mater, the University of Sheffield, among others.[7]

What's one of the best-kept secrets of our alumni citizenship? It's university affinity partnerships.[8] And why shouldn't alumni citizens take advantage of these offers? From special health, car, and home insurance rates to faculty-led trips to exotic locales. Flashing our alumni pride in our wallets, a percentage of our affinity credit card spend goes to our alma mater. Affinity partnerships are a win-win-win: for alumni, a business partner, and our alma mater.

The university can be a natural or even comfortable place to start our client pitch. Firecloud365 and Summer can attest to this university client success. Founded by Yale alumni, Summer is a free financial management app for students. The Yale School of Management talk about the start-up in their alumni magazine: 'Summer partners with colleges and universities – in fact, Yale was its first partner – to offer students an easy-to-use app, as well as loan counselling.'[9] These aren't one-off success stories; universities often support lifelong alumni entrepreneurship. Take, for example, the story of Rupert Forsythe.

A name is called. Applause. The graduate steps onto stage to receive a parchment and handshake. Then, the same in slow motion. This creates a shareable moment captured in an instant, individualized graduation video clip. This is Rupert Forsythe's most recent venture: StageClip. When I interviewed Forsythe, he described himself as "a serial entrepreneur in alumni-land". Campus clothing, graduate bags, and graduation videos are all his previous university-connected ventures. Forsythe draws on his own alumni capital from the University of Birmingham to support StageClip. "I get heavy weight support and strategic direction from thought leaders for the business," he says. The COVID-19 pandemic forced the cancellation of graduation ceremonies at universities worldwide. StageClip pivoted its operations. Within weeks, StageClip generated over 1,100 virtual graduations for university clients worldwide.[10] These businesses show ingenuity to offer solutions for the university, students, or alumni markets. Firecloud365 offers the institution a robust fire safety system. Summer supports students to manage the mounting college debt. StageClip provides newest alumni a way to show their university pride, while peppering social media with the university's brand.

Is our product or service perfectly suited to become a campus essential? As a city, the university connects with hundreds of businesses and suppliers: management consultancy, lab and office equipment, gardening supplies, catering, travel agencies, career coaches, and more. Procurement might be tough, but the trade-off is the cachet of a university client. Where do we start? This is where we can play our alumni card. Start with a known university contact and let the introductions unfold. Our business partnerships or sponsorship might be with the main institution. Instead, it could be better suited to the wider university network: student government, alumni association, residence halls, federated colleges, English languages schools, or conference centres.

Earlier in the book, we met Teo Salgado, founder of VerveSmith independent educational consultants. VerveSmith's clients are families and young people who seek unbiased, expert advice to secure college admission based on their personalized needs. The university isn't the client. Businesses like VerveSmith form part of the wider higher education ecosystem. The same could be true of businesses with prospective students, students, or alumni clients such as tutoring or proofreading services.

All these alumni businesses can also benefit from loyal alumni customers. Driving through Nova Scotia, I loved seeing the 'Acadia Alumni owned and operated' signs outside of business premises. Acadia University alum Cindy James displays the sign outside her Halifax business Petite Urban Pooch: 'I'm a proud alumna,' James says, 'I wanted to identify with other Acadia alumni.'[11] Even without a displayed notice, we can be intentional about seeking out and supporting alumni businesses. Check the university's website for an online alumni business directory. The Bauer College of Business at the University of Houston supports an active, online directory of Bauer alumni businesses.[12] When I met Giovanni Roselli, Director of Alumni Relations online, he informed me it was Cougar Red Friday and he was wearing the college colours. "It's a tight-knit community centred around the city of Houston," Roselli explains. "We hope that Bauer alumni will consult the directory when seeking an accountant, restaurant or micro-brewery, gravitating to businesses of fellow alumni."[13] Bauer followed up with a #bauerloveshouston campaign on social media to gather alumni support for Bauer alumni businesses in Houston. It's like having a Cougar Red Friday every day, all over the city. With or without a formal directory or campaign, we can take our curious spirit to offer alumni-led businesses exposure and our custom.

What happens when our company needs to attract top talent? Universities have us covered on this one too. Work placements, internships and career fairs are a common, and often still effective, solution to find entry-level employees. Boot camps and executive education programmes serve as professional development options for business too. Learning partnerships with industry is also a way to identify key talent and upskill current employees. For instance, Jaguar Land Rover, teamed up with the Institute of Technology, Sligo to design the world's first Master of Engineering in Connected and Automated Vehicles course.[14] Kevin Boylan of Firecloud365 worked with his former lecturers and his alma mater to develop a short, accredited course in fire safety management. With his extensive industry expertise, Boylan ensured that the course design meets the needs for staff with a fire safety responsibility in their organization. These examples demonstrate the creative and agile potential of university-industry partnerships.

A thriving industry indeed. According to the National Centre for Universities and Business reported on over 100,000 interactions between universities and businesses in a single year across the United Kingdom. This staggering figure shows the sheer breadth of potential for these innovative partnerships.[15] This includes over 85,000 university-SME (small and medium enterprises) interactions, demonstrating that this isn't only a big business activity.[16] One key university-business collaboration is in research and development (R&D). Apart from support for business product development discussed earlier in this chapter, R&D projects can build on significant challenges facing our planet, including climate change. For instance, Unilever is working with seven universities across the United Kingdom to reuse waste materials across the chemical industry. The partnership, including other industry partners, secured significant government investment to adopt circular economy principles for end-of-life projects while reducing carbon footprint from the chemicals industry.[17] Through the Sustainable Earth Institute, the University of Plymouth collaborates with businesses, social enterprises, and the wider community to consider local to global sustainability challenges.[18] How can our employer, our own business, or our community benefit from an injection of university connection?

Activity 13: Leverage alumni capital for business by remembering the university as a city – and as a potential client

Think back to your time as a student. Chances are you waded through crowds to get free stuff. From notebooks and keychains to ice cream and pizza, students are drawn to free swag. Consider the demographic advantages of marketing on campus. Identify three brands that you love and consider how they might be able to grow their market share with a campus presence or online university-targeted campaign. Think beyond the traditional student demographic to include staff and faculty, even cohorts of alumni in different age groups, in various ethnic and religious groups, regional locations, and other demographic segments. If you have your own business, complete this exercise for your own business product or service. Consider how your alma mater may play a part to scale your market.

Alternative activity

Think back to an event you participated in on campus, whether it was your graduation, an alumni reunion, or even an online course or webinar. Consider the businesses and suppliers the university needs to deliver the event. Think florist, musicians, catering company, software, sign makers, tent rentals. The list can be long or even silly, to allow you to stretch your mind to all the potential alumni capital business relationships.

11

Curiosity trait summary: Shining a light

We may feel that we are entering 'alumnihood' with little. We didn't maximize our university experience as we hoped. With other life responsibilities, the time for exploration at college was a challenge. Don't fret. Our alumni capital is available now to prime the pump,[1] to initiate the process of curiosity. This is the time to ask questions and gather information. We can illuminate a pathway to grow our career and our business.

Ronit Avni, co-founder of LocalizED, is no stranger to networking and alumni capital. LocalizED is democratizing online alumni and diaspora mentorship for career growth, with a focus on the Middle East and North Africa region. Universities are among LocalizED clients. Avni is a seasoned speaker, including at a plethora of university-sponsored events. As a guest for a Brandeis University podcast, Avni spoke about networking as a relational – not transactional – activity. She offered advice to the students and alumni: 'You're establishing relationships with people. You're trying to learn. You're trying to be generous where you can,' Avni says. 'You're trying to be polite and respectful of people's time.'[2]

How do you reach out for career advice? Avni believes students – and by association alumni – need to be authentic, empathetic, and respectful in the ask. 'If you're a student', she says, 'some of the best networkers are those that may reach out and say, "Hey, Ronit", or "Hey, Whoever. I see that you're working on X. I am looking to learn more about this field. I don't want to take up too much of your time. Could we jump on a 15-minute call?"' To get the most from an informational interview, career advice, or time with a mentor, Avni reminded us to think of it from their perspective. 'Try to see it from their vantage point because chances are, they're getting a lot of requests.'[3] Avni summarizes many of the key messages from this section: applying our curiosity, ensuring we are thoughtful in our preparation, taking the leap. Our fellow alumni and our university are the game changers for our professional advancement.

Let's not discount our own 'alumni intelligence'[4] in this process. As we navigate through life, we build our own career and business wisdom. We can pay it forward to current students, fellow alumni in the classroom or on a video chat. Our careers will be filled with achievements and failures. Let's embrace them as growth-minded learning experiences for ourselves and for fellow (and future!) alumni.

As we peer in the darkness, we see little. Our curiosity is our light. By chance, we catch a glimpse of sparkle in the dim light. This is a career gem falling into our lap. With careful planning, serendipity awaits. With this serendipity and our constant enquiry, we can then share it with fellow alumni. The aim of this section is to pique our curiosity. This anchors our thinking on the lifelong connection between our alma mater and our professional life. How can we think of our alumni citizenship in all facets of our work?

Key messages from Part III

- We can leverage our alumni capital to support our career aspirations. With something as simple as requesting an informational interview, we can learn more about the careers of fellow alumni to enhance our own.
- Mining our alumni capital is a crucial part of networking. Our alumni hypernetwork is first and foremost a relationship building exercise.
- To assemble our own alumni story, we need to spend time listening to other career stories from our alumni capital – fellow alumni and special connections on campus.
- Universities offer a wide variety of campus careers, business partnerships, and relationships, rivalling that of a city.

- Universities support and foster business in many creative ways, and as alumni we can maximize this position as we grow, foster, and build our own business.

Disengaged alumni with the fixed mindset will:

- focus only on narrow group of friends or a small network to help with their career;
- think they are alone after graduation, especially to launch their career;
- believe their knowledge and network within the university is fixed, especially if they had a negative student experience; they feel this relationship can't be erased or changed;
- think that with sheer talent and brilliance at what they know (from their degree), opportunities will fall into their lap with no effort;
- close off to career stories, especially 'success' stories as this diminishes their own brilliance.

Dynamic alumni with the growth mindset will:

- engage with their wider alumni network to advance their career or their business;
- recognize that it takes effort to activate alumni capital towards impact on their career;
- approach networking as hard work that yields excellent positive results;
- be open to listening and learning from the career stories of others, including the 'success' stories;
- learn from the setbacks, mistakes, and failures in our career and business life; they will also learn from the challenges in the stories of fellow alumni;
- approach networking with alumni and members of the university with curiosity, as a key component to building lifelong relationships;
- view the university as a lifelong resource of learning for their career and their business.

Checklist for Part III

To build your Alumni Way, especially your ability for curiosity don't forget to:

- ☐ follow your university, school, or department social media channels (see Activity 9);
- ☐ create a profile on your online alumni community and/or career community (see Activity 9);
- ☐ join alumni professional, affinity and identity groups that interest you (see Activity 9);
- ☐ block out 30 minutes for an Alumni Friday each month (see Activity 9);
- ☐ invite an alum for an informational interview (see Activity 10);
- ☐ ask (or offer) an introduction (see Activity 10);
- ☐ invite a faculty member or administrator for an informational interview (see Activity 11);
- ☐ maintain an active career story (see Activity 12);
- ☐ review career profiles of fellow alumni for ideas and inspiration (see Activity 12);
- ☐ begin to write your own career profile for the career services or alumni office (see Activity 12);
- ☐ reflect on how your favourite brands, your own company or your employer could benefit with a connection to the university (see Activity 13);
- ☐ list the suppliers and business partnerships needed for a major university event (see Activity 13).

Building the Alumni Way: Questions following Part III

- *Recent graduates and alumni*: What three new ideas will you implement to boost your career or business after reading this chapter?
- *Students*: How will you try to connect with alumni to learn more about your career or business interests?
- *University administrators*: How can you make the relationship between the university and local businesses a better one, becoming truly curious and supportive to our alumni's professional endeavours?

- *Advancement professionals*: How can you create the conditions to foster curiosity in our alumni and in your advancement team about our alumni?
- *Parents/career advisers*: What questions can you ask that can foster curiosity about alumni capital and building a career?

PART IV

The Alumni Way trait: Passion

12	Immersing in our passions: The alumni dimension	105
13	Passion signpost: Nourish our wellness through our alumni capital	109
	• Alumni Action 14: Fostering lifelong learning to sharpen the mind	110
	• Alumni Action 15: Nurturing our body	114
14	Passion signpost: Watch our alumni-self flourish	119
	• Alumni Action 16: Following our heart to guide our passion	120
	• Alumni Action 17: Leading with the soul	126
15	Passion trait summary: Our lives, our alma mater	131
	• Key messages from Part IV	132
	• Checklist for Part IV	134
	• Building the Alumni Way: Questions following Part IV	134

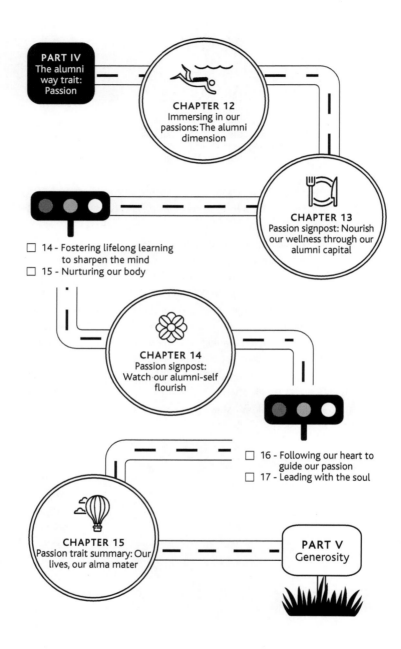

PART IV
The alumni way trait: Passion

CHAPTER 12
Immersing in our passions: The alumni dimension

CHAPTER 13
Passion signpost: Nourish our wellness through our alumni capital

☐ 14 - Fostering lifelong learning to sharpen the mind
☐ 15 - Nurturing our body

CHAPTER 14
Passion signpost: Watch our alumni-self flourish

☐ 16 - Following our heart to guide our passion
☐ 17 - Leading with the soul

CHAPTER 15
Passion trait summary: Our lives, our alma mater

PART V
Generosity

12

Immersing in our passions:
The alumni dimension

Don't skip this section. Life is beyond our careers. We make time for our family and friends, leisure activities, travel adventures, spiritual nurturing, and healthy pursuits. As students, we found ourselves in a place to discover the essence of ourselves. As alumni, how can our alma mater contribute to our lives? This section isn't about becoming passionate about our alma mater per se. It is identifying those things in life that bring us joy.

Researchers suggest that passion plays a key role in contributing to that elusive fulfilling life.[1] While we can associate passions with negative traits, psychologist Robert Vallerand and his colleagues describe harmonious passion in an article entitled *Les Passions de l'Âme* (Passions of the Soul): 'Such passions become central features of one's identity and serve to define the person. ... Those who have a passion for playing the guitar, for reading, or for jogging do not merely play the guitar, read, or jog. They are "guitar players", "readers", or "joggers". Passionate activities are part of who they are.'[2] Being passionate integrates our quality of life and our development as a person. We exert effort to learn a new language, hike a mountain, or volunteer to care for animals. The Alumni Way trait of passion complements the trait of generosity discussed in the next section. We often see our passions thrive when we give of ourselves. Our alumni capital connects us to our wider identities and shared communities too: ethnic and cultural groups, religious faiths, being from one place and living in another.

Our alma mater appears everywhere: the bio of our favourite blogger, an introductory speech, front and centre on our social media profiles. The words 'he graduated from … ', or 'she completed her degree at … ' or 'they studied at … ' are common. This tells us something about the person. It anchors them to something familiar. What is the fourth indicator on Wikipedia? Alma mater. This form of *identification* is different to *identity*. J Travis McDearmon explores the nuance of difference through alumni role identity.[3] We may recognize and identify our alma mater as exactly that, the place we went to school, but we may not see it as part of *who we are*. McDearmon describes this as a forming our 'own sense of self'.[4] As we identify ourselves as alumni in all types of situations, we open to the value our alma mater brings beyond our professional lives.

In his book *The Element: How Finding Your Passion Changes Everything*, Sir Ken Robinson reveals that a natural talent is not always our passion: 'I know many people who are naturally very good at something but don't feel that it's their life's calling,' Robinson explains. 'Being in your Element needs something more – passion. People who are in their Element take a deep delight and pleasure in what they do.'[5] We can hide behind something that comes easy, but it may not make us happy. When we draw on our passion, we also draw on our growth mindset. This puts our desire to learn at the core to enable us to reach the incredible heights of our potential.

Passion describes both positive and negative outcomes. Classical scholars Plato and Aristotle both cautioned that reason should control our passion.[6] Obsessive or addictive tendencies can draw from passion.[7] In this book, we focus on the positive nature of passion and becoming passionate. I am drawn to Vallerand's definition for the Alumni Way: 'Passion is defined as a strong inclination toward a self-defining activity that one loves, values (finds important), and devotes a significant amount of time and energy to.'[8] In this section we explore how the flows of people, knowledge and resources of our alumni capital are the conduit to finding (or fostering) our passions.

A significant amount of our drive and motivation may come from immersing ourselves in our passion. 'When we are truly passionate about something, it's contagious,' says Keith Ferrazzi, bestselling author of the networking book *Never Eat Alone.* 'Our passion draws other people to who we are and what we care about. Others respond by letting *their* guard down.'[9] We can foster meaningful relationships linked to our passions. Our face lights up in conversation. We have this ability to present our authentic self.

We can also tailor our own alumni experience to fit our interests and our lifestyle. The university can present options, but only *we* know the breadth of our preferences. *We* become our best resource to our individualized alumni experience. To capitalize on this, we need to become more proactive. We need to identify areas of our alumni capital to engage where we can. Our university offers so many conduits to plug into our passions beyond alumni relations programming. As the growth mindset suggests, as we invest our efforts, we see a significant return.

Our universities focus on passion too. They achieve certain accolades, awards, or designations. These are like labels (yes labels!) that align to the university's mission, vision, and values. The university's associated projects and activities point to institutional passion. Here's a broad snapshot of examples as a case in point:

- Universities in the United Kingdom and Ireland have signed a charter to become Universities of Sanctuary. These universities commit to supporting asylum seekers and refugees to access post-secondary education.[10]
- University of Canterbury in Christchurch was New Zealand's first Fair Trade university.[11]
- Trinity College Dublin designed a higher education programme for people with intellectual disabilities. Programme participants and their supporters are passionate about the course (and the graduation that follows!). University academics and administrators deliver course curriculum. External partnerships include philanthropic organizations and leading businesses. These collaborative efforts are all

anchored by the vision for people with intellectual disabilities 'to enhance their capacity to fully participate in society as independent adults'.[12]

- Heidelberg University in Germany achieved a Family Friendly University certification. The university met criteria as a supportive employer and offers family programming.[13]
- The Age Friendly University is Dublin City University's designation. The university engages people in the 'Third Age' with intergenerational opportunities and activities.[14]
- The University of Auckland achieved the top spot twice in the *Times Higher Education* Impact Rankings. This is an evaluation of universities set against the 17 United Nations Sustainable Development Goals. These annual rankings 'shine a light on those institutions that are working hard to tackle global issues such as gender inequality, quality education for all, climate change, achieving peaceful societies and economic growth'.[15]

Alongside labels are common taglines: ' "the engaged university"; "the borderless university"; "the accessible university" … "the research intensive university" even the "entrepreneurial university"'[16] that might resonate with many of us. What is our university's distinct features? How can this complement our own interests and passions in life?

Business scholar Stephen Covey reminds us of the four key components of our lives: our mind, body, heart, and soul. When we focus too much on one aspect in our lives, the others become neglected. This imbalance disrupts our well-being. 'Although renewal in each dimension is important,' Covey says, 'it only becomes optimally effective as we deal with all four dimensions in a wise and balanced way.'[17] Universities are well positioned to be lifelong places to nurture this balance in our lives, *for life*. This section looks at mind, body, heart, and soul in turn. We'll cover rock star memorabilia, researchers-turned-comedians, doctors on boats, pets, mindful practices, and grandparents at university. Some journey! Suffice to say there is incredible breadth and depth in these examples. If these examples fit, so do our passions in life. This is our chance to tighten the connection between our life passions and our alumni capital.

13

Passion signpost: Nourish our wellness through our alumni capital

My young daughter adores all living creatures. When I read an article in the University of Sheffield alumni magazine, I sensed a teachable moment. Entitled 'The Professional Birdwatcher',[1] the article detailed Tim Birkhead's study of guillemot birds on the uninhabited Skomer Island. We watched videos on guillemots and an interview with Birkhead. We learned how his research impacts the well-being of the sea life ecosystem. We were enthralled. I explained that the professor's bird watching began as a child. His passion continued throughout his life as a researcher and will continue after his retirement.

I am cautious not to overstate the potential for passions to become careers. My love of swimming won't take me to the Olympics. Nor will my knitting projects lead to a knitwear business. Not all our hobbies or passions become our careers. I explained as much to my kids. We can enjoy these leisure and recreational activities throughout our lives. Universities are such places to discover knowledge and nourishment. How do we inject a sense of passion in our lives? At my house, we learned new things about birds and the natural ecosystem. The passion for animals remains, binoculars perched on the windowsill.

Alumni Action 14: Fostering lifelong learning to sharpen the mind

Our growth mindset is viewing obstacles or failures as learning opportunities. This is also our chance to seek out new platforms for learning. What better setting for learning throughout our life than a university? An underlying value of all universities – stated or not – is lifelong learning. When we first graduate, we may set our sights on advanced study. We might hope to specialize to a master or doctoral level. We might opt for continued professional development to extend our career-based knowledge and skills. The focus here is learning for learning's sake. We pursue learning because we are curious. We have a passion for the subject or for the debate. The knowledge connects us to a hobby, interest, or recreational activity. Our alma mater, or other universities of interest, help us to stop scrolling mindlessly through information. We can take the time for depth over breadth.

Our thirst for lifelong learning is the essence of our humanity. It is our ability to apply knowledge for creative, caring, and passionate purposes. This is a refreshing perspective, with such an emphasis on automation and technology, including artificial intelligence. Our alma mater provides us with a distinctly human dimension to our lives: learning opportunities over our lifetime to make us dynamic, alumni citizens.[2] We are in a state of constant enquiry (or at least we should be!). We can be reflective, curious, and creative. What are these leftfield moments of esoteric learning? Get your pen ready, immersing ourselves in this learning enables new ideas to flow!

Universities are masters at designing events anchored in passion. As alumni, we are welcome attendees at public seminars, webinars, colloquiums, and conferences. Every topic imaginable might be covered, from current affairs to scientific discoveries, pop culture to historical fiction. These events attract international speakers or involve prestigious faculty. They encourage open high-spirited debate and share thought-provoking research. University TEDx evenings are also common, like the regular event coordinated by the University of Malta.[3]

Indeed, TED talks continue to put university academic research into the public spotlight. With millions of views, Brené

Brown isn't a YouTube influencer. Her TED talk, 'The power of vulnerability', draws on her years of research as a University of Houston professor.[4] Sharpening our mind is part of the university's raison d'etre. Case in point, over 80 universities in the United Kingdom alone signed up to the *Manifesto for Public Engagement*.[5] This is a public acknowledgement of a university's commitment to sharing 'knowledge, resources and skills with the public'.[6] Public engagement goes two ways. As alumni, we can actively participate in these learning and knowledge sharing sessions. We might be the lively audience participant, university TEDx curator, or the next speaker.

Universities get very creative to present their knowledge to the masses. I liken it to parents attempting to get a child to eat broccoli. Tell them to bite and swallow quickly. The university equivalent? A competition to challenge graduate students to distil their research into a three-minute talk. Make them laugh and sneak in the green vegetable? The comparable academic initiative could be Bright Club. This is the comedy club night inviting academic researchers in the UK and Ireland to produce stand-up comedy routines. 'We wanted something with content that would attract an audience beyond those already working and studying in universities,' explains Bright Club founder Steve Cross. 'The thing we came up with was stand-up comedy ... because you can make anything funny.'[7] Bright Club can boast the claim 'researchers become comedians for just one night'.[8] What we discover is that broccoli isn't so bad after all − it's delicious! That's the kind of appetite (and attitude) we need to delve into in our learning, to nourish our mind.

Universities also offer a wide range of learning opportunities − for free. The University of Melbourne surpassed the one million enrolments to their MOOCs from over 200 countries worldwide.[9] The Australian university boasts a broad spectrum of courses 'from animal behaviour and the French Revolution, to citizen journalism and corporate financial decision making'.[10] What's a MOOC? It's a Massive Open Online Course. This is a free, online course designed and delivered by university faculty. A visit to platforms like EdX, Coursera, or FutureLearn, showcase the tens of thousands of courses available. Why are universities giving away their knowledge for free? Among the reasons, the research suggests, it's 'extending the reach of the institution and access to education'.[11] University of Melbourne reports that about one third of the learners of their MOOCs are from countries with emerging economies.[12] MOOCs can broaden learning and curiosity.

MOOCs offer thousands of courses from some of the world's most renowned universities. While the enthusiasm to sign up to a free online course is swift, MOOC completion rates remain low,[13] even referred to as 'education voyeurism'.[14] Don't be discouraged. We can embrace the MOOC flexibility. We might pick up a snippet during one course. Another might spark new ideas or prompt us to enrol in a full accreditation. When I wanted to learn more about the GDPR coming into force across Europe in 2018, I signed up for a MOOC offered by the University of Groningen. I took another, 'Babies in Mind', from the University of Warwick to support my role as a new parent. MOOCs are quenching our thirst for lifelong learning. They complement – not replace – formal higher education.

'Sip, sip hooray!' is the theme for the Alumni Wine Program at UC Davis.[15] These are tasting and educational events that bring together the university's wine and beer partners. The university also boasts: '80% of winemakers throughout the globe are connected to UC Davis.'[16] It's an impressive claim. Wines and craft beers produced especially for or by universities is also not that unusual. Pairings, cooking demonstrations, and baking workshops satisfy our inner sommelier and aspirations for culinary greatness.

Sometimes, instead of venturing out, we would rather curl up with a good book. Book clubs are making a comeback with an alumni twist. An online book club allows us to reconnect with our alma mater even if we live far from campus. Some alumni book clubs select books by fellow alumni authors. Others, like the Massachusetts Institute of Technology (MIT) Alumni Book Club, involve faculty members to lead online discussion.[17] Pace University summarizes the benefits of the alumni book club as being good for career growth, leading to positive health outcomes, and providing fellow alumni with a way to connect 'across industries, generations and geographies to help improve your network'.[18] These book clubs tend to attract alumni who have seldom connected with the university in the past. This might be the gateway to fostering our passion for reading or finding other alma mater activities of interest.

Special university anniversaries or commemorations are another platform to sharpen the mind. In September 2019, Solent University marked 50 years of yacht design. To celebrate this milestone, the university organized a weekend of events to bring together the entire university community. Alumni, former design staff, students, key corporate sponsors, and interested members of the community gathered on campus with a shared passion for world-class yacht design.[19] When I interviewed Robert Wayman, the elation of the sold-out events hadn't yet abated. As Alumni Relations and Philanthropy Manager at the university, Wayman spoke of the buzz of learning in these events. Alumni marvelled over the developments on campus since their studies. They set out on a maritime simulation tour. The learning extended into the evening gala dinner. Guests received an insightful address by fellow alum Matthew Sheahan, a leading sailing journalist.[20] These events bring it all together: people, knowledge, and resources to create a synergy of alumni capital.

Our mind tingles with excitement at these events – the times when learning happens, and we don't even notice. What are the passion points that we might share with fellow alumni? Even without the yacht (or broccoli!), we can approach our alumni capital with a sharpness of mind.

Activity 14: Nourish our wellness through our alumni capital by fostering lifelong learning to sharpen the mind

Return to the Alumni Capital diagram in Chapter 2 (Figure 2.1). What are the flows of knowledge, people, and resources around you? After the learning so far in this book, you're ready to map out your alumni capital.

Draw the three overlapping circles. Set yourself to alumni mode. In the first circle, consider the key people that immediately come to mind – alumni, professors, lecturers, students, staff members, coaches. These people may have inspired you during your studies and/or continue to connect with you today. In the second circle, map out the university and alumni resources available to you – both the resources you might use regularly or ones you intend to use in future. The third circle focuses on the flows of knowledge within your institution. This one might take a little research. Visit the university's website for ideas of things that interest you from a professional – and a passion – perspective. Check out the university's most recent news stories and publications to get a sense of the research, partnerships, courses, and projects that might be of interest.

Voila! This is your own alumni capital framework. This is a work in progress. Revise as you discover other elements of interest.

Next, sharpen your mind by focusing on lifelong learning opportunities. Given the right conditions – time, location, even financial resources – what would you want to learn more about right now? Professional development to progress your career may come to mind first. What else? Perhaps you want to learn a new language. You may want to be better at interior design. Set a timer for 15 minutes. Search online for formal accredited programmes, MOOCs, webinars, or conferences in your area of interest. These courses might be at your own alma mater or other institutions near and far, nudging out the boundaries of your alumni capital. I suggest limiting the time because chances are your search will open you to a world of interesting learning opportunities at your fingertips!

Alumni Action 15: Nurturing our body

For the new year, I had great intentions to embrace a healthy new regime. The email from my alma mater was perfectly timed. I signed up immediately to the University of Sheffield's Couch to 5K. Within days, the sign-ups from fellow alumni and members of the University community exceeded expectations. The university smashed their fundraising goal for Parkinson's research, before our training began in earnest. I enjoyed feeling part of a university community, all striving towards the same goal. My jogs were a little less isolated on my rural, country trails. Time travelling back to my early alumni days, I participated in many recreational activities. I continued my regular swimming sessions and took up squash. One incentive was a special alumni membership rate at Hart House, one of University of Toronto's extra-curricular hubs. It conjures up great memories with friends, at the pool, even several court defeats. This is my little nod to nostalgia, a necessity for an alumni book!

Caught up in life after graduation, it's easy to shelve our connections to sports facilities, teams, and fitness classes at the university. When a university football team made it to the city league, Kate Burgess, in the Alumni Relations Office at the University of Suffolk put out an appeal. 'The team will be made up of current students and alumni,' Burgess said in her LinkedIn post, 'Whether you are looking to get started, get back into the game, improve your fitness or make new friends, please let us know if you are interested in joining!'[21] Her quote reminds us of all the reasons to participate in team sports, along with the merits of a campus connection. Burgess also reminds us how important it is, as alumni, to follow key social media accounts of our alma mater. This way, we don't miss any of these opportunities. Do campus or student societies – canoe clubs, intramural sports, or outdoor adventure groups – welcome alumni members? Even virtual yoga, Pilates, or fitness classes streaming from university centres now abound. Hiking clubs for alumni are popping up in universities or even corporate alumni circles too. There is no harm in asking the question or seeking them out. It could be a natural and gentle start into finding a new sports interest, keeping up your fitness, or enjoying the great outdoors.

There are physiotherapy and sports injury clinics on many campuses, often open to students and alumni as clients. Massage therapy, personal training, health screenings and even dental services (usually by dental students under supervision) might be available too. We can repurpose those curiosity skills to investigate the campus services that help to keep us in peak physical condition (or at least healthy!). As alumni, we can be on alert for creative ways to weave a passion for wellness into our lives.

Staying in shape may also involve our four-legged friends, with alumni events to match. The best canine inspired event titles? The Yappy Hour Social organized by Old Dominion University,[22] and the Dog Days of Summer, the campus dog walking session at Kent State University.[23] University College Dublin's Woodland

Walkies event offers guided walks, pup orienteering, and agility courses for the canine friends of alumni.[24] This is a chance to meet other alumni passionate about their pets. Don't see this as a perk at our alma mater but passionate about pets? We can always start an alumni dog-walking group of our own.

Nurturing our body requires our listening along with our lively participation. We can gather information to improve our physical health. 'In order to be happier, you don't have to go out and run a marathon,' reports Jason Rentfrow, lead researcher on an exercise-happiness study at the University of Cambridge, 'all you've really got to do is periodically engage in slight physical activity throughout the day'.[25] Phew! Universities are masters at promoting research on physical well-being to a public audience. From obesity research to cleanliness, caring for our skin,[26] and benefits of exercise, the media draws on university research for provocative, reliable, and informative content. Will we change our habits? Try a new exercise routine? Eat differently? Alumni-inspired action is possible!

'Wellbeing: Not Just Jogging and Broccoli.'[27] This headline appeared in Iowa State University's alumni magazine. In the article, alumni and university experts present a holistic view of well-being. The article highlights the university's student wellness programme, featuring peer wellness educators. For alumni well-being, ISU promotes a 'Living a Life' podcast and an archive of wellness webinars.[28] Our alumni communications – magazines, blogs, podcasts – are valuable sources of provocative and digestible information on improving our well-being.

When we follow our passion – for sport, for wellness, for healthy cooking – we build our arsenal to keep learning, getting better in the process. We can become discerning about the sources of our information and how we apply this to our lives. 'Many growth-minded people didn't even plan to go to the top,' Dweck reminds us, 'They got there as a result of doing what they love.'[29] We don't need to obsess about these unachievable goals like a perfect body or reaching the top in our sport; we can enjoy the journey, be open to learning, and through this growth mindset see that we can reach unintended heights of wellness.

Let's not forget glorious food! Campuses are a hive of culinary delights, from fast food to slow food. Cafés, food trucks, restaurants, farmers markets, and exclusive bistros dot the university landscape. Our favourite late-night haunt or event caterer might be an alumni-owned business too. We can keep our eyes open for the alumni cookbooks, food blogs, and recipe videos. New food product lines pass through university research centres, before adorning our supermarket shelves. Foodies unite! The discerning palates and conscientious nature of alumni and our alma mater communities see food as more than a consuming activity. Food has the potential to nourish us, repair us, and unite us through culture and traditions. Campuses are open places for alumni too. We are welcome to indulge on the run, on the patio, or even with online orders.

Activity 15: Nourish our wellness through our alumni capital by nurturing our body

We all have good intentions to nourish our physical health. Identify three things – a sport, an activity, a new nutrition regimen, even tackling some home cooking – you are curious about or that aligns with your passions. Consider how your university and your alumni capital can help you to engage in the activity of your choice. Complete this as a reflection and do some research online to see how your alma mater – or other institutions – offer a gateway to better health!

14

Passion signpost: Watch our alumni-self flourish

What tugs at our heartstrings? What renews our soul? Sometimes in this hectic, always-on world, we set aside our passions. We forgo the things that make us truly happy and joyful. Perhaps as we completed the reflection and curious questioning something surfaced. A university memory. A moment of clarity. A shared connection to make us smile. These initial points of reference can point us to our passion. Sir Ken Robinson spoke of The Element. I believe these are the elements with a small 'e'. These elements lead us to our purpose and our passion. These are the values that anchor our lives.

Entrepreneur Jessica Huie beamed when I met her in London on a spring afternoon. Her new book, *Purpose*, published only weeks earlier, embodied the elements of a growth mindset. Huie's book charts her setbacks and struggles: she was a school dropout and a teenage parent. She also points to her public success: working with celebrities at a top public relations firm, founder of the multicultural greeting card company Color Blind Cards. After a personal epiphany, Huie decided to share her deeply personal story. 'An incredible convergence happens when you share your message or brand with the world from the authentic space,' Huie says. 'Your tribe finds you … Those who believe the same things that you believe and who care about the things you care about.'[1] Through retreats and workshops, Huie assembles a community and helps people find their voice.

From this authentic space comes a community of supportive purpose-driven businesses. How can we find a community that nurtures our passion? What *are* our passions? Sometimes even after reflective questions and curious conversations, we aren't there yet. We need to find our voice.

This might seem like a tall order. How does our alumni identity contribute to our flourishing selves? Maureen Gaffney, in her aptly titled book, *Flourishing*, explains: 'We all know people who seem to be deeply and enjoyably involved in their lives,' she writes. 'Some have a single overriding passion – soccer, science, theatre, teaching – that completely absorbs them. Others seem to have the knack of consistently finding many things that give them scope to develop their talents and skills.'[2] She presents the key strategy to this success as 'the art of vital engagement'. Gaffney describes this concept as 'the joy of losing yourself in everything you do'.[3] We can lose ourselves. Let go. Resist the temptation of finding a practical reason for it in our lives. Be masters of the moment. As we allow a hidden passion to surface, we bring more dimension to our lives. This enhances our whole self. We search for our north star – or constellation of stars – to follow. Our alumni capital, through our alma mater and alumni network, are a great place to begin our navigation. It's also a great community to mobilize further support. This is a reflective and curious audience, a passionate like-minded community.

Alumni Action 16: Following our heart to guide our passion

The Cabaret of Dangerous Ideas is The University of Edinburgh's contribution to the Festival Fringe. As the largest international celebration for the arts in the world, the university is also a key venue for the festival. At the Cabaret, university researchers, without the crutch of slides, present on outrageous themes like 'The Politics of the Tooth Fairy'[4] and 'All News is Fake News.'[5] Not all of us can make it to the Fringe to see this show. We can turn instead to our own alma mater, a long-standing patron of the arts. From drama festivals and theatres, to art collections and galleries. We can explore concerts, poetry readings, book launches, symphonies, dance recitals, and art exhibitions. Residency programmes for artists, poets, dancers, musicians, and writers abound, ranging from dance classes and music programmes to writing workshops and shelves of books by famous alumni. These special events and virtual opportunities allow us to celebrate the artistic success of fellow alumni or faculty from all over the world. My parents are season ticket holders for theatre productions at Dalhousie University. My holiday baking was infused by my university's alumni festive playlist.[6] As alumni, we can promote *our* artistic achievements to *our own* alumni audience. We can also join our fellow graduates to revel in these cultural experiences.

The arts are diffused across the university. In some cases, universities *are* the arts. There are architectural feats of wonder, controversy, and campus folklore. There are beautiful buildings, centuries old, and modern buildings of glass, timber, steel, and concrete. Atriums and staff offices display paintings from the university's collection. Music composed for the university is played at the graduation ceremony. I love visiting universities to see the eclectic artwork hanging from the walls and across open spaces indoor and out. They make statements and often hold a deep meaning to place and to the values of the institution. Even the gifts given to university visitors are often the art or craftwork created by students or alumni. They have a special place in preserving arts heritage too. The Muppets are part of a video archive at University of Maryland Libraries, creator Jim Henson's alma mater.[7] Want to peruse the collection of Bruce Springsteen memorabilia? Visit Monmouth University, near the New Jersey town where 'the Boss' got his start in music — it is home to over 35,000 items. With this immense collection, Monmouth offer public events, and they digitized the collection for online access.[8] Universities take this role of stewardship to heart, for meticulous preservation, for study, and for us to enjoy for years to come.

We might underestimate the role universities can play in what we watch, what we buy, and even what we wear. Naturally, universities foster the next generation of performers and production across all genres, that often began with a course or campus production. What a frisson of excitement when filming takes place on campus! Alumni like us continue to find inspiration from their university experience by depicting it on screen or published in novels. We can participate in much of this celebration of the arts too. Passionate for the arts we can become members of the theatre or musical productions, attend art gallery openings, or celebrate artistic process of students or alumni.

Universities are also known as bastions of freedom of speech and freedom of expression. A location to ignite social movements and explore issues of equity, diversity, ethics, ethnicity, and identity. The Bike Kitchen, a non-profit community bike shop at the University of British Columbia is one such place. Through bike education, members of the university community get the know-how to fix their bike. With this new skill set – and recycled parts – they are empowered to make environmentally conscious transportation choices.[9] The values of accessibility, social justice, education, and fun (there *is* free pizza at volunteer nights!) permeate from the Bike Kitchen. Access nights enable women, queer and LGBTQ2I+ community members to use the shop in a relaxed, supportive environment.[10] Like-minded people congregate with a shared passion for sustainable living. Through the passionate volunteer efforts of students and alumni, the Bike Kitchen is a mobilizing community action.

How can alumni encourage and engage in work with heart? Universities are always looking for volunteer student mentors or classroom guest speakers. We can also *be* the role models of diversity for students and the university community. Greenwich Portraits strive to match the demographics of the University of Greenwich community with alumni stories.[11] The outcome is beautifully curated photographs of alumni, reflecting the diversity of the community with the distinction of an iconic place on campus. Some of the photos have gone viral, including grime MC artist JME (Jamie Adenuga), a well-known figure photographed in the vice-chancellor's office. Featured alumni are now inspiring students to show pride in their alma mater and to aspire to be a portrait of the future. The institution has found its voice through alumni citizenship: one of diversity, outstanding potential, inclusion, and creativity. What can we do to support our university's role to ignite social change?

Universities *are* often leading this change. They are reviving minority languages or researching problems in our health system. Often alumni lead this work with heart. When I heard Benjamin La Brot on the radio, he was explaining origins of the Floating Doctors, an organization he founded in 2009. The Floating Doctors brings urgent medical attention to rural island communities that would otherwise not have access to quality healthcare.[12] La Brot was in Ireland speaking at the Royal College of Surgeons in Ireland (RCSI) alumni event 'showcasing RCSI alumni as healthcare innovators and global thought-leaders'.[13]

La Brot and fellow alum Ryan McCormick raised awareness of the work of Floating Doctors to an alumni audience while reflecting on how their own RSCI experience enhanced their current work. Current RCSI students continued to raise funds for the cause.[14] RCSI celebrated alumni living their passion for accessible healthcare. Our challenge as alumni engaging with our university is formidable and global. There is immense potential for alumni to actively embrace and address the United Nations 17 Sustainable Development Goals. 'These goals have the power to create a better world by 2030', states the challenge set on the Global Goals website, 'by ending poverty, fighting inequality and addressing the urgency of climate change'.[15] How can we collectively, as alumni, address some of the greatest challenges facing humanity and our planet?

Community outreach programmes give us a whole lifetime – and across our life stages – to enjoy connection to our university. Alumni programming is intuitive to our lives if we seek it out. During the COVID-19 pandemic, the family-friendly programming pivoted to include online kids' camps, virtual story times, and parental advice for schooling at home. In the family-focused spirit, the University of Wisconsin-Madison started Grandparents University (GPU) an alumni association-supported grandparent-grandchild weekend camp. The event includes 'staying in a residence hall, touring the campus, going to class, participating in engaging and hands-on activities in a major – and earning a GPU "degree!"'[16] What a strategic way to introduce the next generation to the university, through the eyes of someone who, decades before, enjoyed the experience. More poignantly, is the suggestion that the alumni dimension to our lives can be central to special family experiences. Don't just bring the kids to the local parade, the university has a dedicated seating for families to enable mingling with fellow alumni and their families too. As our lives add and shed identities – as parents, new homeowners, even grandparents – we can return to our alma mater to see what it offers us at different touchpoints in our lives.

Take Nika Shakiba's experience with DEEP, the Da Vinci Engineering Enrichment Programme, a University of Toronto pre-university outreach programme.[17] "I've been privileged to come full circle with DEEP," Shakiba said. "I attended as a high school student, volunteered as a teaching instructor for the programme, and I have now been lucky enough to design and teach a DEEP course during my graduate career." I caught up with Shakiba when she was a post-doc at MIT. She attributes DEEP to introducing her to the world of engineering as a high school student. She opened her eyes to the curiosity and problem solving that the discipline allows across a range of sectors. "DEEP is a playground to test the boundaries of engineering," Shakiba recalls.

As a PhD candidate, she taught her popular 'Stem Cell Talks' course before passing the baton of teaching to her brother, a fellow graduate student. Shakiba is passionate about engineering, and, as a DEEP alum, she gained mentorship skills, curriculum development, and teaching skills. She also had fun inspiring the next generation of potential engineers. I heard about Shakiba's story on Twitter, after the university highlighted her leadership award for her work. When universities identify and highlight these stories of active alumni engagement like Shakiba's, they serve as inspiration for others. Outreach programmes act as the catalyst to spark the core passion we have for a topic or discipline. As research suggests, STEM (science, technology, engineering, mathematics) outreach programmes serve a tripartite mission. First, involve universities in enhancing science education and public literacy in STEM. Second, outreach programmes prepare graduate students actively within service elements of academia. Finally, to create two-way interactions between universities and the community (instead of one-way transmission of university resources outwards).[18] As Shakiba's story shows, alumni have immense potential to be involved and promote outreach programmes. We can wear our many hats in this work as former participants, as parents of current participants, as public educators, as graduate students, or members of the wider university community.

The Serengeti of Tanzania, ancient Greece, mystical India, and Antarctica, are some incredible destinations to share with fellow alumni. No longer is a trip simply meandering through tourist traps or must-see sites. Alumni affinity travel programmes enable us to become informed and enlightened travellers. At the Johns Hopkins University's Alumni College, faculty or alumni experts lead weekend trips to special excursions, like jazz festivals, sampling food and wine across North America.[19] Universities have also diversified their travel programmes to include alumni trips for families or adventures like white water rafting or ambitious hikes up some of the world's most challenging peaks. We can broaden our alumni capital to include travel too. Cost-effective tours and experiences through tourism websites are often led by expert guides who are either completing their graduate studies or are alumni of a local university. This was my experience with Big Onion walking tours[20] when I toured Harlem in New York City. My tour of hidden Porto was also led by a local university graduate. Involving alumni brings heart to our experiences.

Activity 16: Watch our alumni-self flourish by following our heart to guide our passion

Take a piece of paper and put a line down the centre to create two columns. List five things on the left side that you are passionate about, starting with values, interests, or activities you enjoy. On the right side, consider the question: how can my alma mater foster these passions? Check out the university's website to see how your university offers programmes, events, or initiatives to ignite your passions. Consult your alumni capital map too for further ideas. Connect to fellow alumni who share the same interests or values.

Don't be afraid to stretch yourself! It might not simply be your *own* alma mater that may be of interest, it could be another institution nearby that shares your passion. Seek out alumni connection at this institution and broaden your alumni capital!

Alternative activity

Complete a Global Goals micro-reflection. Review the Global Goals – the 17 United Nations Sustainable Development Goals.[21] Write down three goals that you are most passionate about and explain why. Consider how your alumni capital – your university and alumni network – can be collaborative partners to these goals. Be reflective and curious about what is already happening at your alma mater or by fellow alumni. Do you want to join an existing Global Goals-inspired university project? Identify and reach out to a fellow alum to hear about their work in a short online informational interview? Finally, write down the steps you intend to follow and take action!

Alumni Action 17: Leading with the soul

We might bring passion, even heart into our projects. To bring soul, though, is much deeper and more profound. When conversations are effortless, the learning is illuminating, and the programmes inspirational; we begin to connect with the essence, the soul of our alma mater. Tick box exercises and government key performance indicators need not apply. Universities have a long relationship with faith and spirituality.[22] In fostering the traits of the Alumni Way, I hope that our passion will also surface, and no passion is deeper than the passion in our soul. The soul is a complex and very individual entity; we each have a different experience of aspects that delve deep into the fabric of our being.

At the risk of this section waxing lyrical about the joys of the soulful in the university, I believe that the passionate element that nourishes our soul can derive from our alma mater. Universities, by their very nature, foster practising academics – the students – creating the ideal environment for this replenishment of the soul. We may have found that at university – or just after graduation – allows the time for soul searching.

There are places of worship and serenity on campus that provide students, staff, and faculty that inner sense of peace – chapels, churches, inter-faith rooms, meditation spaces, peace gardens. As alumni, we can join the celebrations, rituals, and faith ceremonies on campus. Often there is a spiritual community connected to these spaces that are open to alumni members. Many larger institutions also have retreat centres or outreach campus spaces that students and alumni can book to have their own time in nature and a connection with self. Soul is also about those once-in-a-lifetime moments, such as a wedding day. Universities often offer us with space for ceremonies, receptions, and photographs, even a celebrant, a dinner venue, even an impressive student string quartet.

In 2015, the National University of Ireland, Galway began a journey to become a Mindful University. The inaugural conference and a series of regular mindfulness and meditation practices on all the university's campuses set the scene.[23] 'The Mindful Way conference was our first step towards understanding the role mindfulness can play in providing a more enriching experience for staff and students,' explains Lokesh Joshi, then the university's vice-president leading this movement on campus, 'There was such an enthusiastic response that we want to build on the momentum to see what can be achieved collectively through a more mindful approach.'[24] As alumni, we can participate in these explorations, these movements on campus towards our own positive, personal discovery.

As our alma mater searches for its soul and creates mindful practices, alumni can be a forgotten shareholder. This isn't a malicious attempt at exclusion. Often, universities are focused on those that are right in front of them: students, staff, and faculty, even the local community. When a university wishes to build a mindful university or embed entrepreneurship, the question I like to ask is, how can alumni support this goal? One example is Harvard Alumni for Mental Health (HAMH), a shared interest group open to alumni with a professional or personal interest in supporting mental health, especially of students and recent graduates.[25] 'The main goals of the group are to connect alumni across schools and years, to facilitate dialogue, and to reach out to current students.'[26] HAMH offers new alumni a 'next step',[27] continuing support for student mental health after their time in peer support groups or peer advising roles. This creates a cohesive community that cares about student mental health. Our alumni connection can also be our participation in large campus events, pilgrimages, retreats, and think-ins. If we find the link that touches our soul, this is the anchor for our holistic development and the chance to ignite our passion through supporting others in our alma mater.

Randy Pausch had a legacy to leave — for his family and for humanity. The Carnegie Mellon Professor and alum was diagnosed with cancer and given only months to live. Pausch wanted to share his wisdom of life in the way he knew best: the university lecture. In his presentation — now watched by millions — Pausch tells his story in an upbeat, humorous and, yes, passionate way.[28] This includes a passion for the academy where he spent his professional life. Pausch points out the role that universities can play in fulfilling childhood dreams stating: 'as you get older you may find that enabling the dreams of others is even more fun'.[29] We can reflect on our own passions in life and we can also enable others to achieve incredible heights, attend university, or secure a dream job. We might need to endure sacrifices and we may need to draw on our inner strength to enable others.

This is not only about the physical university but also the soulful connection with our fellow alumni. We might feel nostalgia for our experience or the people we met who had a profound connection with us during our time on campus, or after graduation. Stories like Pausch's, and his last lecture, remind us of our humanity and our place to make a difference while we are here. In his book *Tuesdays with Morrie*, author Mitch Albom rekindles a relationship with his former professor from Brandeis University, remembering the lessons he learned about 'being human and relating to others'.[30] Sometimes our time at university and after university is so transactional that we forget the relational and even the transformational.

For some of us, our alma mater permeates so many aspects of our life. Rupert Forsythe of StageClip described to me the significance of the University of Birmingham on all aspects of his life: "That's where I met my wife and I started my first business," he said. Forsythe maintains his alma mater as a loyal client for his business, and his son also maintains a campus connection. Perhaps not all of us are as intertwined with our alma mater, but it may still be a deep and soulful relationship that plays a significant role in the milestones of our lives. Shehu Sani, author and Nigerian senator calls alumni associations 'a reunion of souls'.[31] This is our opportunity to ensure that all alumni feel they can participate to what Sani calls 'unconditional love and celebrate the wrinkles, baldness and the grey hairs that marked our mileage'.[32] We might all not be there (yet!), but we move towards these wide celebrations of our alumni connections in our lives. A reunion with fellow alumni can be less about nostalgia and more about rekindling a relationship with like-minded people. At the Middlebury Institute of International Studies, a group of International Environmental Policy (IEP) alumni organized a gathering described as 'living lives of passion'.[33] As alum Cynthia Yeh, explained, 'I left the event feeling inspired by that my IEP colleagues are in the world implementing changes from grassroots to international waters.'[34]

Activity 17: Watch our alumni-self flourish by leading with the soul

There are several ways that you can connect directly with your alma mater or alumni capital to find spiritual meaning. In this activity, identify a fellow alum, recent graduate, former professor, or even a current student and request an informational interview. Once again, be prepared and follow a formal informational interview format. This discussion is as important as your career questions. Explain when you make the request that the focus of this meeting is to explore how the person copes with the stresses of life, draws comfort, and even finds spiritual or mindful practice in their daily life. Ask them to recommend books, podcasts, or even blogs – and of course university resources – to draw another level of inspiration.

15

Passion trait summary: Our lives, our alma mater

Our universities are often viewed as and rated on their instrumental purposes, such as graduate employability. This section reminds us that our institutions also have a greater purpose: as higher education and philosophy scholar Mala Singh succinctly states, 'higher education itself *as* a public good and higher education *for* the public good'.[1] Yes, our alma mater is a valuable part of our educational community. As alumni, we are an important part of this public good within the university ecosystem. As alumni who wish to pursue a passion – whether it is recreation, social justice activism, travel, and beyond – the university can help us pursue our passion to its fullest.

We need to be open to the alumni dimension of our lives to support our passions. Our alma mater, fellow alumni, even a favourite professor, may support us in identifying and fostering our passions. They sustain us or also prove to be obsessive or challenging aspects of our lives. Carol Dweck reminds us that passion is also an important trait of resilience: 'The passion for stretching yourself and sticking to it', she says, 'even (or especially) when it's not going well, is the hallmark of the growth mindset'.[2] When we try something new, venture somewhere novel, or get involved in something that hasn't gone entirely as we hoped, we can draw on our passion for our own tenacity to try it until it works – allowing us to build our passionate arsenal.

In her book *The Rocket Years: How Your Twenties Launch the Rest of Your Life*, Elizabeth Segran argues that it is in our 20s that we often develop our lifelong hobbies.[3] It may seem counterintuitive, as our time in university or immediately after graduation for many of us was a time to focus on our career. 'We sometimes seek out hobbies that reflect our values and our sense of self,' Segran says. 'But we occasionally stumble into hobbies entirely by chance and discover a new passion ... The hobbies we settle on, as random as they are, end up defining us.'[4] Whether we develop a passion for photography, sewing, or windsurfing this can add another dimension to our lives.

Recent research shows the positive health effects of regular participation in recreational activity, in which the researchers concluded, 'when individuals engaged in leisure, they also reported better mood, more interest, less stress, and exhibited lower heart rate than when they were not engaging in leisure activity'.[5] This reinforces what we already know: engaging in activities we are passionate about *does* improve our lives and our well-being. Part IV reminds us to be a proactive sleuth. We find ways to apply our wider alumni capital to immerse ourselves in things to which we derive a deep sense of satisfaction, align to our purpose, and even inject a little fun in our lives.

Key messages from Part IV

- Our alma mater appears everywhere, and it has a lifelong impact beyond our professional life.
- Our alma mater, and institutions near us, can foster a wide array of the passions in our life.
- By following our passions, we can create mind, body, heart, and soul balance.
- We learn throughout our life and the university can offer a breadth of accessible courses, research, and initiatives. These are available to alumni and the public to sharpen our mind and satisfy our interest in learning.

- From leisure activities to sports, healthy physical fitness to culinary delights, our body can be nourished through our lifelong connection to our alma mater.
- As we follow our heart and values, we can see alignment with our alma mater. We can find, follow, and participate in heartfelt outreach and activities at our alma mater.
- The university is a place of soul. Spirituality and mindful practice are embraced to enable us to flourish.

Disengaged alumni with the fixed mindset will:

- avoid putting in any effort to seek ways the university can nourish mind, body, heart, and soul;
- consider their talent and intelligence is static and does not seek out new opportunities for learning;
- ignore recommendations from fellow alumni on an invitation directly from their alma mater to join an alumni or university activity they feel might be of interest;
- become critical of the successful initiatives at another university instead of thinking how this could be enjoyed or initiated at their own alma mater.

Dynamic alumni with the growth mindset will:

- embrace new challenges and put in effort to try ways to nourish the mind, body, heart, and soul;
- consider the university has a lifelong place to enable their passions to flourish;
- seek out ways the university can support life outside of work;
- share interesting alumni capital-infused activities or initiatives with fellow alumni;
- take charge of their own lifelong relationship with their alma mater and alumni capital to impact themselves, values they care about and support society;
- find inspiration in successful initiatives in other universities; take the lead in finding ways for these initiatives to be available in their own alma mater or for fellow alumni and students.

Checklist for Part IV

To build your Alumni Way, especially to foster your life passions don't forget to:

☐ complete your own Alumni Capital diagram as an ongoing work in progress (see Activity 14);

☐ discover lifelong learning opportunities to fuel your passions (see Activity 14);

☐ identify areas to nourish your physical health (see Activity 15);

☐ reflect on the things you are most passionate about in your life and consider how your alma mater and fellow alumni can support this passion (see Activity 16);

☐ review the Global Goals and complete the micro-reflection to take action (see Activity 16);

☐ conduct an informational interview that focuses on questions of spiritual and mindful well-being (see Activity 17).

Building the Alumni Way: Questions following Part IV

- *Recent graduates and alumni*: What activities did you participate in during university that allowed you to identify your values and passions in life? How can these activities be extended today?

- *Students*: How do you maintain a balance of involvement that allow your mind, body, heart, and soul to flourish, especially with the pressures of academic study?

- *University administrators*: How do you integrate our alumni into the heart and soul of our university community aligned to the mission, vision, and values of the institution?

- *Advancement professionals*: What initiatives and programmes does the university offer (or could offer) that supports alumni to nourish their mind, body, heart, and soul?

- *Parents/career advisers*: How can you support students and recent alumni to maintain a balance between mind, body, heart, and soul in their lives?

PART V

The Alumni Way trait: Generosity

16	When giving back has new meaning	137
17	Generosity signpost: Recognize we are all philanthropists	139
	• Alumni Action 18: Giving our time as an active alumni citizen	142
	• Alumni Action 19: Celebrating our talents with our alma mater	146
18	Generosity signpost: Understand the power of giving	151
	• Alumni Action 20: Transforming our thinking on giving our treasure	153
	• Alumni Action 21: Connecting generously with our ties	161
19	Generosity trait summary: Our generosity as service	169
	• Key messages from Part V	170
	• Checklist for Part V	172
	• Building the Alumni Way: Questions following Part V	172

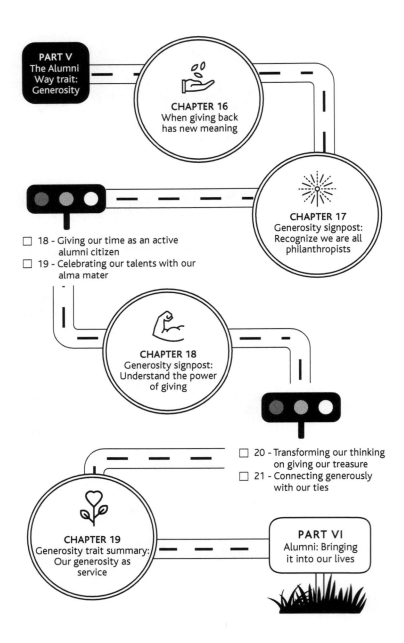

PART V
The Alumni Way trait: Generosity

CHAPTER 16
When giving back has new meaning

CHAPTER 17
Generosity signpost: Recognize we are all philanthropists

☐ 18 - Giving our time as an active alumni citizen
☐ 19 - Celebrating our talents with our alma mater

CHAPTER 18
Generosity signpost: Understand the power of giving

☐ 20 - Transforming our thinking on giving our treasure
☐ 21 - Connecting generously with our ties

CHAPTER 19
Generosity trait summary: Our generosity as service

PART VI
Alumni: Bringing it into our lives

16

When giving back has new meaning

The word 'alumni' is synonymous with generosity. Part V is a special gift. We don't trek alone. We spend so much time focused on ourselves that we can forget the people who helped us to reach graduation. As we develop our Alumni Way, as with active citizenship or networking, there is give and take. Giving back is almost cliché, viewed as an expectation or duty. We need to reclaim the value of giving back to our community. The giving of our time, our talent, our treasure, even our ties is key to our full alumni citizenship. This is the true and comprehensive definition of philanthropy. Our philanthropy is giving back.

In his book *Why Good Things Happen to Good People*, Stephen Post reports on his research that reinforces the spirit of generosity. According to Post, we live healthier and longer when we give: 'The remarkable bottom line of the science of love is that giving protects overall health twice as much as aspirin protects again heart disease.' Post says, 'If giving weren't free, pharmaceutical companies could herald the discovery of a stupendous new drug called "Give Back" – instead of "Prozac".'[1]

Generosity *is* good for our health. We can live longer and reduce stress in our lives.[2] Giving back is not a luxurious activity. We can decide to be generous. What better place to concentrate our efforts than the comforts and familiarity of our alma mater. If giving is so good for us, shouldn't we all make time every week to give? We recognize the value of regular exercise and eating a healthy diet. We are full of good intentions. Giving should be as much about our passion and interest in the cause as it is about our own health. However, we are time poor. We fill our time with so much complexity online and offline. Fitting one more thing in – good for us or not – can be a challenge. In this section, we navigate through the give-take parameters of life. How can we, as university shareholders, reinvest in our alma mater? How can this investment yield dividends for us and for the campus community?

The origins of the word 'generous' denoted exclusivity reserved for nobility.[3] Aristotle viewed generosity as a key virtue of a leader.[4] There are hangovers of this thinking in society today. Generosity is for the extraordinary not the ordinary person.[5] Yet, it *is* in each one of us to be generous. Generosity of spirit is something that, when practised, fosters well-being. Imagine the bounty we generate if we 'give value, give opportunities, give satisfaction, give praise, give encouragement, give joy'.[6] What would it be like if we received this level of generosity from our alma mater? More poignantly, what would it be like if we *gave* this level of generosity to our fellow alumni and our alma mater?

17

Generosity signpost: Recognize we are all philanthropists

We started this journey together under one premise: we are all alumni. We are all philanthropists too. Philanthropy is not an exclusive term for the mega wealthy. It is giving of our time, talent, treasure, *and* our ties. 'Philanthropy comes in so many forms,' says Deborah Goldstein in her TEDx talk on the universal nature of philanthropy, 'and we, as a society, should validate and honour each of these contributions and the difference they make to the world'.[1] Time, talent, and treasure is a common definition of philanthropy. Adding ties is particularly relevant to our alumni citizenship. Ties are our alumni capital. Our external networks – employers, friends, companies, children, neighbours – can also benefit from our university connection. This definition of philanthropy is radical. It means giving isn't limited to fundraising appeals from the university's development office. The entire university has a responsibility to enable the philanthropic giving by alumni.

'The only time I hear from the university is when they ask for money', declares the alumni grinch. Our cynicism is stirred when stories emerge of major donors steering the direction of the academy. When I am bombarded by a fixed mindset perspective, I reread 'The College is a Philanthropy, Yes a Philanthropy.' This article, in *The Chronicle of Higher Education*, was written by Dick Merriman, then the President of Southwestern College.[2] 'This college exists as a philanthropy because thousands of people, many of whom you and I will never know, have built it,' Merriman writes. 'They built it for your benefit, knowing they would never meet you. The college's facilities, our endowment for scholarships, our mission – all of these have been built, and protected and sustained, for your benefit.'[3] He sets us this challenge: 'They were built so you can gain a college education, find and pursue your passion, and commit yourselves to living a valuable life. In short, this college exists so you can become a better person, and, in turn, help make the world a better place.'[4]

Merriman's sentiment may seem utopian. Yet, he makes an impassioned argument on the purpose of an education and why to support it. It may sway opinion. University contributes to our knowledge, skills, networks, and ideas. Our university experience equips us to live the lives we want to live and to help others in the process. As a student, we receive professional and personal growth through the generosity of others.[5] These people may include government officials who provide state funding, university administrators, academics, programme leaders, support staff, student representatives, alumni volunteers and, yes, even donors.

As alumni shareholders, we are all invested in our education. When our alma mater's reputation grows or international rankings rise, so does the credibility of our degree. New graduates are struggling to find jobs in the face of mounting university debt. Giving may not seem a priority or a possibility. However, the shares in lifelong alumni investment are more important than ever. As the saying goes, the more you put in, the more you get out. The same is true for the alumni-university relationship.

Let's look at the alternative. If a customer service view saturates student life, then the student-turned-alum expects nothing less than a product outcome. Questions like this surface: Where is my degree? What can the university *do* to help *me* get *my* career off the ground? As I argued earlier in this book, as alumni we need to reject this customer position. By exercising the Alumni Way traits of reflection, curiosity, passion, and generosity, we create a healthy balance. As an alumni shareholder, we *invest* in our alma mater. This investment is not for the institution's sake. It is to share and support this experience for others.

What is essential is our personal connection with our alma mater. Our fondest memories at university are likely relational: meeting lifelong friends, an inspiring professor, a kind administrator, a motivating sports coach. Conversely, it is also the absence of these moments: feeling lonely and isolated, having no one to turn to after a bad grade, and feeling like 'a number' in a large class. Through our curiosity, we reached out to fellow alumni for career stories. We asked a faculty member to write a reference letter. Our professional lives thrive through the support of these connections.

The relational is also the foundation of our passions. We feel connected immersing in our favourite hobby, or sport. When we support a cause we care about, we feel a renewed sense of energy. In our interconnected world, it is easy to put ourselves at the centre. We focus on our needs, our profession, our career, our interests. Universities offer programmes, initiatives, even networking events to meet these needs. What attracts us to re-engage with our alma mater? It's not the stellar programming. It's the promise of the relational. Eventually, the goodwill from taking can run out. 'It's a constant process of giving and receiving – of asking for and offering help,'[6] Keith Ferrazzi advises. 'You can't amass a network of connections without introducing such connections to others with equal fervour.'[7] Selfishness and entitlement crumbles the relational. Leadership comes from generosity. Love of humanity is at the core of philanthropy and we can all be a part of it.

Instead of complaining or feeling powerless, we can choose a growth mindset – invest our efforts in giving activities. We can decide to live a life of service, aligning to the generosity trait of the Alumni Way. As university evolves, so do our opportunities to give. We can give to causes that are important to us or to the educational mission of the university itself. The University of Toronto is a different institution in size and scope to the one I attended over 20 years ago. It is different again from the university my dad attended 30 years before me. It continues to evolve through the generosity of others – the philanthropy. The major benefactors – many proud alumni – are only part of the story. The university thrives because of the generosity of its staff, students, alumni, and the wider community. They gave – and continue to give – their time, talent, treasure, and ties. Focusing philanthropy only on the treasure – the financial donations – unduly diminishes our value to our universities.

Alumni Action 18: Giving our time as an active alumni citizen

Volunteers permeate the university. Some student volunteers coordinate events or become class representatives. Other students volunteer for causes they care about, mentor fellow students, or organize clubs. Giving our time to support these projects underpins the university's mission. Volunteer recognition programmes and community engagement initiatives reinforce the university's active citizenship agenda. Graduation doesn't erase our appetite for active citizenship. Our lives *do* change after graduation. Our volunteering focus should evolve too. We can become active alumni volunteers.

Let's start at the top. The university maintains a robust governance structure. With a central governing body, the university also has dozens of committees, task forces, sub-committees, boards, councils, and advisory groups. They meet to steer academic programmes and build new initiatives. They support recreational activities, seek advice, and conduct wide consultation. Many of these structures depend on broad representation – including alumni – to operate effectively. Alumni representatives at a governance, management or operational level need to prepare to actively take part in meetings (in person or virtually). We bring a special insider-outsider perspective to these meetings. As insiders, we understand the nuances of university operations as former students. As outsiders, we can contextualize the decisions from our place in the wider world. Our diversity enhances the university. In return, we learn about corporate governance in action and build our leadership skills. Some governance positions for alumni require nominations, or even elections. Others may be appointed by deans or heads of department. Again, this is a time to scour our alumni capital. Who do we know (and who knows us!) that might be able to help steer us in the direction of a committee position?

Alumni leaders. This is the powerful language often used by our alma mater to entice us to volunteer. Establishing an alumni regional chapter is alumni leadership. So is serving on an alumni association board. Reviewing scholarship applications or interviewing student applicants is alumni volunteer leadership too. We take a leap so many other alumni like us *could* take. For many reasons they don't or can't put themselves forward. Be warned: the road of alumni leadership is long but rewarding. We will often be called on by our alma mater to do more. When the experience is positive and enjoyable, we will want to *participate* more too.

Active alumni volunteers are essential university citizens. Our alumni volunteering is often casual and informal. We are the invisible, volunteer superheroes. It's our super senses when we recommend a course at our alma mater to our neighbour. Our super strength when we speak at our former school about our career and university experience. Our super speed when we make a quick introduction between two fellow alumni on LinkedIn. With our super vision we share or tag in our university's social media posts. Why? Our hope is that with our efforts others connect to the opportunities we see in our university. This isn't micro-volunteering,[8] as it is often unknown to our university, rather we are being informal alumni ambassadors.

There is a misconception out there, however, that the alumni volunteer is not as valued as the major donor. Remember we *are* all philanthropists. We offer immense benefit to the institution in our own way. Ron Cohen, a seasoned alumni strategist, caught my attention with his article headline 'What if an Alum Generated $200,000 Dollars for Your Institution, without Writing a Check?'[9] Cohen goes on to detail the story of one alum, who actively met prospective students in his region, leading to 20 student enrolments. This volunteering holds as much value – if not more – as a major donor. This could be any of us.

As alumni, we also need to channel our formal volunteering to its best use. We might organize a class reunion, or we might 'takeover' the university's alumni Instagram posts for a day. Writing an article for a university blog might be more our style. Cohen's vignette reminds us that we represent our alma mater in everything we do. When we're asked 'what was university like for you?' it's easy to give the polarized, 'it was good' or 'it was bad', response. Instead, in our ambassador role, we can draw on our new Alumni Way superpowers. We can reflect on the *learning* from our university experience and offer a more considered reply. A reply that might persuade others to attend or engage in our alma mater.

Our university may also coordinate once-off, episodic alumni volunteering opportunities. The hashtag #flashesgiveback charts Kent State University's annual Alumni Day of Service. Alumni posts vary from cuddling puppies, creating capes for children in hospital, cleaning up a playground, or preparing food for people in need. The day-long volunteering projects spanned almost 40 locations and involved over 800 alumni.[10] During such events, alumni networking occurs naturally, creating stronger local alumni communities.

Is there more we can do? Citizen Alum founder and scholar Julie Ellison thinks so. She challenges universities to look 'beyond the tokenism and the momentary feel-good payoff of the standard alumni association day of service'.[11] Ellison argues that universities should shift to long-term, meaningful engagement of alumni. Sustained involvement of alumni opens up the opportunity to create greater societal change. An alumni day of service still has great merit. These events could be integrated into a greater university civic engagement strategy involving alumni. Many of us can give more than one day of our time. We crave involvement that generates lasting, long-term impact. Campus or community projects supported by our alma mater that contribute to impact on the United Nations Sustainable Development Goals (SDGs) might be the answer. Imagine participating in the university's access to quality education initiative. As alumni, we can be online ambassadors for prospective international students from countries with emerging economies, or participate in a sustainability committee to support the university's efforts to be rated on the Sustainable Campus Index or the *Times Higher Education* Impact Rankings. These activities require our sustained volunteering to see transformational results.

As open, inclusive civic spaces – even in a virtual sense – the university is an excellent place to offer our time. Our alma mater might emphasize supporting student mental health or reducing single use plastic on campus. Major festivals spilling onto campus or the university's signature events – open day, homecoming – all seek volunteers. Alumni – with all our superpowers – are welcome volunteers.

Alumni ambassador programmes are a starting point to foster our volunteering efforts. Often, the volunteering roles are narrowly focused alumni relations, student recruitment, or career services roles. I believe there are ways to engage alumni volunteers right across the university. Scholar Jessica Vanderlelie's initiative Engaging Alumni provides a clear framework for universities in Australia to consider alumni volunteering roles in every stage of the student lifespan, from prospective student to post graduate. In this case, Vanderlelie's framework recognizes that supporting positive outcomes for students begins with authentic, active alumni participation diffused across the institution.[12]

As a radical solution, imagine an alumni-university volunteering matchmaking app. We create our profile featuring our interests and attributes (and stunning photo!). We scroll through a robust list of volunteer roles on boards or committees. We pause on event volunteer roles on campus, virtual events, or positions abroad. We save some interesting student support roles to review later. All centrally coordinated by the institution. The match is made by alumni volunteers indicating their interest in a volunteering role (swiping involved of course). This is where our reflection, curiosity, and passion can be genuinely applied in seeking a meaningful volunteering role with our alma mater. Even in the absence of an app to manage broad alumni volunteering activity, we can ask our key university contacts: how can I give my time?

Activity 18: Recognize we are all philanthropists by giving our time as active alumni citizens

Drawing on the examples in this section, consider one or two ways you may consider giving your time volunteering on campus or with your alma mater. Seek a list on your university website to help with some inspiration (and potential real roles available!).

Create a pro/con list on becoming an alumni volunteer. Consider all the benefits of volunteering – contribution to the university community, the extra experience on your CV or résumé, the warm and fuzzy feeling, building your leadership skills. Consider all the deal breakers to taking on volunteering: timing, location, other life responsibilities, and so on.

Reflect on the list. If the pros outweigh the cons, forge ahead to start the process of seeking a volunteer role at your alma mater. Scan your alumni capital to see who might be able to help. If the cons outweigh the pros, consider the ideal scenarios or changes in circumstances that, if in place, would change your mind. Review the list again in three months' time.

Alumni Action 19: Celebrating our talents with our alma mater

Do universities ask too little of us as alumni? According to research based on millennials and giving patterns, 86 per cent of millennials wish to give back their talent to their alma mater.[13] Without scrutinizing this claim specifically, imagine this: what if each one of us could give our talent to our alma mater in a meaningful way?

The classroom is a familiar space to start. As a guest speaker, you can apply your reflection skills to construct a compelling university story or use real-life examples to bring a concept to life. With our curiosity, we might anticipate any questions *we* might ask alumni if they came to *our* lecture. This can extend to our direct involvement on a curriculum course committee or participate in course design. Henry Onukwuba of the Lagos Business School in Nigeria describes two other defining roles that alumni can play that impacts the classroom. Onukwuba describes these as:

- curriculum development – source of local case studies and teaching resources;
- curriculum refinement – providing feedback to the school on the right curriculum and pedagogy; improving the teaching standards.[14]

From the curriculum development perspective, research suggests that a real-life dimension to case studies in entrepreneurship designed by alumni resonates with students more than abstract, generic examples.[15] What better strategic partner is there to help set up a service learning project to balance student learning with the needs of a real-life community project?[16] For example, we might be tasked with designing a rain harvesting system for a community building. Alumni act as advisers, guiding students through the environmental or engineering requirements of the design. We might organize study visits to our place of work or offer a virtual tour. Our experience in our careers − even and especially early on − supports course curriculum refinement in other ways. We can offer feedback from our sector, pointing to the concepts applied in our daily work. We can participate in quality assurance reviews, teaching evaluation, or take on adjunct teaching assignments.

Alumni can also draw on their expertise to offer student work placements, apprenticeships, graduate internships, or job shadowing programmes. We might organize study visits to our place of work or offer a virtual tour. Our contributions to student learning and career discovery foster our role as alumni leaders. We become the enablers of experiential learning for students. This learning by doing − and the reflection on the learning − is a clever strategy on our part. We flex our own growth mindset muscles, reflect on our learning, and overcome our challenges with effort. We impart this growth-minded thinking with hands-on, real-world experiences for students too. Win-win!

As we navigate our relationship with our university, it is easy to fall under the spell of this large institution. The university holds gravitas. Even when we are giving our talent as an adviser or guest speaker, the experience may be intimidating at first. We need to reconceptualize this power relationship. With a genuine stake in the institution's well-being, we can view it through a stewardship lens. 'Stewardship is a way to use power to serve through the practice of partnership and empowerment,' explains Peter Block in his book on the subject, 'The intent is to redesign our organizations so that service is the centrepiece and ownership and responsibility are strongly felt among those close to doing the work.'[17] When we serve our alma mater with our expertise, we get closer. We create a genuine partnership to empower fellow alumni and students to enhance the overall educational experience, for instance, when we are thoughtful in designing a meaningful learning opportunity so students on placement are 'no longer just making the tea'.[18] By extension, we feel we have a responsibility to consider hiring fellow alumni too when internships or employment opportunities in our company arise.

As civically minded students-turned-alumni, we haven't lost our interest in social justice or supporting the community. What's the value of pooling our alumni talent for social change? Alumni from the University of Pennsylvania can apply to participate in PennPAC. As a non-profit organization, independent from the university, PennPAC offers pro bono alumni consulting on short-term projects with non-profit leadership. Operating since 2010, PennPAC mobilized over 1,000 alumni volunteers for business consulting in over 150 non-profits across New York, Pennsylvania, and the Bay Area.[19] 'It's incredible that we are able to put together the intellectual capital of Penn alumni and put it to good use,'[20] explains PennPAC founder and Penn alum Jackie Einstein Astrof. ImPACt events offer team-based 'deep dive'[21] one-evening mini-consultancies in branding or mission statements to the leadership of non-profits. Special ImPACt events offer interactive panels of alumni for non-profit constituents (youth, skilled immigrants and refugees) with job search, résumé writing, and interview skills.[22]

Penn alumni remain growth minded during their volunteering experience. Even while bringing talent to the non-profit table, alumni volunteers find that the process is one of learning and self-discovery. 'The Power of PennPAC'[23] charts the stories of alumni volunteers with personal and professional impact, thanks to the rewarding volunteering experience. Alumni joined non-profit boards, shifted their career from the corporate to non-profit sector, expanded their network, and even secured new career opportunities. Programmes like PennPAC show that giving our talent involves immense growth for others and for ourselves.

Activity 19: Recognize we are all philanthropists by celebrating our talents with our alma mater

Make a list of your talents and strengths. As an alum with the growth mindset, your talents are constantly improving throughout your life. Complete the following micro-reflection: How can engaging in activities with your alma mater share your talents with others? How could volunteer work help to build your strengths and develop your talents?

18

Generosity signpost: Understand the power of giving

One of the biggest challenges in presenting a book with broad appeal is the cultural differences in financial giving to the university. Experiences of alumni donations vary by country and size of institution. Other factors also affect financial giving, such as if the university is publicly or privately funded, tuition paid by students (if any), debt at graduation (if any), or even if the word 'alumni' is commonly used at all. One common thread transcends all of this: funding dominates the discussions, policies, and decision making across higher education. From the debates on who pays for higher education, to diversifying income streams, regardless of the system or funding structure, money is on the agenda. Alumni, enter stage left.

The alumni and philanthropy are intertwined, especially alumni financial donations to their alma mater. So much so that it's ubiquitous. 'Most universities maintain a fairly active alumni network,' writes David Burkus in his bestselling book on networking, *Friend of a Friend*. Burkus continued his point with the explanation: '(they see it as a source of future donations)'.[1] Burkus is saying what many of us are thinking: universities are engaging with us, as alumni, ultimately to solicit a donation from us in the future. The add-on 'T' – ties – to the common time, talent, and treasure definition of philanthropy, is not far behind. Alumni also give from their personal or professional network. The main beneficiary becomes our alma mater or fellow alumni.

With an overall theme of generosity, we will examine treasure and ties from a slightly radical perspective.

Have fundraising campaigns taken over our campuses? There are banners, brochures, and social media posts promoting the impact that private donations have on the university. The messages of 'giving back' or 'being part of the campaign' invite us to join the crusade of advancing the institution. Behind the scenes, these calls are the strategic collaboration of many university departments, including communications, marketing, alumni relations, and development (fundraising). We can decide to be generous in a multitude of ways that encompass our time and talent discussed earlier, or our treasure and ties. This is one of many powerful positions we find ourselves in as alumni.

As learning organizations, universities are in a constant race to get better, *to advance*. It's a cyclone of courses, research, facilities, access, infrastructure, scholarships, and resources are all possible through university advancement. To realize this advancement requires commitment and vision along with strategy, careful measurement and, yes, increased income. Alumni can get swept up in this storm. How does an alumni relations function or alumni association fit in? Often, the ultimate measure of alumni involvement is financial gifts.[2] We sell ourselves short to equate our only value to our alma mater as a nominal, annual donation. As a self-confessed alumni romantic,[3] I believe our alumni contributions to our alma mater are often intangible or even immeasurable. Especially if we indulge as philanthropists, giving our time, talent, treasure, and ties with equal fervour.

Funding seeps into the institution's psyche – and ours too. This commodifies our relationship with our alma mater. We need to reposition our thinking from funding-centric, to alumni-centric. This is not to discount or negate the importance of money to the institution or the investment required to attend post-secondary education; it's a refocus. Our Alumni Way journey helps us to become growth minded, discerning, and informed alumni. As savvy alumni, we can slowly change the culture in our institutions. When we are generous towards our alma mater to show our gratitude, we exert immense power. As alumni, we hold agency, that is, free will to invest our generosity as we see fit in our alma mater.

The more we understand the role we consciously play in the generosity of treasure and ties, the better we can apply our power, energy, and agency to make informed choices to participate meaningfully in this activity. I should be clear that this isn't an either/or prospect. Our university may measure alumni as donors and non-donors, but this shouldn't impact or devalue our decision to engage with our alma mater. There are gradients of generosity in treasure and ties, all valid contributions to the institution. Rob Reich, in his book *Just Giving* argues 'philanthropy is a form or exercise of power'.[4] He argues that the mega wealthy wield this power of giving to a public cause to steer and change public policy. Reich and others are calling for a wider democratization of philanthropy: a call for all of us to be philanthropists, to question and better understand the power of philanthropy so we can participate on our own terms.

Alumni Action 20: Transforming our thinking on giving our treasure

I want to put my cards on the table from the start. After graduation, I became an accidental fundraiser. This wasn't a career path by design. Since then, this serendipity positively affected my advanced studies, my career options, and even contributed to my initial motivation for writing this book. I hope to offer you a glimpse into the power of treasure and ties from this insider perspective.

Let's set the scene. In 2017–18, giving to American post-secondary education from private sources – alumni and non-alumni – exceeded US$45 billion dollars.[5] I'll let that sink in. US$45 billion dollars. What's fascinating is that the number of donors has *decreased*, while the amount given per donor has risen. When donations reach millions, even tens of millions, it becomes abstract. It is easy to disconnect from this side of the university. Throughout our time at university, it's hard to ignore how much these gifts to the university had an impact on us. Whether that's in the classroom, lab, or lounge, there is likely to be a connection to these gifts. A scholarship or bursary we received, the sports facilities we used, or the research that we participated in, may also have a connection to private – and often alumni – donations.

'The true meaning of life is to plant trees, under whose shade you do not expect to sit.'[6] This well-known quotation appeared on a card seeking a donation from my alma mater. There is something poignant about this quotation. Today there is a focus on ourselves, our personal brand. We record everything that we do from posting our lunch to documenting our every move. It's difficult to imagine doing something that might not be attributed to us or recognized as our deed. Giving a donation can seem anonymous, joining a nondescript group. Unless we are giving significantly large donations, we aren't given wide public acknowledgement of our donation. Yes, universities publish a donor list. Our alma mater undertakes stewardship activities, showing us how our money is spent. At the same time, I see the allure and increased popularity of online crowdfunding sites. We can donate, put our name down, and make a public comment of support. Often, we want to give money where we feel we can make the greatest social change.

Offering a special legacy that may go beyond our lifetime – that shade from planting seeds – is something special. Spanning centuries and all ways of life, giving is as much of a pleasure for the giver as the benefit is to the receiver. *Tzedakah* is the Hebrew word for philanthropy, and Jewish origins of philanthropy are rooted in social justice, charity, and building relationships.[7] Fundamentally, financial giving should not simply be transactional; it should be based on a foundation of a relationship. This is not a gift *to* the university; it is a gift *with* the university. We have consciously decided to give to a cause. We give our money because we stand by its worth and importance. We want to see it advance and thrive.

'We believe that philanthropy is a way of fulfilling dreams,'[8] explains the Pa'lante Caribe campaign to increase access to higher education in the Colombian Caribbean region. Four universities, Universidad de los Andes, the Universidad del Norte, the Universidad Tecnológica de Bolívar, and the Universidad Pontificia Bolivariana (Montería campus) joined forces in 2018 to address the inequalities in higher education access. In the region, only 10 per cent of young people enrol in an undergraduate programme. 'We are breaking down inequality through education,'[9] reads the campaign tagline. The Pa'lante Caribe public outreach campaign shared the vision of raising US$2.5 million dollars for undergraduate scholarships with this impassioned call: 'We believe philanthropy is a way of fulfilling dreams. Understanding higher education as a tool for social mobility, which is a country's main development driver ... The model of the programme is fundamentally a solidarity chain.'[10] Students currently supported by the Pa'lante Caribe campaign pledged to donate once employed to help fund scholarships for future students in the region. This cycle of giving and extending the cohesion – the solidarity – reinforces the power of the campaign to increase access to quality higher education.[11] This campaign presents a compelling case for support, that is, a clear vision of its aims, motivating giving by alumni and even beneficiaries.

Being generous with our treasure – our money – should be based on a convincing case for support: Does it align with our values? We may wish to target our giving to create transformational impact.[12] Alternatively, we may give an unrestricted donation to our alma mater to enable them to decide the area of greatest need. Ultimately, when we give, we have trust and confidence in our alma mater. I became a first-time donor to one on my alma maters on Giving Tuesday. This is a day designated for giving to charities at the beginning of the holiday shopping season. The University of Victoria initiated its #AddSprinklesUVic campaign, a fund for small student projects such as hosting conferences or volunteering overseas. 'Together, those experiences are what makes the UVic student experience extraordinary,' exclaims the campaign materials that secured my donation, 'much like added "sprinkles" are to a cupcake or cookie.'[13] What struck me was the widespread university engagement with the campaign, including students enjoying hot chocolate – with sprinkles – on campus. This also reinforces the message that small financial gifts like mine are appreciated and used to directly support students.

What motivates giving? Giving is individual. As much as the university tries to predict our giving, we can decide to give to a compelling need, a value we truly support.[14] We speak volumes when we support – and when we don't. Scholar Noah Drezner's research on 'philanthropic mirroring'[15] offers insight into potential giving habits. 'I found that philanthropic mirroring within marginalized populations did not result in giving only to those who shared the same identity (eg Blacks supporting other Blacks);' writes Drezner, 'rather, I found a greater propensity to support others with marginalized identities (eg Blacks supporting LGBT students)'.[16] The inspiration for our giving is linked to our ability to identify with the cause. Our ability to see our donations, perhaps small in size but loud it its volume in the statement it makes. We loudly amplify our commitment to a cause, whether it is social justice, reducing inequalities in education, or another value we hold dear.

The sun beams down on a stone wall alcove with entangled green leaves at Mount St Vincent University (MSVU) in Halifax, Nova Scotia. This isn't another typical ivy clad university building. Each of the leaves is a marbleized green plaque, adorned with the names of hundreds of women honoured for their leadership. This is the Riva Spatz Women Wall of Honour, where alumni and members of the wider community can purchase leaves to celebrate special women. 'We were each mentored, guided, encouraged, challenged, and shaped by the remarkable women in our lives – our mothers, aunts, teachers, mentors, friends,' explains the webpage, listing the names and inspirational stories of the women honoured on the wall. 'These women believed in us and raised our sights. They cheered us on, sacrificed for us, and encouraged us to follow our dreams.'[17] The wall is nestled in sight of the Margaret Norrie McCain Centre for Teaching, Learning and Research at MSVU, a building dedicated to honouring women.[18] This philanthropic giving at MSVU aligns directly with the values of the university and its history as a place for the continued education for women. The deeply personal reasons for giving a leaf to honour a special woman, becomes part of interconnected vines, which goes to support MSVU's higher education mission. A personal tribute becomes public support to the future of education. How can our gift be part of a wider ambitious vision?

The words donation and gift are often interchangeable. Universities can often become a platform to make this gift in memory of someone special, to make a tribute, or honour someone with a special milestone. Gift planning is another way that we can leave a legacy donation to the university in our will, or through giving of stocks, shares, or securities. Imagine for instance, a law graduate who leaves a legacy to the university in their will. The legacy funding creates a free legal aid clinic at the university, offering pro bono services to the community; or a substantial gift in memory might fund research into new cancer treatments. These *are* gifts. These are gifts that go beyond the confines of the university creating wider community impact.

Giving a donation is cultural too: American alumni are more predisposed – or were – to expect the donation 'ask' at some stage after graduation. In some cases, donation requests start with parents of current students. In other parts of the world, giving is a new cultural construct. When I first moved to Ireland as a Canadian university fundraiser, I was asked at my new job, 'How soon can you raise millions for the annual fund here?' Even early on, I knew the giving culture was different across the Atlantic.

I don't want to get into a philosophical debate on higher education funding, public good, and advancement.[19] Suffice to say that these concepts can impact the alumni-university relationship – for better and for worse. For better when universities and alumni possess a shared vision for higher education. The stars align when the call for student aid, scholarships essential programmes, or facilities is answered. Alumni mobilize with donations to a cause they care very deeply about. Our donation can have an impact on the lives of others. The fundraising campaign distils this vision. Giving to this campaign is one way to show solidarity for this wider vision. It is easy to become cynical about the large donations by wealthy donors: how can the average alum compete? This is not a competition: large or small, the purpose is to show an expression of support.

For worse, is the positioning of alumni only as future donors. There is a lot of cynicism out there. We may feel our university is only warming us up for the financial ask. When universities make alumni and donors synonymous, then university administrators begin to view alumni value through a financial donation lens. Friend-raising before fundraising.[20] This is a dangerous phrase when taken to its extremes.[21] Positioning our relationship with our alma mater – getting involved, giving back our time or talent or even our ties – only towards the ultimate outcome of securing our donation. *Friend-raising can be a positive, transformational, and significant end in itself.* Alumni engagement can support the institution in so many other meaningful ways outlined throughout this book.

How can our donation of whatever size have a significant impact? Some fundraising appeals are matched through government incentive programmes or a special private fund. For instance, a donation of 50 becomes 100, enhancing its impact. When giving to the university, our donation might also be matched by our employer, through a corporate matching gift programme. Giving piecemeal, that is, donations to several different causes, can disperse its effect. We may find it beneficial to audit our giving habits. We can concentrate our investment in one area of our alma mater or a cause we feel has the greatest impact on students, research, or another area we deem a priority.[22]

This is not to say giving a donation to our alma mater should be a given. On the contrary. By drawing on our savvy Alumni Way traits, we can reflect on our own past university experience. We can consider our current circumstances. We can ask, how did we benefit from someone else's giving when we were at university? We can be curious as to *why* the university is asking for money. We consider whether the appeal is convincing and compelling to us. We can assess whether the appeal aligns with our passions and values, such as enhancing access to education or equality. It is then that we can decide if, when, and how we express our generosity to our alma mater.

University advancement work is a sophisticated operation. There are usually dozens, sometimes hundreds of advancement professionals that work in alumni relations, data analytics, marketing, communications, student recruitment, career services, affinity services, and more. Fundraising itself can be sub-categorized into so many areas: annual giving, legacy or gift planning, major gifts, prospect management, donation processing, and stewardship. Through training and professional associations, the treasure side of advancement looks quite

Figure 18.1: The Donor Bill of Rights[23]

Philanthropy is based on voluntary action for the common good. It is a tradition of giving and sharing that is primary to the quality of life. To assure that philanthropy merits the respect and trust of the general public, and that donors and prospective donors can have full confidence in the not-for-profit organizations and causes they are asked to support, we declare that all donors have these rights:

I. To be informed of the organization's mission, of the way the organization intends to use donated resources, and of its capacity to use donations effectively for their intended purposes.

II. To be informed of the identity of those serving on the organization's governing board, and to expect the board to exercise prudent judgement in its stewardship responsibilities.

III. To have access to the organization's most recent financial statements.

IV. To be assured their gifts will be used for the purposes for which they were given.

V. To receive appropriate acknowledgement and recognition.

VI. To be assured that information about their donation is handled with respect and with confidentiality to the extent provided by law.

VII. To expect that all relationships with individuals representing organizations of interest to the donor will be professional in nature.

VIII. To be informed whether those seeking donations are volunteers, employees of the organization, or hired solicitors.

IX. To have the opportunity for their names to be deleted from mailing lists that an organization may intend to share.

X. To feel free to ask questions when making a donation and to receive prompt, truthful, and forthright answers.

Reproduced with permission from the Association of Fundraising Professionals, December 2018

similar from institution to institution, even across systems and countries. This means there can be some predictability in what we can expect from the donor experience. What *are* our rights as a donor? It is best summed up in Figure 18.1, the Donor Bill of Rights, adopted by over 3,600 educational institutions worldwide through membership to CASE.[24]

I received permission to reproduce the Donor Bill of Rights[25] here to give us the opportunity to read the fine print, to offer us more power and knowledge, as it is likely our alma mater aligns to this list for its fundraising work. What strikes me about the Donor Bill of Rights is the transparency we can expect when we donate and the confidence we can have about the process of our donation. As a donor too, or someone who elects *not* to be a donor, our wishes need to be respected by our alma mater.

Cynical as we might be about all this, fundraising is a relationship. We can be enrolled automatically into alumni giving clubs. These usually kick in once we give a certain amount, give monthly, or give to a certain campaign. Through stewardship, the university shows us the responsible ways the university values our donation and shows the progress. This is to foster our loyalty. The more persuasive the stewardship – the personalized postcards from current students, the thank you letters, the donor reports – the more likely it is that we will decide to give again. In fundraising, it is more cost effective to keep an existing donor than to try to attract a new one. Therefore, as donors, we *are* in a privileged position. We can evaluate whether the financial investment we made was worth it. Sometimes, the second time is not so persuasive. Giving is individual, and there could be a change in our personal circumstances since our last gift. The project we are passionate about could come to an end. We may decide that the university is no longer the priority for our giving.

Now, I am going to suggest something radical. When we get the next appeal for a donation, don't ghost the university. Take a few minutes – write a few lines in an email to the contact person on the appeal – to explain our reasons for giving – or not giving. A solicitation is a good opportunity for reflection. It also provides some feedback for the university. Think of this as an exercise in diplomacy – how to write a message with leadership, constructive criticism, even positive comments, to help shape future appeals.

As prospective or current donors, we can play an active part in the fundraising relationship. We are in control. We can decide whether we want to receive fundraising appeals at all – we can ask the university to put a 'do not solicit' code on our database record. This is a powerful exercise in leadership. If we are not satisfied with the university on how they are using donations, say so. Have our priorities for giving changed? Going to grad school? The university will be happy to hear our feedback and wish us well. Philanthropy is for the love of humankind. Let's bring humanity back into the response. Impressed by the ask? Tell the university why it was so compelling that it prompted our giving. Not impressed? Tell them why and what might motivate you to give another time. Being generous with our responses, we can come from a place of giving to support, nay, transform humanity in the philanthropic space.

Activity 20: Understand the power of giving by transforming our thinking on giving our treasure

Revisit a fundraising appeal you received from your alma mater. If you haven't received one yet, go to your alma mater's website and find some of the priority fundraising areas. Is the case for support (the purpose and vision for the fundraising call), convincing to you? Persuasive? Why or why not?

Next, make a list of causes that you give to informally – sponsorship cards, online fundraising efforts, bucket collections, events – and formally – regular giving to charities or causes. Tally up roughly how much money you give to these causes in a year. Could your giving be more strategic and focused? Does the list align with your passions and values? In this activity, you can also consider whether a donation to your alma mater is or will remain a strategic choice.

Alumni Action 21: Connecting generously with our ties

We won't put away our tights and cape just yet. Our superhero powers will be called upon in philanthropy that is not part of the traditional definition: ties. Ties *is* our alumni capital. To give of our connections, to the university or to fellow alumni we need to establish trust.[26] We need trust in our alma mater, to ensure that these connections will be treated with respect and care. Even when we recommend a course, we are entrusting the university with a duty to offer a high-quality programme.

In March 2018, Tony Coote, a parish priest, was diagnosed with Motor Neurone disease. He decided to mobilize his network to raise money for research and to support people with the disease. Five months later, Coote began his Walk While You Can journey across Ireland, raising over half of the €250,000 goal within the first week. How did he manage to inspire individuals across Ireland to support the cause? With his passion and generosity, Coote touched so many lives as Chaplain at University College Dublin (UCD). Student volunteers in Haiti sent messages of support for his walk. These students benefitted from a formal system in the university for international development work – UCD Volunteers Overseas, which Coote established in 2003. With his passion for supporting students to overcome mental health challenges, Coote also founded PleaseTalk, now a national movement to support student mental health initiatives.[27]

I first heard of his walking campaign in a message from a friend and former UCD colleague. I suspect this was one of dozens of such emails and social media shares from students, alumni, and staff who met Coote in their travels, as I did. Without even realizing it, he leveraged his own alumni capital to raise awareness, money, knowledge, and resources for a cause he held dear. UCD also shared the campaign to reach even wider university and alumni communities. Coote is not the first person to mobilize a community and apply crowdfunding to generate support for a cause. Crowdfunding, by virtue of its name, needs a crowd, and Coote leveraged his networks – his university connections, his parish, his communities – towards realizing his fundraising and engagement goals. Coote died in August 2019. Walk While You Can raised almost €700,000 for Motor Neurone Disease support including Trinity College Dublin's naming of the Tony Coote Assistant Professor in Motor Neurone Disease.[28] At the funeral, Coote's brother described him as 'the ultimate connector'.[29]

In December 2018, UCD conferred an honorary doctorate to Coote for his outstanding service to the university and fundraising for Motor Neurone Disease.[30] Honorary degrees are a way that institutions create new ties – and support special ones. Typically, honorary degree recipients are recognized for their service to their respective fields. There are thousands of honorary degree recipients at universities worldwide who inspire and epitomize the values of the institution.[31] There are cynics of this practice with good reason. With controversies of honorary degrees being awarded to celebrities or those deemed later to be less than honorary, universities have been known to revoke these honours. For our purposes here, universities often open the honorary degree nomination process, to the wider community, including to alumni. We can suggest someone worthy – like Tony Coote – that show integrity and leadership throughout their life.

Being generous with our ties, that is, our broad network connections, can be a transformational gift to others. In her book *Build Your Dream Network*, J. Kelly Hoey reminds us that 'networking is a two-way street'.[32] It is as much about giving as receiving in the relationship. She advocates for listening carefully to fully understand the needs of others . This allows to us to have others on our own radar, sharing with them things that might be of value – information, influence, or resources. Hoey describes this as 'cultivating a "network-minded" reputation'.[33] As we become expert prospect miners, we become more knowledgeable in what is happening at our own alma mater. We can then unearth the nuggets of opportunities that could be valuable for our network. An advertisement for a STEM summer camp? Maybe a work colleague may be interested in this for their children. Campus concert? Share the social media post with a friend. Job vacancy at our alma mater? We might share it with a member of our network with the right skill set and experience. Our small efforts sharing information or network contacts can yield incredible personal and professional transformation for others. We can begin to show our wider network – our ties – the value of alumni capital, and opportunities for themselves.

When I reconnected with Melanie Eusebe in London a few years ago, we reminisced and laughed over our shared times at the University of Toronto. Eusebe is the Founder of the Black British Business Awards (BBBA). She squeezed our walk down memory lane between informal interviews with potential BBBA nominees. One such nominee, Jessica Huie, joined us. Of course, hearty introductions ensued, and I heard about Huie's feverish work on her book. I had just started writing mine. We connected, and eventually I interviewed her for this book. I often thought about this chance meeting, and more importantly, the crucial role Eusebe played as a *boundary spanner*. What's a boundary spanner? Borrowing liberally on the definition, boundary spanners are people who act as 'exchange agents between the organization and the environment'.[34] An alumni boundary spanner is someone who stretches the outside networks from shared experiences to support fellow alumni. In my case, fellow alum Eusebe connected me with Huie, someone from her BBBA network. She saw two aspiring authors and passionate writers in her network. She made the connection. Eusebe is thoughtful and generous with making valuable connections for others, a serial boundary spanner across her networks. What would it be like if we were all boundary spanners with and for our alumni capital?

Consider boundary spanning from a different angle. Global engagement specialist Gretchen Dobson also recommends alumni academic networks. Alumni, who are scholars or administrators in other institutions, can connect back to their alma mater to explore opportunities. Dobson suggested the potential for collaborative research, mentorship for current graduate students or to 'help build virtual and hybrid partnerships for today's reimagined study abroad programmes'.[35] We might be these academics and administrators working at one institution, but our alma mater is another. Or we might be the student or recent graduate who might benefit from intra-institutional boundary spanning. We can even extend Dobson's original idea to our corporate networks – these precious employment related ties – to offering work placements, internships, apprenticeships, even graduate level jobs. While Dobson advises for formal alumni academic networks, let's not be afraid to begin this outreach first informally – with a former professor, a key contact – to watch it grow organically, partnerships and collaborations abound.

There are innovative ways to give treasure that begin with ties. Giving circles, for example, are growing in popularity. This is a way for groups of people, who pool their earmarked funds to collectively give larger amounts of money or time to causes. 'Some have described giving circles as "democratizing" philanthropy', explains Angela Eikenberry and Beth Breeze, scholars that study philanthropy trends, 'because they seem to attract people not typically engaged in philanthropy – such as the less wealthy, women and young professionals'.[36] What is also new about giving circles is the 'hands-on' nature of this type of giving. Members are eager to be involved in the process of social change, and by pooling resources and giving more impactful gifts, they have a chance to be part of this change. For instance, the Arizona State University's Women & Philanthropy group pools donations from alumni women towards agreed priorities for the group.[37] If this is about treasure, why is this in the ties section?

Giving circles, like online start-up funding, has relationships at its core. For this group of Arizona State University (ASU) women, 'the group has a dual purpose', reports Marjorie Valburn in her article for *Inside Higher Ed*, 'to reduce barriers to higher education for women students and to cultivate women philanthropists'.[38] There is a desire to grow the ASU group to include more members and to create further impact. These women cultivate their alumni ties to network and identify other giving circle members. Philanthropic culture, like others, runs deep with nuance, trends, lingo, and practice that might seem daunting to some people. The university may be a safe place to begin navigating our ties, our connections that we can give – or receive – as points of generosity to make the world better. The core of many of these ideas, like that of the giving circle, is that these ideas translate into wider social impact.

Ties also means another dimension of service to our alma mater. Alumni and donors can be invited to sit on university committees or campaign boards to steer the direction of the fundraising strategy. Have you ever noticed the same names often appear on hospitals, community centres, libraries, and university buildings? These donors and their foundations also form interconnected networks. Volunteer alumni donors often accompany professional fundraisers to meet an alumni prospect to ask for a significant donation. These meetings are the culmination of years of building a relationship of mutual trust. Having a peer involved in the process, a fellow alumni donor, reinforces the confidence others have in giving to the institution. These donors give freely of their time because they believe in the cause. The university seeks this form of campaign leadership to ensure that the ambitious fundraising priorities can be met and that they realize the university vision. This process might seem very far from our own reality. However, understanding the nuances of the philanthropic giving that happens within our institutions – in charitable organizations too – gives us a sense of the leadership and the relationship building that is involved in philanthropy. This may also be a leadership path we may wish follow in the future.

As informed, savvy alumni, we become the ambassadors for our alma mater. We encourage others to reconnect and potentially become generous alumni too. We might not have the means or inclination to give financially, but we can be generous in our strategic knowledge. The university might call on us to give country-, region-, or city-specific insights, valuable when our alma mater is recruiting new students or arranging a new student send-off event in our local neighbourhood. Recent alumni are particularly desirable for these initiatives, as they offer the most up-to-date experience for new or prospective students. We may also know fellow alumni not as keen to embrace the growth mindset strategies of the Alumni Way. We can chip away at their cynicism and negativity and promote opportunities of interest for our former classmates, friends, and family. We can help them to see the value in reconnecting with their alma mater.

Julia Freeland Fisher researches innovative ways to rebuild our education system. She believes that the sharing of our networks is a crucial factor in the process. In her book *Who You Know: Unlocking Innovations that Expand Students' Networks*, she describes that we are all born with a network. These are the ties she calls an inherited network based on our inherited circumstances. 'Inherited connections are by no means negative or bad influences,' Freeland Fisher explains. 'They can provide all sorts of critical supports, love and care ... but as students grow older, they may find that the reach of their inherited network is limited.'[39] The importance of expanding our own ties, and generously connecting others to ties that may be valuable to them is crucial to expand the networks of others. Online social media platforms, though giving us a glimpse into the wider world, are not enabling people to expand their networks, only to reinforce the networks they already have in person.[40] Therefore, we become the keepers of ties that can support others to expand their network. We may hold the flows of people, knowledge, and resources in our alumni capital to support others. We may also seek the support of others to expand our own inherited networks. Networking is a kind, generous, and balanced activity. We can identify alumni to enhance our network and opportunities. At the same time, we need to dig deep in our own ties to give of our network to others to achieve a healthy balance.

Activity 21: Understand the power of giving by connecting generously with our ties

Identify a prospective university student, a current student, recent graduate, or alum, and invite them for a reverse informational interview. Consider ways that your ties can support and help this person as they navigate the next stage in their life. Ensure that part of this conversation is also a chance to learn more about their experience and their perspective of university life, aspirations, and career interests, and reflect how this is different from your own experience at this stage in your life.

Alternative activity

How have you been a boundary spanner with your alumni capital? Perhaps you have:

- introduced two people in your network because you knew the connection would be mutually beneficial;
- referred a business owned by a fellow alum to a friend or to your employer;
- connected two fellow alumni from your different alumni capital circles, say, a student you mentor with a fellow alum who works in a career sector that interests the student as a future career path?

Consider a situation where your alumni capital could be beneficial to someone else you know. Orchestrate the introduction or situation to enable the boundary spanning activity to occur. What was the result of this connection? How did this benefit both sides involved? How did you feel using your ties to help others? Imagine some ways your boundary spanning alumni connections could contribute to addressing some of the world's biggest challenges: what kind of alumni connections from around the world collectively with different experiences, academic expertise could address a chosen challenge? Be creative – the possibilities to bring together these alumni synergies are endless!

19

Generosity trait summary: Our generosity as service

'I will leave you with one challenge,' says astronaut Chris Hadfield in his honorary degree speech at the University of Waterloo, 'You have an obligation to give this opportunity to someone else.'[1] This is a formidable challenge. When we spent our time and energy on our own progress, we forget that we have had this incredible opportunity. We amassed a network of connections and opportunities with our alma mater. It's easy to become narrowed in our focus. We all may not have the financial means to offer the financial freedom to someone else in university that we may have had ourselves.

Research suggests that generation X and millennial donors, emphasize giving to create impact. Thanks to the technology available and their use of it, these alumni are highly networked.

> They learn about causes and strategies from their peer networks and enjoy sharing their own knowledge and experiences with their peers. They believe that collaborating with peers makes them all better donors, and extends their impact. Put simply, they want to give their full range of their assets – their treasure, of course, but also their time, their talents, and even their ties, encouraging others to give their own time, talent, treasure, and ties.[2]

This is a current and future challenge for universities and for us too to diversify our giving patterns based on impact. In Sharna Goldseker and Michael Moody's bestselling book *Generation Impact: How Next Gen Donors are Revolutionizing Giving*, they suggest that 'impact', by this next generation's standards, is not one single definition.[3] It's individual. Institutions are then challenged to identify and promote impact as part of their appeal for support. It's then up to us to assess whether this is impact that aligns with our values.

We need to reflect on our own identities as philanthropists, and how this may evolve over time, and whether the university will play a part in our philanthropic giving. We are the products of our networks.[4] We can share the university's campaigns, insights and research that might be of value or interest to others.

We might have worked hard and think others can do the same to get their break. There *were* breaks for all of us: an inspiring professor who provided additional guidance, a bursary, a solid contact that helped secure a summer job. We don't live our lives in a vacuum. When we are generous, we can open more of the same opportunities for others. It can be as simple as meeting a prospective student who is a neighbour back home. It could be suggesting a motivational speaker for a student induction event, or a donation to an important cause. We all have the potential for a life of service.

Key messages from Part V

- We are all philanthropists. We can decide to give our time, talent, treasure, and ties to our fellow alumni and to our alma mater as we are past beneficiaries of the generosity of others.
- Giving is good for our health and our learning, while activating our role as alumni citizens.
- Alumni volunteers are viewed by their alma mater as leaders. Once we start to volunteer, we are called to take on more leadership roles within our alma mater.
- We can bring our talent to contribute to the learning environment for students and actively enhance the university's ability to create social change.

- We can become savvy university donors, consciously deciding whether to give a financial donation with our alma mater, to a cause or campaign we feel will make an impact.
- We can mobilize our alumni capital – our ties – to enact philanthropic impact at our alma mater or to a cause we hold dear.

Disengaged alumni with the fixed mindset will:

- consider only a fixed view that the university's appeal for money is the only purpose for alumni relationships, dismissing opportunities to engage with their alma mater;
- believe their genius or natural talent cannot be developed, especially not through giving generously to their alma mater;
- hold a sense of superiority and entitlement to giving; consider this is something for others not for them;
- rationalize the need to hold back from giving because they can't identify with others giving to their alma mater;
- distance themselves from their university experience and from giving back – this requires their acceptance that they weren't as successful as they had hoped;
- lay blame on external circumstances for these failings in their lives.

Dynamic alumni with the growth mindset will:

- stretch their thinking to the challenge of giving in different ways to their alma mater to find the way that they feel represents the best value;
- become motivated to be generous in giving their time, talent, treasure, and ties;
- believe in the transformative power of effort, and through the hard work of generosity, support university initiatives, fellow alumni, and students towards reaching their potential;
- draw inspiration from the success and generosity of other alumni and to the alma mater, deciding to make their generous contributions within their own capabilities, hard work, and effort.

Checklist for Part V

To build your Alumni Way, especially generosity, don't forget to:

☐ review potential volunteering opportunities at your alma mater (see Activity 18);

☐ make a list of your talents and strengths (see Activity 19);

☐ undertake the micro-reflection on talent (see Activity 19);

☐ provide feedback on the most recent fundraising appeal you received (see Activity 20);

☐ audit your financial giving to charitable causes and to your alma mater (see Activity 20);

☐ invite a student or recent graduate for a reverse informational interview (see Activity 21);

☐ complete a boundary spanning activity and reflection (see Activity 21).

Building the Alumni Way: Questions following Part V

- *Recent graduates and alumni:* Are there ways you could give generously to your alma mater right now?

- *Students:* How have you already benefitted from the generosity of alumni?

- *University administrators:* How can you reconceptualize alumni not simply as donors, but as lifelong alumni citizens of the institution? How can your strategy point to meaningful ways to enable alumni to give of their time, talent, treasure, and ties to the entire campus?

- *Advancement professionals:* How do you create giving opportunities that are compelling to our alumni?

- *Parents/career advisers:* In what ways could alumni that you know (eg friends, former classmates, neighbours, colleagues) enhance your work of supporting students and young people in/into higher education?

PART VI

Alumni: Bringing it into our lives

20	Our potential: Building our Alumni Way	175
	• Believe the Alumni Way is universal, transformational, and inclusive	176
	• Alumni Action 22: Exploring the breadth of our shared experiences	178
21	Our alumni call to action	185
	• Final checklist	186
	• Building the Alumni Way: Questions following Part VI	186
	• Bonus Alumni Action 23: Generating momentum for our Alumni Way health check	187
	• The final word: The Alumni Way journey continues ...	189

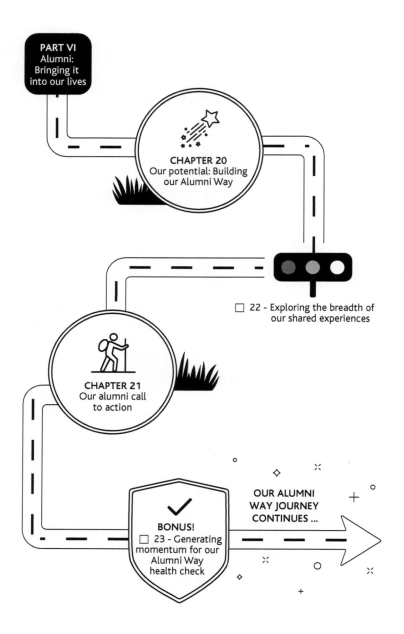

PART VI
Alumni:
Bringing it
into our lives

CHAPTER 20
Our potential: Building
our Alumni Way

☐ 22 - Exploring the breadth of
our shared experiences

CHAPTER 21
Our alumni call
to action

BONUS!
☐ 23 - Generating
momentum for our
Alumni Way
health check

OUR ALUMNI
WAY JOURNEY
CONTINUES ...

20

Our potential: Building our Alumni Way

We are alumni to all our shared experiences. This book navigates us through the alumni identity most familiar to us: our university experience. What would it be like if our alumni experience was quantum instead of linear? Becoming savvy, informed alumni citizens, we apply this learning across our whole life. We can ask:

- How can we *reflect* on our formal, shared experiences as alumni experiences?
- Where can *curiosity* add a new dimension to our lives?
- What *passion* can we follow and foster?
- Where can we channel our *generosity*?

Let's promote our Alumni Way thinking across *all* our shared experiences. We may have attended or graduated from several different alma maters. Within our alma maters, there may be colleges, departments, subject of study, sports, clubs, activities that shaped our university experience. It's the same for our shared experiences outside the university. We can extend our Alumni Way thinking to the networks that together form our full identity. Our wider alumni capital holds even more transformative power. It can transform our personal and professional lives. It can create positive impact in our communities.

We are all connected by one word: Alumni.[1] This was the title of my TEDx talk in 2018. It wasn't my first choice. I was challenged to present a talk to resonate with the wider audience. I needed to rethink the power of alumni beyond the academy. These traits and ideas are easily adaptable elsewhere. We have alumni-ness in so many avenues of our life. That's the universal nature of these ideas in my TEDx talk and along the Alumni Way.

Believe the Alumni Way is universal, transformational, and inclusive

We are all alumni. We reclaimed this word as inclusive not exclusive. We are all welcome members of our alumni communities. While it is inclusive for our own personal experience, the term 'alumni' is also universal. Universities don't own a patent on alumni connection. It's open to anyone who wishes to reconnect with their past, formal shared experiences of life. We belong to dozens of alumni groups, whether we acknowledge them or not. The Alumni Way is a special paradigm. In describing paradigms, Stephen Covey offers a simple explanation: 'It's the way we "see" the world – not in terms of our visual sense of sight, but in terms of perceiving, understanding and interpreting.'[2] We have an opportunity to view our own world from this wide vantage point, through an alumni lens. As alumni, we hold many other roles in life – parent, sibling, university administrator, student, partner, friend, neighbour, volunteer. We can take the alumni lens to this rich outside environment. We can also remind others that this alumni paradigm is available for them too. The Alumni Way isn't a secret. It's a non-competitive journey. The beauty of the Alumni Way is the universality of the ideas. We can all experience the joy of imagining our alumni selves in so many ways and the spread the word of this potential to others.

There is inclusivity in embracing our alumni selves. We connect with more people; we are genuine and authentic in this pursuit. Our connection is with people of all ages, backgrounds, ethnicity, social status, gender, diversity, creeds, and location. Our shared experience is with a summer camp, scouts, or award. Our link is with anyone – and everyone – that has ever participated too. This is our special bond. Our alumni status is the great leveller. When I see that an organization has set up a formal alumni group, I smile. It's a victory for connection. The reconnection is not necessarily with the experience itself but with the rich community of other alumni citizens with this shared experience.

The university degree makes many lofty promises: it will open doors, attract opportunities; create a path to financial freedom. There is the allure of gaining independence too: getting out of our parents' house, starting our own business, securing a fabulous job on the way up the career ladder. As we journey along the path of our Alumni Way, it is obvious that one parchment alone cannot deliver on these ambitious promises or hopes of independence. Our education is part of our university experience; it forms our bond to our alumni capital. It is this alumni capital – the flows of people, knowledge, and resources – that can help us take up the megaphone to amplify the next phase of our lives. In fact, it is not independence at all; our alumni capital fosters our potential *interdependence*. We can gather the threads of our shared experiences of our life and weave a rich tapestry. This woven cloth of our shared experiences drapes over us. It is comforting and warm, especially when we are open to interactions and lifelong learning that we gain from others around us.

Not convinced of the full power of our alumni capital yet? When entrepreneur and venture capitalist Peter Thiel announced the Thiel Fellowship in 2011, young people under 23 were enticed with a US$100,000 dollar stipend to skip the college experience and 'build new things instead of sitting in a classroom'.[3] The foundation funded young people across the globe to create companies, work on new software or hardware ideas, even to start non-profit organizations. This is a radical form of experiential education: learning by doing. In fact, the Fellowship adopted the famous Mark Twain quote: 'I have never let my schooling interfere with my education.'[4]

The great experiment began. The media followed closely to see if this education (without an education) would yield success. True, some fellows raised millions for their new tech companies. What is clear is that the success of Thiel Fellows is due to one important factor: the network.[5] This revelation on the power of the network for these young fellows should not come as a surprise. The Fellowship itself was described as 'the alumni network without a formal alma mater?'[6] This is the Alumni Way in action. The Fellowship *is* an alma mater, a nurturing parent drawing together these young people who have undertaken the same shared experience.

It's time for us to reclaim *all* our alma maters – sports teams, summer camps, conferences, and yes, even fellowships – along with many other formal shared experiences. What this story illustrates is that the education is not nearly as important as the experience.

Alumni Action 22: Exploring the breadth of our shared experiences

This multitude of alumni identities in our lives also extends us. It is easy to become insular, and to be so absorbed in one thing that we forget we are part of an intricate web. I'm not talking about the internet. This online web is one where we can easily get trapped in the narrowing of ourselves. We spend so much of our lives staring into a screen. Whether we are on the bus, waiting in the doctor's office, or at home after a long day, it has become a default position. We are no longer lost in thought. We are lost in a virtual world. What's worse is that the online world *seems* interactive.

Our language has shifted too. Only a few years ago we described many of the platforms like Facebook, Instagram, Twitter, and LinkedIn as social networking sites. Today, it is more common to call this social media. Yes, we can broadcast our recent holiday photos for our thirsty scrolling followers. Ten seconds later, all is forgotten, caught in this web. The shift to social media is powerful. It's telling us that the main reason for these sites is now *not* for networking – unless we are actively doing so – it is for our consumption. We become passive, online consumers. Engaging with the Alumni Way lets us reclaim these online spaces for ourselves and for our networks. We can become active online alumni citizens.

To reclaim this true web online, we need to understand ourselves. Who we are and what makes us who we are. A good place to start is the shared experiences from our lives. The milestones that we shared with others. These can be schools, sports teams, conferences attended, awards, summer camps, past employers, volunteering experiences, committees – this list is endless! It is a fallacy that our online time connects us. For authentic connection, we need a genuine purpose for this connection.

In Part II of this book, we imagined how our university experiences created part of who we are – our affiliations, by our *reflection* on these experiences. Now, we can expand our reflection towards all the other shared experiences in our lives asking:

Through self-reflection, what did we learn about ourselves?

Next, in Part III, we adopted *curiosity*, to ask questions, be inquisitive about the vast network in our alumni capital, fellow alumni, and key connections within the university. Now, we can build our curiosity to all aspects of our shared experiences, wondering:

How can we become curious about our wide shared experiences to help us with our personal and professional journey?

In Part IV, we identified, followed, and fostered our *passions* through our alma mater. Now, our wider alma maters beyond the university also offer insights and opportunities that align with our values, saying:

In what ways can our wider alma maters allow us to engage deeply in our passions?

Finally, we explored our giving in Part V, the *generosity* to support others on their university journey, building on the earlier Alumni Way traits as a foundation to identify the place to focus generosity energy. Now, we can consider the potential of our generosity strategically channelled to the causes that we care about to other places too, considering:

Where can our giving have the best impact for the alumni capital of others?

It is through this journey of the Alumni Way that we become authentic, informed alumni citizens. As we navigate through the possible alumni experiences of our lives, we need to think deeply and creatively. 'The basic foundation of alumni community', writes Andrew Shaindlin, 'derives from a group of individuals sharing a lived experience that has helped to shape their identity, and/or contributed to their accomplishments over time'.[7] Others cannot create our alumni connections for us. They might remind us that we have them, but we must *want* to seek them out to include them as part of our identity. We need to see ourselves as alumni of many of these other shared experiences to extend our alumni capital. This list of our alumni affiliations is fluid. While we may not feel we have a strong affiliation with our university at all, there might be an extra-curricular experience, a specialized professional programme, a club, sport, college, faculty, department, or campus that is important to us at this time of our lives. Philip Conroy, with decades of experience in advancement, likens the alumni-university relationship to an onion: the different layers represent the different sections of the university, and the closer to the centre, the closer the experience to the individual alum.[8] Only *we* can truly determine which layers are the closest to us. This is the same with our external alumni identities: only we know which of these identities is important right now. We have more inspiring affiliations than we realize if we cast our net wide.

We can identify our alumni-ness everywhere and anywhere. The word alumni may not be used at all. Network, friends, or past pupils, award winners, participants, former athletes, past employees are all collections of alumni by another name. Many organizations recognize the benefit of starting alumni groups, corporate alumni networks, or high school alumni associations. They seek alumni to offer mentorship to the next generation, or referrals to secure new talent in their organization. Even in these alumni networks outside our university, they can spark our generosity.

InHive recognizes the immense power of strong alumni networks. The organization partners with schools and youth structures to increase access to these crucial alumni networks across the globe.[9] For instance, InHive partners with Pakistan Youth Change Advocates to support young women in Pakistan to continue their education. The partnership enables the setting up of alumni networks in rural schools 'so that girls can get exposure to relatable role models who are successful university students and young professionals.'[10] Alumni networks for broader social impact are popping up all over the world. The InHive model focuses on addressing inequality and improving life chances,[11] anchoring values that resonate with other organizations building alumni networks for social impact. For schoolchildren, international scholarship participants, or other social impact project participants to thrive, relatable role models from alumni networks are not a nice to have, they are essential.

To sustain alumni participation in local schools, InHive ensures alumni benefit from the experience too. Alumni leadership development is embedded in these programmes. Alumni gain experience delivering training and offering alumni-alumni mentorship. The alumni leadership networking creates intra-alumni relatable role models too.[12] When we hear of an inspiring alumni story stemming from a scholarship, youth initiative, or social impact project, this is a pebble dropping in a pond. The ripples formed from this one alumni story are far reaching with an alumni network in place. As active global alumni citizens, our challenge is to recognize, celebrate, promote, and even establish these networks to be the ripple multipliers.

The breadth and depth of alumni networks are everywhere. In my interview with Kevin Boylan of Firecloud365, he discussed the value of the supportive network from the enterprise accelerator programme New Frontiers: "Some of us are still connecting on a daily basis," Boylan says. Once, a fellow New Frontiers alum was meeting someone he thought would be an ideal client for Firecloud365. "He wanted me to make the pitch to the client almost on the spot." Boylan remembers. This aligns with the research evidence that suggests the power of alumni networks in business accelerator programmes. These specialist alumni networks allow active participants to refine their funding pitch to a knowledgeable network, offer strategic business support and even camaraderie.[13] To find and activate these alumni components of ourselves, in many cases we need to seek them out, formally with the organization or create them informally within our own alumni capital.

All alumni networks should aspire to be a 'High-Energy Network'[14] , but only CERN, the European Organization for Nuclear Research, can claim the title. As the largest particle physics laboratory in the world, located in Geneva, Switzerland, CERN attracts researchers from all over the world, at all stages of their career to advance 'science for peace'.[15] The alumni network prioritizes activities that support career advancement and opportunities. CERN alumni respond with great zeal by attending some events and volunteering as speakers at others. With a curious fascination about CERN, alumni can access standard presentation materials to be both ambassadors and advocates of CERN in their universities and organizations around the world.[16] Whether by accident or design, we *are* the ambassadors and advocates for so many of our shared experiences. From returned volunteers with the Peace Corps to Global Undergraduate Award winners, these experiences, although a short point in time, have shaped part of who we are. We can continue with a lifelong, mutually beneficial relationship.

Along our career journey, we also collect other alumni networks that are worthy of celebration. Corporate alumni networks are popping up everywhere. In his book *Under New Management*, David Burkus reminds us that we are still valuable to our past employers too – and they are still valuable to us. 'Current employees and clients become the close-knit ties with whom the company interacts frequently,' explains Burkus. 'At the same time, former employees scattered across industries and sectors provide arm's-length ties that can relay important information and serve as important connections.'[17] As corporate alumni, we might offer client referrals or industry insights to our former employers. Why should our former employer get all the perks? In a world where it is unlikely that any of us will have the same job for life, alumni networks matter. A corporate alumni network means we have this network to draw on when we seek our next career move, or need to identify new clients. These are arm's length ties for us too.

The corporate alumni network trend is also our chance to promote our career success, socialize with other former employees, or even become a mentor to inspire others with our leadership story. We understand our former employer's corporate culture. We can recommend suitable candidates for vacancies – or become a boomerang, the affectionate term for people who re-apply for a job with their former employer. Leaving a company is no longer a negative, as talent research analyst Robin Erickson asks, 'What if organizations treated their former employees as long-term assets?'[18] Indeed, what if universities and all organizations remained curious and considered alumni as a long-term asset for future advancement?

As we embrace our wider alumni identities, we will become curious. Attend a sports event to see how the old team is doing, attend an elementary school reunion, follow a former club on social media. This is about *us*. Then, there's the leap from about *us* to *them*. We give of ourselves in this experience because we know that others can benefit the way we did. We can join the committee for our team gala fundraising event. We can return to participate as a corporate alum to the company's day of volunteering in the community. We can become a speaker or mentor at our former secondary school. The 'remember when' moments become 'remember why' moments of action. This is not about being sappy, this is simply part of the strategic component of our lives: we are, we learn, we take, we give.

Activity 22: Building our Alumni Way by exploring the breadth of our shared experiences

Take 20 minutes to list all the formal shared experiences over your lifetime. Consider your past and present.

- *Educational experiences*: schools, study abroad experiences, exchange programmes, conferences, study visits, research fellowships.
- *Employers*: organizations, non-profits, and companies, both full-time and part-time casual work, internships, apprenticeships, job shadowing experiences.
- *Professional connections*: associations, networks, and societies; start your own business, enterprise accelerator, or development groups.
- *Leisure activities*: sports teams, activities, clubs, summer camps, scouting
- *Awards*: academic, sports, scholarships, fellowships, service-based and volunteering awards.

- *Volunteering experiences*: service on boards and committees, international development service.
- *Religious, spiritual and diaspora affiliations*: retreats, spiritual, or religious events or trips, pilgrimages, cultural groups, diaspora outreach for countries, regions, cities, or cultures, nationally coordinated global alumni networks.
- *STEAM (science, technology, engineering, arts, and mathematics activities)*: STEM initiatives, coder dojo or coding clubs, bands, theatre troupes, musical societies, painting groups, math Olympiads, hack-a-thons.
- *Social impact*: programmes, initiatives, interventions, social change movements, change maker projects.

Be creative! Consider all your formal, organized shared experiences.

Next, rate the experiences. Three stars for those experiences you enjoyed the most and which had a transformational effect on your life; two stars for those experiences that were good but not something you consider often; one star for those experiences that are not a priority to re-engage with now.

Place a tick beside any of these shared experiences with a formal alumni network and/or ways for alumni to stay in touch or get involved. Prioritize the three-star and even the two-star shared experiences for reconnection. Reach out to the formal networks or informal social media groups for these shared experiences. Consider starting an alumni network or group for your top-shared experience if one doesn't exist. Approach the organization to see if they would support a formal alumni network or have fun setting up your own informal group.

Next, for your top three shared experiences, complete an Alumni Capital diagram (Diagram 2.1). This allows you to recognize the broader picture of the flows of people, knowledge, and resources at play within your alumni capital and community. With more practise in this quantum Alumni Way thinking, we can connect these circuits of our networks as second nature.

21

Our alumni call to action

The Alumni Way allows us to build our growth mindset. We open up to new opportunities and draw on our learning experiences. We invest hard work and effort on the journey. Developing an Alumni Way mindset is more than something *to do*. It is something that we have, something that *we are*. The Alumni Way challenges us to think beyond our titles, identities, and personas, or, at the very least, adds an extra one: alumni. By developing our alumni capital, we can explore other parts of ourselves. We can examine networks and ideas that connect us. We find our passion and place to give service.

Once we embark on the journey, our alumni citizenship serves us. We can think of *all* our formal, shared experiences differently. Our connections to institutions, organizations, sports teams, associations, and schools are all different. Relationships are meaningful exchanges. We can draw from institutions and they can draw from us. We are not alone. We are empowered to choose the experiences in our lives that hold the most meaning in our lives.

Our alumni citizenship is as fluid as we are. Our university alumni identity may be strong early in our career. As our needs change, we may develop a yearning to seek our ancestral home, to reconnect with childhood friends, to dust off the tennis racquet. Another alumni identity takes prominence.

It is easy to remain in the status quo and to decide not to change. 'Many people with the fixed mindset think the *world* needs to change not them,' Carol Dweck cautions. 'They feel entitled to something better — a better job, house or spouse. The world should recognize their special qualities and treat them accordingly.'[1] This fixed mindset stunts our growth. It takes special effort to embrace challenges we may encounter after university: a new career path, a fledgling business, finding a healthy balance in life and our go-to place to find inspiration, our alma mater and our networks. We all have shared experiences that impact and shape our lives. Some examples on how to seize our alumni status are in this book. Some aren't. The alumni actions and activities in this book help with this process of discovery. Be creative. Be a miner, a detective. With the Alumni Way we can reconceptualize these connections as universal, transformational, and inclusive!

Final checklist

To build your Alumni Way, drawing on your shared experiences you need to:

- ☐ devise and rate a list of all your shared experiences in your life (see Activity 22);
- ☐ map out an alumni capital diagram for three shared experiences outside of the university (see Activity 22);
- ☐ be creative in building your alumni capital!

Building the Alumni Way: Questions following Part VI

- *Recent graduates and alumni*: What other shared experiences do you value that can support the next stage in your life?
- *Students*: Before you were a student, what were your shared experiences? What does this tell you about the kinds of activities to actively explore while at university?
- *University administrators*: How do the institution's structures promote universal, inclusive, and transformative experiences for alumni?
- *Advancement professionals*: How can you inform alumni on the power and benefits of a lifelong relationship with their alma mater?
- *Parents/career advisers*: How do you model the Alumni Way across the multitude of alumni-shared experiences in your own life?

Bonus Alumni Action 23: Generating momentum for our Alumni Way health check

The aim of this book is to give thought to becoming, being, and engaging with alumni. This is our alumni health check. What's the proactive approach we take to embracing our alumni status, our alumni capital, and our alumni experience? Some may not agree with all the advice and the strategic nature that alumni and institutions play in our lives. The reality is that our alumni status is, if enacted, very powerful. We all have alumni capital: this is a valuable prospect that enables us to have the life we want.

We will all engage and tackle the alumni dimension of our lives differently. Overall, this book is an allegory for thinking of our lives as an epic journey. Throughout our lives, we hit milestones. These are times when we share and celebrate with others. We won't all become president of the alumni association. We can approach our alumni network in our own way.

Evan Mandery wrote his provocative article in *The Huffington Post* called 'Why I'm Skipping My Harvard Reunion (A Call to Action)'.[2] Mandery leveraged his alumni status as a platform to discuss equality in admissions to his Ivy League alma mater. The purpose of presenting this here is not to debate whether we agree or disagree with his points for ending legacy entrance into Harvard. What is poignant is that Mandery applies his alumni status to open a conversation towards enacting change. In the article, Mandery is reflective on the university experience he gained at Harvard. He described himself as 'as middle class as it gets' when he arrived at Harvard and immediately recognized the immense social divide between him and his classmates. It sparked his curiosity to identify a career that satisfied his passion for access to education and social justice. Mandery is a professor at the Jay John College of Criminal Justice, City University of New York (CUNY). He continues to write about addressing the inequalities and access to education.[3] He devotes time to supporting students and alumni at CUNY and his secondary school.[4] This is an example of the Alumni Way in action.

Now it's our turn. As a student, how can alumni help us to explore important life lessons? How can we prepare to be active alumni in the future? The Alumni Way challenges us to reflect on our past and connect to values meaningful to us, distilled in so many of those books on life purpose. Be curious to ask questions about our shared experiences; stay informed on this work. Identify our passions. Consider how these shared experiences shaped our interests and how they can be fostered throughout our lives. Decide how we can be of service as alumni. The dividends we receive in so many ways from giving is immense. Our shared experiences, our alma maters, our fellow alumni can be the beneficiaries of this — including the next generation of alumni.

Bonus Activity 23: Our alumni call to action by generating momentum for our Alumni Way health check

This bonus activity is a chance to take stock of the Alumni Way ideas shared in this book. Create a final action list for yourself, to follow the principles of the Alumni Way towards fostering a lifelong investment in your education. What are the three key takeaways from this book?

This is not just a personal exercise for you; it's not a secret. Alumni capital is non-competitive, so share it with your friends, family, co-workers, and beyond. Be an ambassador for the Alumni Way *in life, for life*.

Recommend the book to others — students, alumni, and others — that support you. Suggest it (or include it) on the reading list for a capstone course or transition year programme. Send it to a career adviser or coach you know who supports other students and alumni. Review the book online (and share your review!).

Use and follow the hashtag #TheAlumniWay to showcase creative ways that you are following this path. Let's celebrate your alumni triumphs! Your results can inspire others. We can create a supportive Alumni Way community to enable each one of us to build value from our university investment.

The final word: The Alumni Way journey continues ...

The Alumni Way isn't wishful thinking. It draws on the best of the growth mindset. All our experiences are learning experiences. The journey is long – lifelong! – our health, wellness, and professional and personal lives can benefit through our efforts. Think alumni in everything that we do. Watch the opportunities unfold. Think and act. To gain immense value from shared experiences requires our action and our efforts. We *are* all connected. The Alumni Way adds a new dimension to our lives. We can start as one alum and one university at a time. Let's build an alumni revolution – its lifelong value awaits!

Notes

Introduction

[1]   Schuster, E. (2018). 'Special Issue: Democracy's Graduates: Reimagining Alumnihood'. *Diversity & Democracy*. Spring, 21(2) [accessed 19/02/2021 https://www.aacu.org/diversitydemocracy/2018/spring]

Chapter 1

[1]   Seuss, Dr (1990). *Oh, The Places You'll Go!* New York: Harper Collins.

[2]   Seuss, Dr (1990). *Oh, The Places You'll Go!* New York: Harper Collins.

[3]   OECD (2019). *Benchmarking Higher Education System Performance: Higher Education and the Wider Social and Economic Context.* Paris: OECD Publishing [accessed 19/02/2021 http://www.oecd.org/education/benchmarking-higher-education-system-performance-be5514d7-en.htm]

[4]   Pettigrew, T. (2012). 'Why You'll Never Be an Alumni'. *Maclean's*. 26 April [accessed 19/02/2021 https://www.macleans.ca/education/uniandcollege/why-youll-never-be-an-alumni/]

[5]   Merriam-Webster Dictionary Online [accessed 19/02/2021 https://www.merriam-webster.com/dictionary/alumnus]. I am keenly aware, like so many other heteronyms, alum is a word spelled identically to the chemical compound with the same name but with a different pronunciation and meaning.

[6]   Please note that a term 'alumnx' as a gender-neutral alternative has been increasing in its usage in institutions, most notably in the United States. However, in this book I use alumni as a generally understood and recognized gender-neutral term employed in institutions worldwide. For further information on the emergence of alumnx, see Wolk, J. (2020). 'What is 'Alumnx'? One of Higher Ed's Newest Social Justice Terms, Explained'. *Campus Reform* [accessed 19/02/2021 https://www.campusreform.org/article?id=15934]

[7]   Favreau, A. (2016). *Stuff Every Graduate Should Know: A Handbook for the Real World.* Philadelphia: Quirk Books. Other popular books include Selingo, J.J. (2016). *There Is Life After College: What Parents and Students Should Know About Navigating School to Prepare for the Jobs of Tomorrow.* New York: William Morrow; Hooley, T. and Grant, K. (2017). *Graduate Career Handbook: Life after Graduation, Maximise Your Employability, Get a Graduate Job.* Bath: Trotman; Milliken, S. (2019). *Learner to Earner. A*

Recruitment Insider's Guide for Students Wanting to Achieve Graduate Job Success. London: Rethink Press.

8 Ellison, J. (2015). 'Happy Graduation, Now What? From Citizen Students to Citizen Alums'. *Change: The Magazine of Higher Learning.* January/ February: 81–83.

Chapter 2

1 Field, J. (2009). *Social Capital* (2nd ed.). London: Routledge.

2 Putnam, R.D. (2000). *Bowling Alone: The Collapse and Revival of American Community.* New York: Simon & Schuster, p 23.

3 Coleman, J.S. (1990). *Equality and Achievement in Education.* Boulder, CO: Westview Press.

4 Woolcock, M. (2001). 'The Place of Social Capital in Understanding Social and Economic Outcomes'. *Isuma: Canadian Journal of Policy Research.* 2(1): 11–17.

5 See for example, Ingham, D. (2016). 'An Answer from Research to the Teaching Excellence Framework – Student Engagement and Graduate Engagement to Evidence Legacy'. *Student Engagement in Higher Education Journal.* 1(1): pp 1–22; and Brooks, R. and Everett, G. (2009). 'Post-graduation Reflections on the Value of a Degree'. *British Education Research Journal.* 35(3): 333–349.

6 Dillon, J.L.R. (2018). 'Alumni Engagement Scoring: What Does the Science Tell Us?' Salesforce webinar 26/06/2018. [accessed 19/02/2021 https://alumniidentity.com/blog/2021/2/15/alumni-engagement-scoring-what-does-the-science-tell-us]

7 Dewey, J. (1933). *How We Think: A Restatement of the Relation of Reflective Thinking to the Educative Process.* Lexington, MA: DC Heath and Company.

8 See for instance, Gallo, M.L. (2017). 'How Are Graduates and Alumni Featured in University Strategic Plans? Lessons from Ireland'. *Perspectives: Policy and Practice in Higher Education.* 22(3): 92–97.

9 Friedman, Z. (2019) 'Is College Worth It?' *Forbes.* 13 June [accessed 19/02/2021 https://www.forbes.com/sites/zackfriedman/2019/06/13/is-college-worth-it/?sh=203b6b8e778d]

10 See for example, Mitchell, J. and Belkin, D. (2017) 'Americans Losing Faith in College Degrees, Poll Finds'. *Wall Street Journal.* 7 September [19/02/2021 https://www.wsj.com/articles/americans-losing-faith-in-college-degrees-poll-finds-1504776601]

11 Morgan, J. (2017). 'Are Graduates Good Value for Money?' *Times Higher Education.* 12 October [19/02/2021 https://www.timeshighereducation.com/features/are-graduates-good-value-money]

12 Ruppell Shell, E. (2018). 'College May Not Be Worth It Anymore'. *New York Times.* 16 May [accessed 19/02/2021, https://www.nytimes.com/2018/05/16/opinion/college-useful-cost-jobs.html]

13 Brooks, A.C. (2020). 'A College Degree Is No Guarantee of a Good Life'. *The Atlantic.* 2 July [accessed 19/02/2021 https://www.theatlantic.com/family/archive/2020/07/will-going-college-make-you-happier/613729/]

14 Anonymous academic article in *The Guardian*: 'My Students Have Paid £9,000 and Now They Think They Own Me'. 18 December 2015 [accessed 19/02/201 https://www.theguardian.com/higher-education-network/2015/dec/18/my-students-have-paid-9000-and-now-they-think-they-own-me]

15 This is a phrase used by Ron Leiber in Leiber, R. (2021). *The Price You Pay for College*. New York: Harper. Kindle edition, Introduction.

16 Bathmaker, A.M., Ingram, N., Abrahams, J., Hoare, A., Waller, R., and Bradley, H. (2016). *Higher Education, Social Class and Social Mobility: The Degree Generation*. London: Palgrave Macmillan.

17 See for example, Ranson, S. (1993). 'Markets or Democracy for Education'. *British Journal of Educational Studies*. 41(4): 333–352; Schwartzman, R. (1995). Are Students Customers? The Metaphoric Mismatch between Management and Education. *Education*. 116: 423–432; and Budd, R. (2017). 'Undergraduate Orientations towards Higher Education in Germany and England: Problemizing the Notion of "student as customer"'. *Higher Education*. 73(1): 23–37.

18 Tight, M. (2013). 'Students: Customers, Clients or Pawns?' *Higher Education Policy*. 26: 293.

19 Gallo, M. (2012). 'Beyond Philanthropy: Recognising the Value of Alumni to Benefit Higher Education Institutions'. *Tertiary Education and Management*. 18(1): 41–55.

20 Dweck, C.S. (2017). *Mindset: Changing the Way You Think to Fulfil Your Potential*. London: Robinson, p 7.

21 Dweck, C.S. (2017). *Mindset: Changing the Way You Think to Fulfil Your Potential*. London: Robinson, p 6.

22 Dweck, C.S. (2017). *Mindset: Changing the Way You Think to Fulfil Your Potential*. London: Robinson, p 48.

Chapter 4

1 I want to acknowledge the use of this phrase from the blog post by Swingle, J. and Willsea, M. (2018). 'Breaking Away from the "Sea of Sameness" in Higher Ed'. WP Campus blog. 18 July [accessed 16/02/2021 https://www.wpcampus.org/blog/2018/07/breaking-away-from-the-sea-of-sameness-in-higher-ed/]

2 Murphy, K.A., Blustein, D.L., Bohlig, A.J., and Platt, M.G. (2010). 'The College-to-Career Transition: An Exploration of Emerging Adulthood'. *Journal of Counseling & Development*. 88(2): 174–181; Silver, B.R. and Roksa, J. (2017). 'Navigating Uncertainty and Responsibility: Understanding Inequality in the Senior-Year Transition'. *Journal of Student Affairs Research and Practice*. 54(3): 248–260; Perry, A. and Spencer, C. (2018). 'College Didn't Prepare Me for This: The Realities of the Student Debt Crisis and the Effect it is Having on College Graduates.' *The William & Mary Educational Review*. 6(1): 8–15.

3 Morgan, M. (2013). 'The Student Experience Practitioner Model'. In: Morgan, M. (ed.). *Supporting Student Diversity in Higher Education: A Practical Guide*. London: Routledge, p 51.

Chapter 5

1. Bula, F. (2017). 'Universities as Real-estate Developers'. *University Affairs.* 28 November [accessed 19/02/2021 https://www.universityaffairs.ca/features/feature-article/universities-real-estate-developers/]

2. UniverCity website (2020). [accessed 19/02/2021 http://univercity.ca/about-us/]

3. Diner, S.J. (2017a). 'How Universities Migrated into Cities and Democratized Higher Education'. Zócalo Public Square website. 31 August [accessed 19/02/2021 http://www.zocalopublicsquare.org/2017/08/31/universities-migrated-cities-democratized-higher-education/ideas/nexus/]; also see Diner, S.J. (2017b). *Universities and their Cities.* Baltimore MD: Johns Hopkins Press.

4. See for example, the note in Selingo, J. (2013). *College (Un)bound: The Future of Higher Education and What It Means for Students.* New York: Houghton Mifflin Harcourt Publishing, p 4.

5. Walker, N. (2018). 'Featured Fellow: Meric Gertler'. *Canadian Geographic* website. 16 February [accessed 19/02/2021 https://www.canadiangeographic.ca/article/featured-fellow-meric-gertler]

6. Florida, R. (2002). *The Rise of the Creative Class.* New York: Basic Books, p 292.

7. McLuhan, M. (2005). *Understanding Media.* Routledge Classics. London: Routledge.

8. See Copenhagen Capacity website – Copenhagen Goodwill Ambassadors [accessed 19/02/2021 https://gwa.copcap.com/]

9. McLuhan, M. (1970). *Counterblast.* London: Pitman Press, p 40.

10. Arnstein, S. (1969). 'A Ladder of Citizen Participation'. *Journal of the American Institute of Planners.* 35(4): 216–224.

11. Arnstein, S. (1969). 'A Ladder of Citizen Participation'. *Journal of the American Institute of Planners.* 35(4): 216–224.

12. Jones, M. (2015). '8 Prerequisites for Successful Alumni Engagement'. LinkedIn Pulse blog. 4 July [accessed 19/02/2021 https://www.linkedin.com/pulse/8-prerequisites-successful-alumni-engagement-mark-w-jones/]

13. Porter, J. (2017). 'Why You Should Make Time for Self-Reflection (Even If You Hate Doing It)'. *Harvard Business Review.* 21 March [accessed 19/02/2021 https://hbr.org/2017/03/why-you-should-make-time-for-self-reflection-even-if-you-hate-doing-it]

14. Boud, D., Keogh, R., and Walker, D. (eds) (1985). *Reflection: Turning Experience into Learning.* London: Kogan.

15. Schön, D.A. (1983). *The Reflective Practitioner: How Professionals Think in Action.* New York: Basic Books.

16. Schön, D.A. (1987). *Educating the Reflective Practitioner: Toward a New Design on Teaching and Learning in the Professions.* San Francisco: Jossey-Bass.

17. Monash Business School website – Alumni Community: Rufimy Khoo webpage [accessed 15/02/2021 www.monash.edu/business/alumni/our-alumni/alumni-stories/rufimy-khoo]

18 This is based on an interview with Teo Salgado, and Neghabat-Wolthoff, N. (2021). 'Q&A with UTM Alumnus Teo Salgado, Founder of VerveSmith Ltd and 2020 Recipient of the UofT Arbor Award for Exceptional Volunteer Service'. UTM University of Toronto website [accessed 15/02/2021 www.utm.utoronto.ca/alumni/news/qa-utm-alumnus-teo-salgado-founder-vervesmith-ltd-and-2020-recipient-u-t-arbor-award]

19 Rhodes College website – Alumni Spotlights [accessed 19/02/2021 https://www.rhodes.edu/alumni-development/alumni-relations/alumni-spotlights]

20 Rhodes College website – Alumni Spotlights [accessed 19/02/2021 https://www.rhodes.edu/alumni-development/alumni-relations/alumni-spotlights]

21 Simon Fraser University website – School of Public Policy – Alumni Reflections webpage [accessed 19/02/2021 http://www.sfu.ca/mpp/alumni/alumni-reflections.html]

22 Azim Premji University website – Student Reflections [accessed 19/02/21 https://azimpremjiuniversity.edu.in/SitePages/students-reflections-2.aspx]

Chapter 6

1 Council for Advancement and Support of Education (CASE) website [accessed 19/02/2021 https://www.case.org/about/case-strategic-plan/looking-future]

2 Gallo, M.L. (2012). 'Beyond Philanthropy'. *Tertiary Education and Management*. 18(1): 41–55.

3 Shaindlin, A. (2012). 'Will the Internet Obsolete Alumni Associations?' *Huffington Post*. 23 May [accessed 19/02/2021 https://www.huffingtonpost.com/andrew-shaindlin/alumni-associations-facebook_b_1375765.html]

4 Haranahan, K. (2015). 'Disintermediation and Alumni Engagement: A Definition'. Switchboard blog. 1 September [accessed 17/02/2021 https://switchboardhq.com/blog/disintermediation-a-definition]

5 Shaindlin, A. (2018) *Alumni Community Whitepaper: Engaging Alumni Outside Academia: Emerging Practices in Foundations, Fellowships and Other Nonprofit Organizations*. Chicago: Grenzebach, Glier & Associates and the Rockefeller Foundation [accessed 11/03/2020 https://www.grenzebachglier.com/wp-content/uploads/2018/07/GGA-Alumni-Community-Whitepaper-Shaindlin-UPLOAD.pdf]

6 Ron Cohen wrote a provocative article on alumni events where he stated: 'Most events don't create urgency or a compelling reason for alumni to attend. People are busy … and these kinds of events no longer carry high enough value to dislodge other things from their calendars.' See Cohen, R. (2018). 'Alumni events: Going, Going, Gone'. LinkedIn Pulse blog. 3 August [accessed 19/02/2021 https://www.linkedin.com/pulse/alumni-events-going-goinggone-ron-cohen/]

[7] Horowitz, J. (2018). 'Digital vs. In-Person Alumni Engagement: The Disparity'. Evertrue blog. 19 July [accessed 19/02/2021 https://www.evertrue.com/2018/07/19/digital-vs-in-person-alumni-engagement-the-disparity/]

[8] Butler, K. (2001). 'Defining Diaspora, Refining a Discourse'. *Diaspora*. 10(2): 189.

[9] Brubaker, R. (2005). 'The "Diaspora" Diaspora'. *Ethnic and Racial Studies*. 28(1): 1–19.

[10] Nilsson, P. (2017). 'Lessons the Alumni Have Learnt'. *The Financial Times*. [accessed 06/03/20 https://www.ft.com/content/44a80fe0-8690-11e7-8bb1-5ba57d47eff7]

[11] Campbell University – Welcome to the City website [accessed 19/02/2021 https://alumni.campbell.edu/engage/events/welcome-to-the-city/]

[12] Campbell University website [accessed 19/02/2021 https://alumni.campbell.edu/engage/events/welcome-to-the-city/]

[13] NL Alumni Network website [19/02/2021 https://www.nlalumni.nl/article/alumni-sharing-session-pre-departure-briefing-jakarta-2018/17/08/2018/344]

[14] Gallo, M.L. (2019). *Global Alumni Networks and Ireland: Learning from International Practice*. Dublin: KITE White Paper [accessed 19/02/2021 https://www.keepintoucheducation.com/resources]

[15] Rincon, S. (2018). 'It's a Small World: How a Global Alumni Association is Benefitting International Alumni and Students – in the Netherlands and abroad'. *CASE Currents*. July/August: 32–37 [also available with a CASE subscription accessed 19/02/2021 https://www.case.org/resources/issues/july-august-2018/its-small-world]

[16] Rincon, S. (2018). 'It's a Small World: How a Global Alumni Association Is Benefitting International Alumni and Students – in the Netherlands and abroad'. *CASE Currents*. July/August: 32–37 [also available with a CASE subscription accessed 19/02/2021 https://www.case.org/resources/issues/july-august-2018/its-small-world]

[17] Council for Advancement and Support of Education (2020). 'Principles of Practice for Alumni Relations Professionals at Educational Institutions'. website [accessed 19/02/2021 https://www.case.org/resources/principles-practice-alumni-relations-professionals-educational-institutions]

[18] Higher Ed Live podcast (2018) 'What will Alumni Relations look like in 2027?' [accessed 16/02/2021 https://www.podbean.com/site/EpisodeDownload/PB7306A1W3YTB]

[19] University College Dublin website (2021). UCD Connections Magazine archive. [accessed 18/02/2021 https://alumni.ucd.ie/magazine-archive/]

[20] University of Limerick website (2021). UL Links Magazine [accessed 18/02/2021 https://www.ul.ie/ullinks/]

[21] Kennedy, J. and Rego, N. (2018). 'How the UNB Alumni Office Re-connected with 6500+ Alumni'. University of New Brunswick blog. 6 September [accessed 09/04/20 https://blogs.unb.ca/marketing/2018/09/how-the-unb-alumni-office-re-connected-with-6500+-alumni.php]

22 Dweck, C.S. (2017). *Mindset: Changing the Way You Think to Fulfil Your Potential*. London: Robinson, p 41.

23 Clark, D. (2019). '3 Ways to Make the Most of Your Alumni Network'. *Harvard Business Review*. 8 November [accessed 16/02/2021 https://hbr.org/2019/10/3-ways-to-make-the-most-of-your-alumni-network]

24 University of Waterloo. *Welcome to the Club Young Alumni Handbook 2018*. Received with permission for quotation from Emily Huxley Osbourne, Senior Alumni Officer, Student-Alumni Bridge 08/01/2019.

25 Granovetter, M.S. (1973). 'The Strength of Weak Ties'. *American Journal of Sociology*. 78(6): 1360–1380.

Chapter 7

1 University of New South Wales Business School website [accessed 19/02/2021 https://www.business.unsw.edu.au/alumni/alum-from-day-one]

2 Lorsch, J. and Tierney, T. (2002). *Aligning the Stars: How to Succeed when Professionals Drive Results*. Boston: Harvard Business School Press, p 202.

3 Precedent (2009). *Alumdergraduates: Aligning the Student and Alumni Experience Online*. London: Precedent.

Chapter 8

1 Krumboltz, J.D. (1998). 'Serendipity is not Serendipitous'. *Journal of Counselling Psychology*. 45(4): 390–392.

2 Mitchell, K.E., Levin, A.S., and Krumboltz, J.D. (1999). 'Planned Happenstance: Constructing Unexpected Career Opportunities'. *Journal of Counselling and Development*. 77(Spring): 116.

3 Drawing on John Dewey's ideas of curiosity in Dewey, J. (1997). *How We Think* (new edition from 1910 original). New York: Dover Publications, pp 30–31.

4 Leslie, I. (2015). *Curious: The Desire to Know and Why Your Future Depends on It*. London: Quercus, p xvi.

5 Kivunja offers a comprehensive synthesis of these Career and Life Skills for the New Learning Paradigm in his article: Kivunja, C. (2015). 'Teaching Students to Learn and to Work Well with 21st Century Skills: Unpacking the Career and Life Skills Domain of the New Learning Paradigm'. *International Journal of Higher Education*. 4(1): 1–11.

6 Harari, Y.N. (2018). *21 Lessons for the 21st Century*. London: Penguin Random House, p 305.

7 OECD (2018). *Preparing Our Youth for an Inclusive and Sustainable World: The OECD PISA Global Competence Framework*. [accessed 19/02/2021 https://www.oecd.org/education/Global-competency-for-an-inclusive-world.pdf]

Chapter 9

1 Brown, P. (2003). 'The Opportunity Trap: Education and Employment in a Global Economy'. *European Educational Research Journal*. 2(1), pp 141–179.

2   Bourdieu, P. (1986). 'The Forms of Capital'. Richardson, J. (ed.) In: *Handbook of Theory and Research in Education*. Westport, CT: Greenwood, pp 241–258.

3   Bathmaker, A.M., Ingram, N., and Waller, R. (2013). 'Higher Education, Social Class and the Mobilisation of Capitals: Recognising and Playing the Game'. *British Journal of Sociology of Education*. 34(5–6): 723–743.

4   Bourdieu, P. (1990). 'The Logic of Practice'. Stanford: Stanford California Press, p 64. Cited in: Bathmaker, A.M., Ingram, N., and Waller, R. (2013). 'Higher Education, Social Class and the Mobilisation of Capitals: Recognising and Playing the Game'. *British Journal of Sociology of Education*. 34(5–6): p 730.

5   McPherson, M., Smith-Lovin, L., and Cook, J.M. (2001). 'Birds of a Feather: Homophily in Social Networks'. *Annual Review of Sociology*. 27: 415–444.

6   See for example, Burt, R.S. (1992). *Structural Holes: The Social Structure of Competition*. Cambridge, MA: Harvard University Press; Granovetter, M.S. (1974). *Getting a Job: A Study of Contacts and Careers*. Cambridge, MA: Harvard University Press. Both cited on the idea of diversity in networks in: de Janasz, S.C. and Forret, M.L. (2008). 'Learning the Art of Networking: A Critical Skill for Enhancing Social Capital and Career Success'. *Journal of Management Education*. 32(5) 629–650.

7   Burkus, D. (2018). *Friend of a Friend: Understanding the Hidden Networks that Can Transform Your Life and Your Career*. New York: Houghton Mifflin Harcourt, p 18.

8   Burkus, D. (2018). *Friend of a Friend: Understanding the Hidden Networks that Can Transform Your Life and Your Career*. New York: Houghton Mifflin Harcourt.

9   Burkus, D. (2018). *Friend of a Friend: Understanding the Hidden Networks that Can Transform Your Life and Your Career*. New York: Houghton Mifflin Harcourt, p 18.

10 Ferrazzi, K. (2014). *Never Eat Alone … and Other Secrets to Success, One Relationship at a Time* (2nd ed.). London: Portfolio Penguin, p 18.

11 Naisbitt, J. (1999). *High Tech, High Touch: Technology and Our Search for Meaning*. London: Nicholas Brealey Publishers.

12 Prichard, M. (2019). Mac's List blog. 'Building a Valuable Network: How To Keep in Touch with Professional Contacts'. [accessed 21/02/2021 https://www.macslist.org/networking/building-a-valuable-network-how-to-keep-in-touch-with-professional-contacts]

13 Cornell Alumni website [accessed 19/02/2021 http://news.cornell.edu/stories/2019/01/cornell-alumni-leadership-conference-opens-all]

14 Cornell Alumni website [accessed 19/02/2021 http://news.cornell.edu/stories/2019/01/cornell-alumni-leadership-conference-opens-all]

15 Auter, Z. and Marken, S. (2019). 'Alumni Network Less Helpful than Advertised'. Gallup website. 15 January [accessed 19/02/2021 https://news.gallup.com/opinion/gallup/245822/alumni-networks-less-helpful-advertised.aspx]

16 Nietzel, M.T. (2019). 'Alumni Networks and the Job Market: Help or Hindrance?' *Forbes* online. 16 January [accessed 19/02/2021 https://www.forbes.com/sites/michaeltnietzel/2019/01/16/alumni-networks-and-the-job-market-help-or-hindrance/#3f7302dfba03]

17 Colgate University – Alumni – Professional Networks webpage [accessed 19/02/2021 https://www.colgate.edu/alumni/campus-events-0/professional-networks]; DeVries, D. (2017). 'Networking with Nuance'. *CASE Currents*. November/December [accessed 16/02/2021 https://www.case.org/resources/issues/november-december-2017/networking-nuance requires professional subscription]

18 Selingo, J.J. (2016). *There Is Life after College: What Parents and Students Should Know about Navigating School and Preparing for the Jobs of Tomorrow*. New York: Harper Collins, p 242.

19 Twigg, K. (2021). *The Career Stories Method: 11 Steps to Find Your Ideal Career – and Discover Your Awesome Self in the Process*. Vancouver: Page Two Books, Kindle Edition, p 138.

20 Twigg, K. (2021). *The Career Stories Method: 11 Steps to Find Your Ideal Career – and Discover Your Awesome Self in the Process*. Vancouver: Page Two Books, Kindle Edition, p 138.

21 McGuire, P. (2018). 'The Misunderstood Art of Networking'. *Irish Times*. 8 May [accessed 19/02/2021 https://www.irishtimes.com/news/education/the-misunderstood-art-of-networking-1.3479288]

22 York University website. 'TASTE Program students, grads for mentorship lunch'. yFiles webpage 9 September 2015 [accessed 19/02/2021 https://yfile.news.yorku.ca/2015/09/09/taste-program-pairs-students-grads-for-mentorship-lunch/]

23 Whittemore, S. (2013). 'Alumni: Includes our Enhance Alumni Engagement Checklist' *Relationship Management*. JISC Online Publication [accessed 19/02/2021 https://www.jisc.ac.uk/guides/relationship-management/alumni]

24 If you were curious enough to come to this note, take the extra five minutes to read this simple and powerful narrative: Longwood University (2020). 'The Hiring Manager's Story'. [accessed 04/02/2021 http://www.longwood.edu/alumni/articles/2020/the-hiring-managers-story/]

25 Passini, R. (1981). 'Wayfinding: A Conceptual Framework'. *Urban Ecology*. 5(1980/1981): pp 17–31.

26 Rancourt, D.W. (2019). 'Wayfinding and Research as Key Work-integrated Learning Strategies'. *University Affairs*. 16 August [accessed 29/02/2020 https://www.universityaffairs.ca/career-advice/career-advice-article/wayfinding-and-research-as-key-work-integrated-learning-strategies/]

27 Berg, M. and Seeber, B.K. (2016). *The Slow Professor: Challenging the Culture of Speed in the Academy*. Toronto: University of Toronto Press.

28 Auter, Z. and Marken, S. (2018). 'Professors Provide Most Valued Career Advice to Grads'. Gallup website. 16 November [accessed 04/01/2021 https://news.gallup.com/poll/244811/professors-provide-valued-career-advice-grads.aspx], drawing on Strada-Gallup (2019). *2018 Strada-Gallup Alumni Survey Mentoring College Students to Success.* Indianapolis: Strada-Gallup. [accessed 19/02/2021 https://news.gallup.com/reports/244031/2018-strada-gallup-alumni-survey-mentoring-students.aspx]. Also see Cownie, F. and Gallo, M.L. (2020). 'Alumni Gratitude and Academics: Implications for Engagement'. *The Journal of Further and Higher Education.* DOI: https://doi.org/10.1080/0309877X.2020.1820457

29 The full list compiled by my children, Luca and Tara, along with my nephew Giacomo included: paramedic, scientist, vet, firefighter, police officer, lifeguard, pony rider, construction worker, musician, palaeontologist, sea search and rescue, shop worker, bus driver, lumberjack, window cleaner, doctor, surgeon, nurse, teacher, secretary, inventor. List compiled on 16/07/18. Can you consider ways each of these jobs can be connected to a university? An exercise in creativity!

30 Selingo, J. (2013). *College (Un)bound: The Future of Higher Education and What it Means for Students.* New York: Houghton Mifflin Harcourt Publishing; Greater Rochester Enterprise (2017). 'Major Employers in the Greater Rochester, New York Region – 2017'. Greater Rochester Enterprise webpage [accessed 11/02/2021 https://www.rochesterbiz.com/Portals/0/Major%20employers%20in%20the%20Greater%20Rochester%20NY%20Region%20-%202017_1.pdf]

31 See for example, Charkrabortty, A. and Weale, S. (2016). 'Universities Accused of "Importing Sports Direct model" for Lecturers' Pay'. *The Guardian.* 16 November [accessed 19/02/2021 https://www.theguardian.com/uk-news/2016/nov/16/universities-accused-of-importing-sports-direct-model-for-lecturers-pay; and Olivier, A. (2016). 'McGill University Casual Support Staff Kick Off 5-day Strike'. Global News website. [accessed 19/02/2021 https://globalnews.ca/news/3033641/mcgill-university-casual-support-staff-kick-off-5-day-strike/]

32 See for example, Staton, B. (2020). 'Universities to Cut Thousands of Academics on Short Contracts'. *Financial Times.* 20 July [accessed 19/02/2021 https://www.ft.com/content/67f89a9e-ac30-47d0-83e7-eba4d1284847]

33 CASE Council for Advancement and Support of Education is the largest professional association for advancement professionals worldwide. The number of advancement professionals is cited from Skinner, N.A. (2019). 'The Rise and Professionalization of the American Fundraising Model in Higher Education'. *Philanthropy & Education.* 3(1): 23–46.

34 Finn, J. (2018). 'The Rise of the Experience Industry on Campus'. *University Affairs.* 13 March [accessed 19/02/2021 https://www.universityaffairs.ca/opinion/in-my-opinion/rise-experience-industry-campus/]

35 See for example, Fearn, H. (2018). 'Take your PhD to industry'. Sparrho Medium blog [accessed 19/02/2021 https://medium.com/sparrho/take-your-phd-to-industry-d9f657beaede]

36 Clark, A. and Sousa, B. (2018a). *How to Be a Happy Academic*. London: Sage.

37 Clark, A and Sousa, B. (2018b). 'Your Biggest Asset for Academic Career Success? A Growth Mindset'. *Times Higher Education*. 21 February [accessed 19/02/2021 https://www.timeshighereducation.com/blog/your-biggest-asset-academic-career-success-growth-mindset]

38 Pan, J. and Kapelke-Dale, R. (2014). *Graduates in Wonderland: The International Misadventures of Two (Almost) Adults*. New York: Gotham Books.

39 Kapelke-Dale, R. (2014). 'The Odd Couple'. *Brown Alumni Magazine*. [accessed 19/02/2021 https://www.brownalumnimagazine.com/articles/2014-09-03/the-odd-couple]

40 Kapelke-Dale, R. (2014). 'The Odd Couple'. *Brown Alumni Magazine*. [accessed 19/02/2021 https://www.brownalumnimagazine.com/articles/2014-09-03/the-odd-couple]

41 Novick, N. (2019). 'Testing the Limits: An Introvert Experiments with Life as an Extrovert'. *Brown Alumni Magazine*. [accessed 04/01/2021 https://www.brownalumnimagazine.com/articles/2019-11-05/testing-the-limits]

42 University of Sheffield website – Alumni Authors webpage [accessed 19/02/2021 https://www.sheffield.ac.uk/alumni/our_alumni/authors]

43 Sanchez, G.J. (2018). 'Curating Career Success for First-Generation College Alumni'. *Diversity & Democracy*. Spring 21(2), pp 29–30 [accessed 19/02/2021 https://www.aacu.org/diversitydemocracy/2018/spring/sanchez]

44 NACE (2020). *Career Services Benchmark Survey Report 2019–20*. Bethlehem, PA: NACE [accessed 29/01/2021 https://www.naceweb.org/store/2020/nace-career-services-benchmark-report/]

45 Busteed, B. and Seymour, S. (2015). 'Many College Graduates Not Equipped for Workplace Success'. *Forbes*. 23 September [accessed 19/02/2021 https://www.forbes.com/sites/brandonbusteed/2019/12/15/importance-of-college-drops-nearly-50-among-young-adults-in-just-six-years/?sh=5f2cfb314b56], reporting on the results of the Gallup-Purdue Index Report: Gallup and Purdue University. (2014). *Great Jobs, Great Lives: The 2014 Gallup-Purdue Index Report*. Washington: Gallup [accessed 26/10/2020 https://www.gallup.com/services/176768/2014-gallup-purdue-index-report.aspx]

46 Twigg, K. (2021) *The Career Stories Method. 11 Steps to Find Your Ideal Career – and Discover Your Awesome Self in the Process*. Vancouver: Page Two Books, Kindle Edition, p 11.

47 University of Greenwich website – Greenwich Snapshots webpage [accessed 19/02/2021 https://alumni.gre.ac.uk/greenwich-snapshots/]

Chapter 10

1 University of Toronto website – Entrepreneurs webpage [accessed 19/02/2021 http://entrepreneurs.utoronto.ca/]

2   Clark, B.R. (1998). *Creating Entrepreneurial Universities: Organizational Pathways of Transformation*. Oxford: IAU Press Pergamon.

3   Fuster, E., Padilla-Meléndez, A., Lockett, R., and del-Águila-Obra, A.R. (2019). 'The Emerging Role of University Spin-off Companies in Developing Regional Entrepreneurial University Ecosystems: The Case of Andalusia'. *Technological Forecasting and Social Change*. 141(April): pp 219–231.

4   Campus Insights website [accessed 19/02/2021 https://www.campus-insights.com/]

5   Daso, F. (2018). 'These Brothers Just Sold Their Market Research Startup to the World's Largest Student-Run Company'. *Forbes Online*. 20 February [accessed 19/02/2021 https://www.forbes.com/sites/frederickdaso/2018/02/20/these-brothers-just-sold-their-market-research-startup-to-the-worlds-largest-student-run-company/#2310bf616fdf]

6   LifeBook website [accessed 19/02/2021 https://www.lifebookuk.com/]

7   University of Sheffield Alumni website – Alumni – LifeBook [accessed 19/02/21 https://www.sheffield.ac.uk/alumni/news_archive/2013/life-book-story]

8   Adams, A. (nd) '7 Alumni Benefits You Should Be Taking Advantage Of'. *The Muse* blog [accessed 19/02/2021 https://www.themuse.com/advice/7-alumni-benefits-you-should-be-taking-advantage-of]

9   Guzman, K. (2019). 'Alumni Startup Helps Students Tame College Debt'. *Yale School of Management Alumni Magazine*. 16 January [accessed 19/02/2021 https://som.yale.edu/news/2019/01/alumni-startup-helps-students-tame-college-debt]

10 Forsythe, R. (2020) LinkedIn post. 4 July [24/07/2020 https://www.linkedin.com/posts/rupertforsythe_pivot-graduation-virtualceremonies-activity-6685225708945457152-dDbe/]

11 After seeing the signs first in Wolfville, Nova Scotia, I found this feature story that illustrates my point about direct alumni engagement. Charlotte Peak, an Acadia alum, wrote the article about fellow grads taking the initiative to show their university pride. See Peak, C. (2013). 'Alumni Business Proudly Put Acadia Front and Centre'. Acadia University website [accessed 24/06/2020 https://www2.acadiau.ca/alumni-friends/alumni/news/alumni-news-reader/alumni-business-owners-proudly-put-acadia-front-and-centre.html]

12 Bauer College of Business, University of Houston – Alumni Business Directory webpage [accessed 19/02/2021 https://www.bauer.uh.edu/alumni/alumni-businesses.asp]

13 Bauer College of Business, University of Houston (2020). Alumni Business Directory webpage [accessed 19/02/2021 https://www.bauer.uh.edu/alumni/alumni-businesses.asp]

14 Institute of Technology, Sligo website [accessed 19/02/2021 https://www.itsligo.ie/courses/meng-connected-autonomous-vehicles/]

15 National Centre for Universities and Business (2020). *State of the Relationship 2020*. London: NCUB, p 9 [accessed 19/02/2021 https://www.ncub.co.uk/index.php?option=com_docman&view=download&alias=479-final-ncub-state-of-the-relationship-report-2020-digital&category_slug=reports&Itemid=2728]

16 National Centre for Universities and Business (2020). *State of the Relationship 2020*. London: NCUB, p 9 [accessed 19/02/2021 https://www.ncub.co.uk/index.php?option=com_docman&view=download&alias=479-final-ncub-state-of-the-relationship-report-2020-digital&category_slug=reports&Itemid=2728]

17 National Centre for Universities and Business (2021). *Showcasing Collaboration: Partnerships for the Planet: Highlighting University and Business Partnerships Formed To Address the Climate Crisis*. London: NCUB, p 3 [accessed 19/02/2021 https://www.ncub.co.uk/index.php?option=com_docman&view=download&alias=484-5044-partnerships-for-the-planet-v9-new&category_slug=reports&Itemid=2728]

18 National Centre for Universities and Business (2021). *Showcasing Collaboration: Partnerships for the Planet: Highlighting University and Business Partnerships Formed To Address the Climate Crisis*. London: NCUB, p 4 [accessed 19/02/2021 https://www.ncub.co.uk/index.php?option=com_docman&view=download&alias=484-5044-partnerships-for-the-planet-v9-new&category_slug=reports&Itemid=2728]

Chapter 11

1 Loewenstein, G. (1994). 'The Psychology of Curiosity: A Review and Reinterpretation'. *Psychological Bulletin*, 116: 75–98.

2 Brandeis University – Podcast with guest speaker Ronit Avni webpage [accessed 19/02/2021 – Transcript of the podcast https://www.brandeis.edu/global/podcast/drbr/transcripts/27-episode.html]

3 Brandeis University – Podcast with guest speaker Ronit Avni webpage [accessed 19/02/2021 – Transcript of the podcast https://www.brandeis.edu/global/podcast/drbr/transcripts/27-episode.html]

4 Aaldernick, W. (2018). 'Alumni Intelligence and the Value of Connecting'. *The Career Leadership Collective Blog*. 20 March [accessed 19/02/2021 https://www.careerleadershipcollective.com/single-post/2018/03/20/Alumni-Intelligence-and-the-Value-of-Connecting]

Chapter 12

1 Vallerand, R.J., Blanchard, C., Mageau, G.A., Koestner, R., Ratelle, C., Leonard, M., Gagne, M., and Marsolais, J. (2003). 'Les Passions de l'Âme: On Obsessive and Harmonious Passion'. *Journal of Personality and Social Psychology*. 85(4): 756–767.

[2] Vallerand, R.J., Blanchard, C., Mageau, G.A., Koestner, R., Ratelle, C., Leonard, M., Gagne, M., and Marsolais, J. (2003). 'Les Passions de l'Âme: On Obsessive and Harmonious Passion'. *Journal of Personality and Social Psychology.* 85(4): 757.

[3] McDearmon, J.T. (2013). 'Hail to Thee, Our Alma Mater: Alumni Role Identity and the Relationship to Institutional Support Behaviors'. *Research in Higher Education.* 54(3): 283–302.

[4] McDearmon, J.T. (2013). 'Hail to Thee, Our Alma Mater: Alumni Role Identity and the Relationship to Institutional Support Behaviors'. *Research in Higher Education.* 54(3): 286.

[5] Robinson, K. (2009). *The Element: How Finding Your Passion Changes Everything.* London: Penguin Books, p 24.

[6] Vallerand, R. (2010). 'On the Passion for Life Activities: The Dualistic Model of Passion'. *Advances in Experimental Social Psychology.* 42: 101.

[7] Vallerand, R. (2010). On the Passion for Life Activities: The Dualistic Model of Passion'. *Advances in Experimental Social Psychology.* 42: 99–193.

[8] Vallerand, R. (2010). On the Passion for Life Activities: The Dualistic Model of Passion'. *Advances in Experimental Social Psychology.* 42: 184.

[9] Ferrazzi, K. (2014). *Never Eat Alone* (2nd ed.). London: Portfolio Penguin, p 107.

[10] Universities of Sanctuary website [accessed 19/02/2021 https://ireland.cityofsanctuary.org/universities-and-colleges-of-sanctuary]

[11] Agnew, M. 'University of Canterbury Recognised as a Fair Trade University'. *University of Canterbury News.* 10 July [accessed 19/02/2021 https://www.canterbury.ac.nz/news/2017/university-of-canterbury-recognised-as-a-fair-trade-university.html]

[12] Trinity College Dublin – Trinity Centre for People with Intellectual Disability website [accessed 19/02/2021 https://www.tcd.ie/tcpid/about/]

[13] University of Heidelberg Family-Friendly University webpage [accessed 19/02/2021 https://www.uni-heidelberg.de/university/family-friendly/]

[14] Talmage, C.A., Mark, R., Slowey, M., and Knopf, R.C. (2016). 'Age Friendly Universities and Engagement with Older Adults: Moving from Principles to Practice'. *International Journal of Lifelong Education.* 35(5): 537–554.

[15] Times Higher Education – THE Student. (2020) 'Top Universities in the World for Global Impact'. *Times Higher Education – THE Student.* 22 April. [accessed 07/02/2021 https://www.timeshighereducation.com/student/best-universities/top-universities-world-global-impact]

[16] Talmage, C.A., Mark, R., Slowey, M., and Knopf, R.C. (2016). 'Age Friendly Universities and Engagement with Older Adults: Moving from Principles to Practice'. *International Journal of Lifelong Education,* 35(5): 542.

[17] Covey, S.R. (2004) *The 7 Habits of Highly Effective People.* New York: Simon & Schuster, p 302.

Chapter 13

1   University of Sheffield. (2018) 'The Professional Birdwatcher' *Your University: The Magazine for Alumni and Friends*. Sheffield: Development, Alumni Relations & Events, University of Sheffield, pp 16–18.

2   Aoun, J.E. (2018). *Robot-Proof: Higher Education in the Age of Artificial Intelligence*. London: MIT Press, p 133.

3   University of Malta TEDx website: [accessed 16/02/2021 https://www.ted.com/tedx/events/33224]

4   Brown, B. (2010). *The Power of Vulnerability*. [video] TEDx Houston [accessed 19/02/2021 https://www.ted.com/talks/brene_brown_the_power_of_vulnerability?language=en]

5   National Co-ordinating Centre for Public Engagement website 'About the Manifesto'. [accessed 19/02/2021 https://www.publicengagement.ac.uk/support-engagement/strategy-and-planning/manifesto-public-engagement/about-manifesto]

6   National Co-ordinating Centre for Public Engagement website 'About the Manifesto'. [accessed 19/02/2021 https://www.publicengagement.ac.uk/support-engagement/strategy-and-planning/manifesto-public-engagement/about-manifesto]

7   Reisz, M. (2011). 'Ionic, Isn't It?' *Times Higher Education*. 20 October, p 41.

8   Bright Club website [accessed 19/02/2021 www.brightclub.org]

9   University of Melbourne – MOOCs page. [accessed 19/02/2021 https://about.unimelb.edu.au/teaching-and-learning/innovation-initiatives/digital-and-online-innovation/moocs]

10 University of Melbourne (2016). 'University Passes MOOC Milestone'. University of Melbourne Newsroom website. 16 May [accessed 19/02/2021 http://newsroom.melbourne.edu/news/university-passes-mooc-milestone]

11 Hollands, F.M. and Tirthali, D. (2014). Why Do Institutions Offer MOOCs? *Journal of Asynchronous Learning Networks*. 18(3): 5 [accessed 11/09/19 https://www.learntechlib.org/p/154185/.]

12 University of Melbourne – MOOCs page. [accessed 19/02/2021 https://about.unimelb.edu.au/teaching-and-learning/innovation-initiatives/digital-and-online-innovation/moocs]

13 Kizilcec, R.F., Reich, J., Yeomans, M., Dann,C., Brunskill, E., Lopez, G., Turkay, S., Williams, J.J., and Tingley, D. (2020). 'Scaling Up Behavioral Science Interventions in Online Education'. *PNAS Proceedings of the National Academy of Sciences of the United States of America*. 117: 27, 14900–14905; Hollands, F.M. and Tirthali, D. (2014). Why Do Institutions Offer MOOCs? *Journal of Asynchronous Learning Networks*. 18(3) 5 [accessed 19/02/2021 https://www.learntechlib.org/p/154185/]

14 Newton, D. (2020). 'The "Depressing" and "Disheartening" News about MOOCs'. *Forbes*. 21 June [accessed 19/02/2021 https://www.forbes.com/sites/dereknewton/2020/06/21/the-depressing-and-disheartening-news-about-moocs/?sh=5ba1037976ed]

[15] UC Davis website. 'Sip, Sip Hooray! UC Davis Alumni Wine Program'. [accessed 19/02/2021 https://ucdavis.imodules.com/s/1768/rd18/index. aspx?sid=1768&gid=2&pgid=2254&content_id=1385]

[16] UC Davis website. 'One Aggie Network: Alumni Wine and Beer Program'. [accessed 19/02/2021 https://alumni.ucdavis.edu/ alumni-wine-beer-program]

[17] London, J. (2016). 'Join the MIT Book Club'. Slice of MIT blog [accessed 19/02/2021 https://alum.mit.edu/slice/join-mit-alumni-book-club]

[18] Professional Book Club webpage: Pace University [accessed 19/02/2021 https://www.pbc.guru/pace/]

[19] Solent University website [accessed 19/02/2021 https://www.solent.ac.uk/ news/life-at-solent/2019/celebrating-50-years-of-yacht-design-at-solent]

[20] Solent University website [accessed 19/02/2021 https://www.solent.ac.uk/ news/life-at-solent/2019/celebrating-50-years-of-yacht-design-at-solent]

[21] Burgess, K. (2018) LinkedIn post [accessed 06/02/2021 https://www. linkedin.com/posts/kate-burgess-03606a121_womens-football-for-both-alumni-and-current-activity-6443372341924888577-hYnH]

[22] Old Dominion University (2019). 'Yappy Hour Social'. [accessed 06/02/ 2021 https://www.odualumni.org/s/1672/bp20/interior.aspx?sid=1672 &gid=2&pgid=2390&cid=4339&ecid=4339&crid=0&calpgid=388&cal cid=1182]

[23] Kent State University website [accessed 16/02/2021 https://www.kent. edu/alumni/event/dog-days-summer]

[24] University College Dublin website [accessed 19/02/2021 https://alumni. ucd.ie/woodland-walkies-2017/]

[25] University of Cambridge. (2017). 'Physical Activity, Even in Small Amounts, Benefits Both Physical and Psychological Well-Being'. University of Cambridge Research webpage. [accessed 19/02/2021 https://www.cam. ac.uk/research/news/physical-activity-even-in-small-amounts-benefits-both-physical-and-psychological-well-being]

[26] Skotnicki, S. (2018). 'A Clean Break: Why Our Society's Obsession with Cleanliness Has Become Too Much of a Good Thing'. *The Globe & Mail*. 25 May [accessed 19/02/2021 https://www.theglobeandmail.com/opinion/ article-a-clean-break-why-our-societys-obsession-with-cleanliness-has-become/?page=all&utm_source=Facebook&utm_medium=Alumni-Facebook&utm_campaign=Alumni-FB-status-post]

[27] Gieseke, C. (2018). 'Wellbeing: Not Just Jogging and Broccoli'. Iowa State University Alumni Magazine. Fall [accessed 07/02/2021https://www. isualum.org/s/565/17/interior.aspx?sid=565&gid=1&pgid=3503&cid= 5247&ecid=5247&crid=0&calpgid=3130&calcid=4805]

[28] Gieseke, C. (2018). 'Wellbeing: Not Just Jogging and Broccoli'. Iowa State University Alumni Magazine. Fall [accessed 07/02/2021 https://www. isualum.org/s/565/17/interior.aspx?sid=565&gid=1&pgid=3503&cid= 5247&ecid=5247&crid=0&calpgid=3130&calcid=4805]

29   Dweck, C.S. (2017). *Mindset: Changing the Way You Think to Fulfil Your Potential*. London: Robinson, p 48.

Chapter 14

1   Huie, J. (2018). *Purpose: Find Your Truth and Embrace Your Calling*. London: Hay House, p 162.
2   Gaffney, M. (2012). *Flourishing*. London: Penguin, p 269.
3   Gaffney, M. (2012). *Flourishing*. London: Penguin, p 269.
4   University of Edinburgh website. [accessed 19/02/2021 https://www.ed.ac.uk/local/projects/cabaret-of-dangerous-ideas]
5   University of Edinburgh website. [accessed 19/02/2021 https://www.ed.ac.uk/local/projects/cabaret-of-dangerous-ideas]
6   Lyn, K. (2018). 'UofT Music Puts Out First Ever Holiday Playlist'. *UofT News* website. 29 November [accessed 19/02/2021 https://www.utoronto.ca/news/u-t-music-puts-out-its-first-ever-holiday-playlist]
7   University of Maryland Libraries Digital Collections website – The Jim Henson Works [accessed 19/02/2021 https://digital.lib.umd.edu/henson/about]
8   Reisz, M. (2011). 'Odds and Quads'. *The Times Higher Education*. 3 November, p 16; Monmouth University website – Bruce Springsteen Archives & Center for American Music [accessed 19/02/2021 https://springsteenarchives.org/]
9   Tansey, L. and Gallo, M.L. (2015). 'Connecting Students on Bikes with Education: Student-led Voluntary Higher Education Bicycle Social Movements as Sites for Informal Environmental and Philanthropic Education'. ERNOP European Research Network on Philanthropy Conference, Paris, July 2015.
10   The Bike Kitchen webpage – Access Nights [accessed 19/02/2021 https://www.thebikekitchen.ca/access-nights]
11   University of Greenwich website [accessed 19/02/2021 https://alumni.gre.ac.uk/greenwich-portraits/]
12   Floating Doctors [accessed 19/02/2021 https://floatingdoctors.com/]
13   Royal College of Surgeons of Ireland website [accessed 19/02/2021 https://www.rcsi.com/impact/details/2019/02/rcsi-alumni-providing-healthcare-to-the-worlds-most-isolated-communities]
14   Royal College of Surgeons of Ireland webpage – Student Life – Boston Marathon webpage [accessed 14/09/2020 https://www.rcsi.com/dublin/student-life/life-on-campus/student-events/boston-marathon]; Royal College of Surgeons of Ireland YouTube channel. [video] 'In Conversation with … The Floating Doctors'. [accessed 21/02/2021 https://www.youtube.com/watch?v=F1hzk2ve2y4]
15   The Global Goals website [accessed 19/02/2021 https://www.globalgoals.org/]

16 University of Wisconsin-Madison website [accessed 19/02/2021 https://www.uwalumni.com/resources-services/alumni-learning/grandparents-university/]

17 Faculty of Applied Science & Engineering, University of Toronto website – DEEP Summer Academy [accessed 07/02/2021 https://outreach.engineering.utoronto.ca/pre-university-programs/deep-summer-academy/]

18 Laursen, S.L., Thiry, H., and Liston, C.S. (2012). 'The Impact of a University-Based School Science Outreach Program on Graduate Student Participants' Career Paths and Professional Socialization'. *Journal of Higher Education Outreach and Engagement.* 16(2): 47–77.

19 Johns Hopkins University webpage Alumni College [Accessed 19/02/2021 https://alumni.jhu.edu/alumnicollege in particular https://alumni.jhu.edu/alumnicollege/2014/napa]

20 Big Onion Walking Tours boast the fact that all their guides are either full-time graduate students or have completed their graduate studies. Big Onion Walking Tours maintains a robust list of alumni tour guides, many of whom are now university professors, researchers, and teachers [accessed 19/02/2021 http://www.bigonion.com/our-guides/]

21 The Global Goals website [accessed 19/02/2021 https://www.globalgoals.org/]

22 For example, McCartney, D. and O'Loughlin, T. (1990). *Cardinal Newman: The Catholic University.* Dublin: UCD.

23 NUI Galway website [accessed 19/02/2021 http://www.nuigalway.ie/mindfulway/]

24 Joshi, L. (2015). 'NUI Galway Embarks on a Mindful Adventure'. *The Irish Times.* 20 October [accessed 19/02/2021 https://www.irishtimes.com/news/education/nui-galway-embarks-on-a-mindful-adventure-1.2393166]

25 Harvard Alumni Magazine (2014). 'SIGnboard: SIG Snapshot'. *Harvard Alumni Magazine.* July–August [accessed 19/02/2021 https://www.harvardmagazine.com/2014/07/the-signboard-sig-snapshot]

26 Harvard Alumni for Mental Health webpage [accessed 19/02/2021 http://mentalhealth.sigs.harvard.edu/]

27 Harvard Alumni for Mental Health webpage [accessed 19/02/2021 http://mentalhealth.sigs.harvard.edu/]

28 Carnegie Mellon University (2007). 'Randy Pausch Last Lecture: Achieving Your Childhood Dreams'. [accessed 19/02/2021 https://www.youtube.com/watch?v=ji5_MqicxSo&vl=en]

29 Pausch, R. (2008) *The Last Lecture: Lessons in Living.* London: Hodder & Stoughton, p 117.

30 Albom, M. (2000). *Tuesdays with Morrie.* London: Little, Brown and Company.

31 Sani, S. (2018). 'Essence of Alumni Association – By Senator Shehu Sani'. *Daily NewsTimes.* 11 November [accessed 19/02/2021 https://dailynewstimeng.com/2019/01/19/essence-of-alumni-association-by-senator-shehu-sani/]

32 Sani, S. (2018). 'Essence of Alumni Association – By Senator Shehu Sani'. *Daily NewsTimes*. 11 November [accessed 19/02/2021 https://dailynewstimeng.com/2019/01/19/essence-of-alumni-association-by-senator-shehu-sani/]

33 Gudbergsdottir, E. (2019). ' "Living Lives with Passion" – Group of Institute Alumni Gather in Monterey'. Middlebury Institute of International Studies. 9 January [accessed 07/02/2021 https://www.middlebury.edu/institute/international-environmental-policy-news/living-lives-passion-group-institute-alumni-gather-monterey]

34 Gudbergsdottir, E. (2019). ' "Living Lives with Passion" – Group of Institute Alumni Gather in Monterey'. Middlebury Institute of International Studies. 9 January [accessed 07/02/2021 https://www.middlebury.edu/institute/international-environmental-policy-news/living-lives-passion-group-institute-alumni-gather-monterey]

Chapter 15

1 Singh, M. (2014). 'Higher Education and the Public Good: Precarious Potential?' In: Munck R., McIlrath L., Hall B., and Tandon, R. (eds) *Higher Education and Community-Based Research*. New York: Palgrave Macmillan, p 203.

2 Dweck, C.S. (2017). *Mindset: Changing the Way You Think to Fulfil Your Potential*. London, Robinson, p 7.

3 Segran, E. (2020). *The Rocket Years: How Your Twenties Launch the Rest of Your Life*. New York: Harper, Kindle Edition.

4 Segran, E. The Rocket Years: How Your Twenties Launch the Rest of Your Life. New York: Harper. Kindle Edition, p 43–44.

5 Zawadzki, M.J., Smyth, J.M., and Costigan, H.J. (2015). 'Real-Time Associations Between Engaging in Leisure and Daily Health and Well-Being'. *Annals of Behavioral Medicine*. 49(4): 605–615.

Chapter 16

1 Post, S. and Neimark, J. (2007). *Why Good Things Happen to Good People*. New York: Broadway Books, p 7.

2 See for example, Dunn, E.W., Ashton-James, C.E., Hanson, M.D., and Aknin, L.B. (2010). On the Costs of Self-interested Economic Behavior: How Does Stinginess Get Under the Skin? *Journal of Health Psychology*, 15(4): 627–633; Poulin, M.J., Brown, S.L., Dillard, A.J., and Smith, D.M. (2013). 'Giving to Others and the Association Between Stress and Mortality,' *American Journal of Public Health*. 103(9) (1 September): pp 1649–1655.

3 University of Notre Dame (2018). 'Science of Generosity – What is Generosity?' webpage [accessed 19/02/2021 https://generosityresearch.nd.edu/more-about-the-initiative/what-is-generosity/]

4   Beck, M.C. (2012). 'Aristotle's Theory of the Virtues of Temperance, Courage, and Generosity as Part of a Universal Model for Leadership Practices Today'. In: Prastacos, G., Wang, F., and Soderquist, K. (eds) *Leadership through the Classics*. Berlin: Springer, pp 147–160.

5   Beck, M.C. (2012). 'Aristotle's Theory of the Virtues of Temperance, Courage, and Generosity as Part of a Universal Model for Leadership Practices Today'. In: Prastacos G., Wang F., and Soderquist K. (eds) *Leadership through the Classics*. Berlin: Springer, pp 147–160.

6   Bogee, L. (2016). '5 Reasons Generosity is the Key to Great Leadership'. *The Medium* [accessed 19/02/2021 https://medium.com/@ljb3/5-reasons-generosity-is-the-key-to-great-leadership-f0d5b62a6a4e]

Chapter 17

1   Goldstein, D. (2014) 'Are You a Philanthropist?' TEDx SantaCatalinaSchool [video]. 14 October [accessed 19/02/2021 https://www.youtube.com/watch?v=1y9EugKh_50]

2   Merriman, D. (2010). 'The College is a Philanthropy. Yes a Philanthropy'. *The Chronicle of Education*. 31 October [accessed 19/02/2021, https://www.chronicle.com/article/The-College-as-a-Philanthropy/125176]

3   Merriman, D. (2010). 'The College is a Philanthropy. Yes a Philanthropy'. *The Chronicle of Education*. 31 October [accessed 19/02/2021, https://www.chronicle.com/article/The-College-as-a-Philanthropy/125176]

4   Merriman, D. (2010). 'The College is a Philanthropy. Yes a Philanthropy'. *The Chronicle of Education*. 31 October [accessed 19/02/2021, https://www.chronicle.com/article/The-College-as-a-Philanthropy/125176]

5   Merriman, D. (2010). 'The College is a Philanthropy. Yes a Philanthropy'. *The Chronicle of Education*. 31 October [accessed 19/02/2021, https://www.chronicle.com/article/The-College-as-a-Philanthropy/125176]

6   Ferrazzi, K. (2014). *Never Eat Alone*. London: Portfolio Penguin, p 15.

7   Ferrazzi, K. (2014). *Never Eat Alone*. London: Portfolio Penguin, p 16.

8   Jones, C. (2017). 'Microvolunteering: What Is It and Why Should You Do It?' *The Guardian*. 13 April Online international edition [accessed 19/02/2021 https://www.theguardian.com/voluntary-sector-network/2017/apr/13/microvolunteering-what-is-it-and-why-should-you-do-it]

9   Cohen, R. (2016). 'What if an Alum Generated $200,000 for Your Institution, Without Writing a Check?' *Academic Impressions Blog* 20th September [accessed 19/02/2021 https://www.academicimpressions.com/blog/what-if-an-alum-generated-200000-for-your-institution-without-writing-a-check/]

10   Kent State University website [accessed 19/02/2021 https://www.kent.edu/alumni/dayofservicefaqs]; Kent State Alumni Twitter (@KSUAlumni) Tweet. 2 May 2019 [accessed 19/02/2021 https://twitter.com/KSUAlumni/status/1123999843926589440]

11 Ellison, J. (2015). 'Happy Graduation: Now What? From Citizen Students to Citizen Alums'. *Change: The Magazine of Higher Learning.* January/February, p 53.

12 Vanderlelie, J.(2015). 'Re-visioning Alumni Relationships to Improve Graduate Employability'. *STARS* – Student Transitions, Achievement, Retention and Success Conference Proceedings, Melbourne, July [accessed 19/02/2021 http://www.unistars.org/papers/STARS2015/07G.pdf]

13 EAB (2015). 'The New Rules of Engagement: Five Strategies for Building the Next Generation of Alumni Leaders and Volunteers'. EAB blog, 14 October [accessed 19/02/2021 https://www.eab.com/research-and-insights/advancement-forum/infographics/new-rules-of-engagement]

14 Onukwuba, H.O. (2019). *Alumni Leadership and University Excellence in Africa: The Case of Lagos Business School.* Switzerland: Palgrave, Kindle Edition, location 625.

15 Finney, S. and Pyke, J. (2008). 'Content Relevance in Case-Study Teaching: The Alumni Connection and Its Effect on Student Motivation'. *Journal of Education for Business.* 83(5): 251–258.

16 Furco, A. and Holland, B. (2004). 'Institutionalizing Service-Learning in Higher Education: Issues and Strategies for Chief Academic Officers'. In: Langseth, M. and Plater, W.M. (eds) *Public Work and the Academy – An Academic Administrators Guide to Civic Engagement and Service-Learning.* Boston: Anker Publishing, p 27.

17 Block, P. (1996). *Stewardship: Choosing Service over Self-Interest.* San Francisco: Berrett-Koehler Publishers, p 63.

18 Berger R., Wardle J., and Zezulkova M. (2013). 'No Longer Just Making the Tea: Media Work Placements and Work-Based Learning in Higher Education'. In: Ashton, D. and Noonan, C. (eds) *Cultural Work and Higher Education.* London: Palgrave Macmillan.

19 PennPAC website. Current Client webpage. [accessed 19/02/2021 https://pennpac.org/our-impact/current-clients2/]; PennPAC website. Our Impact webpage [accessed 19/02/2021 https://pennpac.org/our-impact/]

20 Stern, C. (2014). 'Consulting for a Cause: Alumni Offers Pro Bono Services'. *The Daily Pennsylvanian.* 13 May [accessed 19/02/2021 https://www.thedp.com/article/2014/05/penn-pac-alum-consulting]

21 PennPAC – ImPACt Events webpage [accessed 19/02/2021 https://pennpac.org/our-impact/impact-events/]

22 Zhong, B. (2017). 'This Group of Penn Alumni Is Helping New American Residents Jumpstart Their Careers'. 9 February [accessed 19/02/2021 https://www.thedp.com/article/2017/02/penn-pac-immigrant-training]

23 Stern, C. (2014). 'Consulting for a Cause: Alumni Offers Pro Bono services'. *The Daily Pennsylvanian.* 13 May [accessed 19/02/2021 https://www.thedp.com/article/2014/05/penn-pac-alum-consulting]

Chapter 18

1 Burkus, D. (2018). *Friend of a Friend.* New York: Houghton Mifflin.

2   See for example, Vlahos, C (2017). 'The Alumni Relations Fork in the Road'. Blog post [Accessed 19/02/2021 https://www.linkedin.com/pulse/alumni-relations-fork-road-christopher-vlahos/]; Fusch, D. (2010) 'The Student-Alumni Transition: Encouraging Meaningful Giving'. *Academic Impressions Higher Ed Blog*. November/December [accessed 19/02/2021 https://www.academicimpressions.com/blog/the-student-alumni-transition-encouraging-meaningful-giving/]; Weerts, D.J. and Ronca, J.M. (2008). 'Characteristics of Alumni Donors Who Volunteer at Their Alma Mater'. *Research in Higher Education*. 49(3): 274–292.

3   Here's my alumni romantic confession in full: Gallo, M.L. (2021). 'Confessions of an Alumni Romantic'. LinkedIn Pulse blog post. 11 February [accessed 13/02/2021 https://www.linkedin.com/pulse/confessions-alumni-romantic-maria-l-gallo-edd/?trackingId=lnmaZZ9K SfK7ES%2BaoxTJtA%3D%3D]

4   Reich, R. (2018). *Just Giving*. Princeton NJ: Princeton University Press.

5   Council for Advancement and Support of Education – CASE (2019). *Voluntary Support of Education: 2017–18*. Washington: Council for Advancement and Support of Education. [accessed 19/02/2021 https://www.case.org/resources/2018-voluntary-support-education]

6   Quote attributed to Nelson Henderson, a Manitoba farmer in the book: Henderson, W. (1982). *Under Whose Shade: A Story of a Pioneer in the Swan River Valley of Manitoba*. Nepean ON: Henderson & Associates.

7   DeGroot, J. (nd). 'Jewish Philanthropy: The Concept of Tzedakah'. Learning to Give blog [accessed 19/02/2021 https://www.learningtogive.org/resources/jewish-philanthropy-concept-tzedakah]

8   Universidad de los Andes website (2019). 'What is Pa'lante Caribe?' 9 October [accessed 19/02/2021 https://uniandes.edu.co/en/news/desarrollo-regional/what-is-palante-caribe]

9   Universidad de los Andes website (2019). 'What is Pa'lante Caribe?' 9 October [accessed 19/02/2021 https://uniandes.edu.co/en/news/desarrollo-regional/what-is-palante-caribe]

10   Universidad de los Andes website. (2019). 'What is Pa'lante Caribe?' 9 October [accessed 19/02/2021 https://uniandes.edu.co/en/news/desarrollo-regional/what-is-palante-caribe]

11   Adolph Fore, A. (2020). 'Joining Forces: Multi-institution Collaborations Are Helping Meet Advancement Goals'. *CASE Currents*. March/April, pp 28–35.

12   Dietlin, L. (2013). *Transformational Philanthropy*. London: Jones and Bartlett Publishers.

13   Lowry, K. (2018). 'Giving Tuesday is Coming to UVic on Nov. 27'. The University of Victoria website. 1 November [accessed 19/02/2021 https://www.uvic.ca/news/topics/2018+giving-tuesday+news]

14   Frumkin, P. (2008). *Strategic Giving: The Art and Science of Philanthropy*. Chicago, IL: University of Chicago Press.

15 Drezner, N.D. (2018). 'Philanthropic Mirroring: Exploring Identity-Based Fundraising in Higher Education'. *The Journal of Higher Education.* 89(3): p 283.

16 Drezner, N.D. (2018). Philanthropic Mirroring: Exploring Identity-Based Fundraising in Higher Education'. *The Journal of Higher Education.* 89(3): p 283.

17 Mount St Vincent University website [accessed 07/02/2021 http://www. womenswallofhonour.ca/en/home/honourawoman.aspx]

18 Boudreau, B. (2013). 'Mount Honours 17 Inspiring Women'. Mount St Vincent University website, *Media Centre News.* 28 March [accessed 19/02/2021 https://www.msvu.ca/mount-honours-17-inspiring-women/]

19 For instance, see Wright, K. (2001). 'Generosity vs. Altruism: Philanthropy and Charity in the United States and United Kingdom'. *Voluntas.* 12(4): 399–416.

20 Weinstein, S. (2009). *The Complete Guide to Fundraising* (3rd ed.). New Jersey: John Wiley & Sons; Tromble, W.W. (1998b). *The Function of the Alumni Office.* In: Tromble, W.W. *Excellence in Advancement: Applications for Higher Education and Nonprofit Organizations.* Maryland: An Aspen Publishers; Wagner, L. (2007). *Achieving Success in a Fundraising Programme.* In: Conraths, B. and Trusso, B. *Managing the University Community: Exploring Good Practice.* Brussels: European Universities Association, pp 99–100; Myran, G., Baker III, G.A., Simone, B., and Zeiss, T. (2003). *Leadership Strategies for Community College Executives.* Washington: American Association of Community Colleges.

21 I acknowledge that friend-raising before fundraising is valid when it means, at its core, that before asking for a financial donation, there needs to be an established relationship – an established relationship through university communications and alumni engagement, which can take months or years to establish such a rapport.

22 For more information on a giving audit, see Lemay, K. (2009). *The Generosity Plan.* New York: Atria, Simon & Schuster.

23 The Donor Bill of Rights was created by the Association of Fundraising Professionals (AFP), the Association for Healthcare Philanthropy (AHP), CASE, and the Giving Institute: Leading Consultants to Non-Profits.

24 Council for Advancement and Support of Education Web site [accessed 19/02/2021 https://www.case.org/about-case/evolution-case]. In 1993, CASE adopted The Donor Bill of Rights abided by its membership (3,600 institutions across 82 countries worldwide).

25 Association for Fundraising Professionals 2018 [accessed 19/02/2021 https://afpglobal.org/donor-bill-rights]. The author received permission on 04/12/2018 to reproduce the Donor Bill of Rights in this book. The website also posts the Donor Bill of Rights in French and Spanish.

26 Lemay, K. (2009). *The Generosity Plan.* New York: Atria, Simon & Schuster.

[27] University College Dublin Web site [accessed 21/02/2021 http://www. ucd.ie/ucdinthecommunity/newsevents/newsevents/upcomingevents/ walkwhileyoucan/]

[28] McGarry, P. (2019). 'New Academic Post at TCD to be Named after Fr Tony Coote'. 2 September. *Irish Times* [accessed 19/02/2021 https://www.irishtimes.com/news/social-affairs/religion-and-beliefs/ new-academic-post-at-tcd-to-be-named-after-fr-tony-coote-1.4005572]

[29] McGarry, P. (2019). 'Fr Tony Coote Was "the Ultimate Connector", Funeral Hears'. 2 September, *Irish Times*. [accessed 19/02/2021 https://www.irishtimes.com/news/social-affairs/religion-and-beliefs/ fr-tony-coote-was-the-ultimate-connector-funeral-hears-1.4005540]

[30] Kearns, D. (2018). 'University Honours Father Tony Coote for His "Outstanding Service to All"'. University College Dublin News. 10 December [accessed 19/02/2021 http://www.ucd.ie/newsandopinion/ news/2018/december/10/universityhonoursfathertonycooteforhisoutsta ndingservicetoall]

[31] Freedman, J.O. (2002). 'An Honor, to a Degree'. *The Chronicle of Higher Education*. 48(37): B10.

[32] Hoey, J.K. (2017) *Build Your Dream Network*. New York: TarcherPerigee Penguin, p 49.

[33] Hoey, J.K. (2017) *Build Your Dream Network*. New York: TarcherPerigee Penguin, p 52.

[34] Zhang, C., Wu, F., and Henke, J.W. (2015). 'Leveraging Boundary Spanning Capabilities To Encourage Supplier Investment: A Comparative Study'. *Industrial Marketing Management*. 49: 84–94.

[35] Dobson, G. (2020). 'Why It's a Good Idea to Build Academic Alumni Communities'. *Times Higher Education*. [accessed 07/ 02/2021 https://www.timeshighereducation.com/career/ why-its-good-idea-build-academic-alumni-communities]

[36] Eikenberry, A.M. and Breeze, B. (2018). 'Growing Philanthropy through Giving Circles: Collective Giving and the Logic of Charity'. *Social Policy & Society*. 17(3): 349–364.

[37] Arizona State University Women & Philanthropy website [accessed 19/ 02/2021 https://giveto.asu.edu/engage/womenandphilanthropy]

[38] Valburn, M. (2018). 'New Era for Women as Donors'. Inside Higher Ed. 11 May [accessed 19/02/2021 https://www.insidehighered.com/news/ 2018/05/11/colleges-are-turning-women-philanthropists-source-new- money-fund-raising-campaigns]

[39] Freeland Fisher, J. (2018). *Who You Know: Unlocking Innovations that Expand Students' Networks*. San Francisco: Jossey-Bass, p 71.

[40] The Johnson Center (2013). *Next Gen Donors Executive Summary Report*. Johnson Center [accessed 19/02/2021 https://www.michiganfoundations. org/sites/default/files/resources/next-gen-donors-Executive-Summary. pdf]

Chapter 19

[1] Chris Hadfield quote from his honorary degree speech at the University of Waterloo Spring 2014 Convocation on 10 June 2014. The quote was reproduced on the University of Waterloo Facebook page: [accessed 19/02/2021 https://www.facebook.com/university.waterloo/photos/honorary-doctorate-chris-hadfield-speaks-on-june-10th-at-the-spring-2014-convoca/10152436036470758/]

[2] The Johnson Center (2013). *Next Gen Donors Executive Summary Report.* Johnson Center [accessed 19/02/2021 https://www.michiganfoundations.org/sites/default/files/resources/next-gen-donors-Executive-Summary.pdf]

[3] Goldseker, S. and Moody, M. (2021). *Generation Impact: How Next Gen Donors are Revolutionizing Giving* (Revised ed.). Hoboken NJ: John Wiley & Sons.

[4] Ferrazzi, K. (2014). *Never Eat Alone.* London: Portfolio Penguin, pp 17–18.

Chapter 20

[1] Gallo, M.L. (2018). TEDx Ballybofey. [video] 'We Are All Connected by One Word: Alumni'. [accessed 21/02/2021 https://www.ted.com/talks/maria_gallo_we_are_all_connected_by_one_word_alumni]

[2] Covey, S.R. (2004). *The 7 Habits of Highly Effective People.* New York: Simon & Schuster, p 23.

[3] Thiel Fellowship website [accessed 19/02/2021 https://thielfellowship.org/]

[4] Constine, J. (2014) 'Correction: 20 Under 20 Thiel Fellowship Did Not Up Age Limit To 23, But Maybe It Should'. *Tech Crunch.* 10 October [accessed 19/02/2021 https://techcrunch.com/2014/10/10/thiel-fellowship-twenty-under-twenty-three/?guccounter=1&guce_referrer_us=aHR0cHM6Ly93d3cuZ29vZ2xlLmNlLw&guce_referrer_cs=SBcLlYp6Bc1gubh34Y4hMw]

[5] Hempel, J. (2016). 'Inside Peter Thiel's Genius Factory'. *Wired.* 7 December [accessed 19/02/2021 https://www.wired.com/2016/12/inside-peter-thiels-genius-factory/]

[6] Constine, J. (2014). 'Correction: 20 Under 20 Thiel Fellowship Did Not Up Age Limit To 23, But Maybe It Should'. *Tech Crunch.* 10 October [accessed 19/02/2021 https://techcrunch.com/2014/10/10/thiel-fellowship-twenty-under-twenty-three/?guccounter=1&guce_referrer_us=aHR0cHM6Ly93d3cuZ29vZ2xlLmNlLw&guce_referrer_cs=SBcLlYp6Bc1gubh34Y4hMw]

[7] Shaindlin, A. (2018) *Alumni Community Whitepaper: Engaging Alumni Outside Academia: Emerging Practices in Foundations, Fellowships and Other Nonprofit Organizations.* Grenzebach, Glier & Associates and the Rockefeller Foundation, p 3 [accessed 19/02/2021 https://www.grenzebachglier.com/wp-content/uploads/2018/07/GGA-Alumni-Community-Whitepaper-Shaindlin-UPLOAD.pdf]

8   Conroy, P. (2015). 'International Alumni Relations: One Size Fits All?' EAIE European Association for International Education blog. 24 February [accessed 19/02/2021 https://www.eaie.org/blog/international-alumni-relations.html]

9   InHive Global website [accessed 19/02/2021 http://www.inhiveglobal.org/]

10   InHive Global website – Partners – Pakistan Youth Changes Advocates webpage [accessed 19/02/2021 http://www.inhiveglobal.org/project/pakistan-youth-changes-advocates-pyca/]

11   InHive Global – Our Theory of Change website [accessed 19/02/2021 http://www.inhiveglobal.org/whatwedo/ourtheoryofchange/]

12   Nokes, A. (2018). *From Cohorts to Communities: A Guide to Working with Programme Alumni*. London: Future First Global, pp 35–39 [accessed 19/02/2021 http://www.inhiveglobal.org/project/inhive-from-cohorts-to-communities/]

13   Kohler, T. (2016). 'Corporate Accelerators: Building Bridges between Corporations and Startups'. *Business Horizons*. 59(3): 347–357.

14   CERN Alumni website: [accessed 19/02/2021 https://alumni.cern/]

15   UNESCO (2014). 'CERN and UNESCO: 60 Years of Science for Peace'. United Nations Educational, Scientific and Cultural Organization website [accessed 13/02/2021 http://www.unesco.org/new/en/unesco/partners-donors/single-view/news/cern_and_unesco_60_years_of_science_for_peace/]

16   CERN Alumni website: [accessed 19/02/2021 https://alumni.cern/page/advocacy]

17   Burkus, D. (2015). *Under New Management*. New York: Houghton Mifflin, p 198.

18   Erickson, R. (2018). 'Alumni: Why Former Workers Can Be Long-term Assets'. LinkedIn blog. 5 August [accessed 19/02/2021 https://www.linkedin.com/pulse/alumni-why-former-workers-can-long-term-assets-robin-erickson-phd/]

Chapter 21

1   Dweck, C.S. (2017). *Mindset: Changing the Way You Think to Fulfil Your Potential*. London: Robinson, p 240.

2   Mandery, E. (2014). 'Why I'm Skipping My Harvard Reunion (A Call to Action)'. *The Huffington Post*. 6 July [accessed 19/02/2021 https://www.huffpost.com/entry/why-im-skipping-my-harvar_b_5246982]

3   Mandery, E. (2020). 'We're About to Have the Longest Summer Vacation Ever. That's Going to Be a Problem'. *Politico*. 17 May [accessed 19/02/2021 https://www.politico.com/news/magazine/2020/05/17/long-summer-students-coronavirus-259201]

4   Mandery, E. (2014). 'Why I'm Skipping My Harvard Reunion (A Call to Action)'. *The Huffington Post*. 6 July [accessed 19/02/2021 https://www.huffpost.com/entry/why-im-skipping-my-harvar_b_5246982]

References

Aaldernick, W. (2018). 'Alumni Intelligence and the Value of Connecting'. The Career Leadership Collective blog. 20 March [accessed 30/07/19 https://www.careerleadershipcollective.com/single-post/2018/03/20/Alumni-Intelligence-and-the-Value-of-Connecting]

Adams, A. (nd). '7 Alumni Benefits You Should Be Taking Advantage Of'. [accessed 24/02/19 https://www.themuse.com/advice/7-alumni-benefits-you-should-be-taking-advantage-of]

Adolph Fore, A. (2020). 'Joining Forces: Multi-institution Collaborations Are Helping Meet Advancement Goals'. *CASE Currents*. March/April: 28–35.

Agnew, M. 'University of Canterbury Recognised as a Fair Trade University'. *University of Canterbury News*. 10 July [accessed 19/02/2021 https://www.canterbury.ac.nz/news/2017/university-of-canterbury-recognised-as-a-fair-trade-university.html]

Albom, M. (2000). *Tuesdays with Morrie*. London: Little, Brown and Company.

Anonymous Academic (2015). 'My Students Have Paid £9,000 and Now They Think They Own Me'. *The Guardian*. 18 December [accessed 19/02/2021 https://www.theguardian.com/higher-educationnetwork/2015/dec/18/my-students-have-paid-9000-and-now-they-think-they-own-me]

Aoun, J.E. (2018). *Robot-Proof: Higher Education in the Age of Artificial Intelligence*. London: MIT Press.

Arizona State University Women & Philanthropy website [accessed 19/02/2021 https://giveto.asu.edu/engage/womenandphilanthropy]

Arnstein, S.R. (1969). 'A Ladder of Citizen Participation'. *Journal of the American Institute of Planners*. 35(4): 216–224.

Association for Fundraising Professionals (2018). [accessed 19/02/2021 https://afpglobal.org/donor-bill-rights]

Association for the Advancement of Sustainability in Higher Education (2018). *2018 Sustainable Campus Index* [accessed 19/02/2021 https://www.aashe.org/wp-content/uploads/2018/08/SCI-2018. pdf]

Auter, Z. and Marken, S. (2018). 'Professors Provide Most Valued Career Advice to Grads'. Gallup website. 16 November [accessed 04/01/2021 https://news.gallup.com/poll/244811/professors-provide-valued-career-advice-grads.aspx]

Auter, Z. and Marken, S. (2019). 'Alumni Network Less Helpful than Advertised'. Gallup website. 15 January [accessed 19/02/2021 https://news.gallup.com/opinion/gallup/245822/alumni-networks-less-helpful-advertised.aspx]

Azim Premji University website – Student Reflections [accessed 19/02/21 https://azimpremjiuniversity.edu.in/SitePages/students-reflections-2. aspx]

Bathmaker, A.M., Ingram, N., and Waller, R. (2013). 'Higher Education, Social Class and the Mobilisation of Capitals: Recognising and Playing the Game'. *British Journal of Sociology of Education.* 34(5–6): 723–743.

Bathmaker, A.M., Ingram, N., Abrahams, J., Hoare, A., Waller, R., and Bradley, H. (2016). *Higher Education, Social Class and Social Mobility: The Degree Generation.* London: Palgrave Macmillan.

Bauer College of Business, University of Houston – Alumni Business Directory website [accessed 19/02/2021 https://www.bauer.uh.edu/alumni/alumni-businesses.asp]

Beck, M.C. (2012). 'Aristotle's Theory of the Virtues of Temperance, Courage, and Generosity as Part of a Universal Model for Leadership Practices Today'. In: Prastacos G., Wang F., and Soderquist K. (eds) *Leadership through the Classics.* Berlin: Springer, pp 147–160.

Berg, M. and Seeber, B.K. (2016). *The Slow Professor: Challenging the Culture of Speed in the Academy.* Toronto: University of Toronto Press.

Berger, R., Wardle, J. and Zezulkova, M. (2013). 'No Longer Just Making the Tea: Media Work Placements and Work-Based Learning in Higher Education'. In: Ashton, D. and Noonan, C. (eds) *Cultural Work and Higher Education*. London: Palgrave Macmillan.

Big Onion Walking Tours website [accessed 19/02/2021 http://www.bigonion.com/our-guides/]

Bike Kitchen, The, website – Access Nights [accessed 19/02/2021 https://www.thebikekitchen.ca/access-nights]

Block, P. (1996). *Stewardship: Choosing Service over Self-Interest*. San Francisco: Berrett-Koehler Publishers.

Bogee, L. (2016). '5 Reasons Generosity Is the Key to Great Leadership'. *The Medium* [accessed 19/02/2021 https://medium.com/@ljb3/5-reasons-generosity-is-the-key-to-great-leadership-f0d5b62a6a4e]

Boud, D., Keogh, R., and Walker, D. (eds) (1985). *Reflection: Turning Experience into Learning*. London: Kogan Page.

Boudreau, B. (2013). 'Mount Honours 17 Inspiring Women'. Mount St Vincent University website – *Media Centre News*. 28 March [accessed 19/02/2021 https://www.msvu.ca/mount-honours-17-inspiring-women/]

Bourdieu, P. (1986). 'The Forms of Capital'. In: Richardson, J. (ed.) *Handbook of Theory and Research in Education*, Westport, CT: Greenwood, pp 241–258.

Bourdieu, P. (1990). *The Logic of Practice*. Stanford: Stanford California Press, p 64, In: Bathmaker, A.M., Ingram, N. and Waller, R. (2013). 'Higher Education, Social Class and the Mobilisation of Capitals: Recognising and Playing the Game'. *British Journal of Sociology of Education*. 34(5–6): 730.

Brandeis University (2018). Podcast with Guest Speaker Ronit Avni [accessed 19/02/2021 Transcript of the podcast https://www.brandeis.edu/global/podcast/drbr/transcripts/27-episode.html]

Bright Club website [accessed 19/02/2021 www.brightclub.org]

Brooks, A.C. (2020). 'A College Degree Is No Guarantee of a Good Life'. *The Atlantic*. 2 July 2020 [accessed 24/07/20 https://www.theatlantic.com/family/archive/2020/07/will-going-college-make-you-happier/613729/]

Brooks, R. and Everett, G. (2009). 'Post-Graduation Reflections on the Value of a Degree'. *British Education Research Journal*. 35(3): 333–349.

Brown, B. (2010). *The Power of Vulnerability*. [video] Houston, TX: TEDx [accessed 19/02/2021 https://www.ted.com/talks/brene_brown_the_power_of_vulnerability? language=en]

Brown, P. (2003). 'The Opportunity Trap: Education and Employment in a Global Economy'. *European Educational Research Journal*. 2(1), pp 141–179.

Brubaker, R. (2005). 'The "Diaspora" Diaspora'. *Ethnic and Racial Studies*. 28(1): 1–19.

Budd, R. (2017). 'Undergraduate Orientations towards Higher Education in Germany and England: Problemizing the Notion of "Student as Customer"'. *Higher Education*. 73(1): 23–37.

Bula, F. (2017). 'Universities as Real-estate Developers'. *University Affairs*. 28 November [accessed 19/02/2021 https://www.universityaffairs.ca/features/feature-article/universities-real-estate-developers/]

Burgess, K. (2018). LinkedIn post [accessed 06/02/2021 https://www.linkedin.com/posts/kate-burgess-03606a121_womens-football-for-both-alumni-and-current-activity-6443372341924888577-hYnH]

Burkus, D. (2015). *Under New Management*. New York: Houghton Mifflin.

Burkus, D. (2018). *Friend of a Friend: Understanding the Hidden Networks That Can Transform Your Life and Your Career*. New York: Houghton Mifflin Harcourt.

Burt, R.S. (1992). *Structural Holes: The Social Structure of Competition*. Cambridge, MA: Harvard University Press.

Busteed, B. and Seymour, S. (2015). 'Many College Graduates Not Equipped for Workplace Success'. *Forbes*. 23 September [accessed 19/02/2021 https://www.forbes.com/sites/brandonbusteed/2019/12/15/importance-of-college-drops-nearly-50-among-young-adults-in-just-six-years/?sh=5f2cfb314b56]

Butler, K. (2001). 'Defining Diaspora, Refining a Discourse'. *Diaspora*. 10(2).

Campbell University – Welcome to the City website [accessed 19/02/2021 https://alumni.campbell.edu/engage/events/welcome-to-the-city/]

Campus Insights website [accessed 19/02/2021 https://www.campus-insights.com/]

CERN Alumni website: [accessed 19/02/2021 https://alumni.cern/]

Charkrabortty, A. and Weale, S. (2016). 'Universities Accused of "Importing Sports Direct Model" for Lecturers' Pay'. *The Guardian*. 16 November [19/02/2021 https://www.theguardian.com/uk-news/2016/nov/16/universities-accused-of-importing-sports-direct-model-for-lecturers-pay]

Clark, A. and Sousa, B. (2018a). *How to Be a Happy Academic*. London: Sage.

Clark, A. and Sousa, B. (2018b). 'Your Biggest Asset for Academic Career Success? A Growth Mindset'. *Times Higher Education*. 21 February [accessed 19/02/2021 https://www.timeshighereducation.com/blog/your-biggest-asset-academic-career-success-growth-mindset]

Clark, B.R. (1998). *Creating Entrepreneurial Universities: Organizational Pathways of Transformation*. Oxford: IAU Press Pergamon.

Clark, D. (2019). '3 Ways to Make the Most of Your Alumni Network'. *Harvard Business Review*. 8 November [accessed 16/02/2021 https://hbr.org/2019/10/3-ways-to-make-the-most-of-your-alumni-network]

Cohen, R. (2016). 'What if an Alum Generated $200,000 for Your Institution, without Writing a Check?' *Academic Impressions* blog. 20 September [accessed 19/02/2021 https://www.academicimpressions.com/blog/what-if-an-alum-generated-200000-for-your-institution-without-writing-a-check/]

Cohen, R. (2018). 'Alumni Events: Going, Going, Gone'. LinkedIn blog. 3 August [accessed 19/02/2021 https://www.linkedin.com/pulse/alumni-events-going-goinggone-ron-cohen/].

Coleman, J.S. (1990). *Equality and Achievement in Education*. Boulder CO: Westview Press.

Colgate University website – Alumni – Professional Network webpage [accessed 19/02/2021 http://www.colgate.edu/alumni/professional-networks/about-professional-networks]

Conroy, P. (2015). 'International Alumni Relations: One Size Fits All?' EAIE European Association for International Education blog. 24 February [accessed 19/02/2021 https://www.eaie.org/blog/international-alumni-relations.html]

Constine, J. (2014). 'Correction: 20 under 20 Thiel Fellowship Did Not Up Age Limit to 23, But Maybe It Should'. *Tech Crunch*. 10 October [accessed 19/02/2021 https://techcrunch.com/2014/10/10/thiel-fellowship-twenty-under-twenty-three/? guccounter=1&guce_referrer_us=aHR0cHM6Ly93d3cuZ29vZ2xlLmllLw&guce_referrer_cs=SBcLlYp6Bc1gubh34Y4hMw]

Copenhagen Goodwill Ambassadors website [accessed 19/02/2021 https://gwa.copcap.com/]

Cornell Alumni website (2019). [accessed 19/02/2021 http://news.cornell.edu/stories/2019/01/cornell-alumni-leadership-conference-opens-all]

Council for Advancement and Support of Education (CASE) website – Donor Bill of Rights webpage [accessed 19/02/2021 https://www.case.org/resources/donor-bill-rights]

Council for Advancement and Support of Education (CASE) website – Looking to the Future webpage [accessed 19/02/2021 https://www.case.org/about/case-strategic-plan/looking-future]

Council for Advancement and Support of Education (CASE) (2019). *Voluntary Support of Education: 2017–18*. Washington: Council for Advancement and Support of Education [accessed 28/02/19 https://www.case.org/resources/2018-voluntary-support-education]

Council for Advancement and Support of Education (CASE). (2020). 'Principles of Practice for Alumni Relations Professionals at Educational Institutions'. [accessed 19/02/2021 https://www.case.org/resources/principles-practice-alumni-relations-professionals-educational-institutions]

Covey, S.R. (2004). *The 7 Habits of Highly Effective People*. New York: Simon & Schuster.

Cownie, F. and Gallo, M.L. (2020). 'Alumni Gratitude and Academics: Implications for Engagement'. *The Journal of Further and Higher Education.* https://doi.org/10.1080/0309877X.2020.1820457

Daso, F. (2018). 'These Brothers Just Sold Their Market Research Startup to the World's Largest Student-Run Company'. *Forbes Online.* 20 February [accessed 25/02/19 https://www.forbes.com/sites/frederickdaso/2018/02/20/these-brothers-just-sold-their-market-research-startup-to-the-worlds-largest-student-run-company/#2310bf616fdf]

de Janasz, S.C. and Forret, M.L. (2008). 'Learning the Art of Networking: A Critical Skill for Enhancing Social Capital and Career Success'. *Journal of Management Education.* 32(5): 629–650.

DeGroot, J. (nd). 'Jewish Philanthropy: The Concept of Tzedakah'. Learning to Give blog [accessed 19/02/2021 https://www.learningtogive.org/resources/jewish-philanthropy-concept-tzedakah]

DeVries, D. (2017). 'Networking with Nuance'. *CASE Currents,* November/December [accessed 01/03/19 https://www.case.org/currents/x73581]

Dewey, J. (1933). *How We Think: A Restatement of the Relation of Reflective Thinking to the Educative Process.* Lexington, MA: DC Heath and Company.

Dewey, J. (1997). *How We Think* (new edition from 1910 original). New York: Dover Publications.

Dietlin, L. (2013). *Transformational Philanthropy.* London: Jones and Bartlett Publishers.

Dillon, J.L.R. (2018). 'Alumni Engagement Scoring: What Does the Science Tell Us?' Salesforce webinar [accessed 19/02/2021 https://alumniidentity.com/blog/2021/2/15/alumni-engagement-scoring-what-does-the-science-tell-us].

Diner, S.J. (2017a). 'How Universities Migrated into Cities and Democratized Higher Education'. Zócalo Public Square website. 31 August [accessed 19/02/2021 http://www.zocalopublicsquare.org/2017/08/31/universities-migrated-cities-democratized-higher-education/ideas/nexus/].

Diner, S.J. (2017b). *Universities and Their Cities.* Baltimore MD: Johns Hopkins Press.

Dobson, G. (2020). 'Why It's a Good Idea to Build Academic Alumni Communities'. *Times Higher Education* [accessed 07/02/2021 https://www.timeshighereducation.com/career/why-its-good-idea-build-academic-alumni-communities]

Drezner, N.D. (2018). Philanthropic Mirroring: Exploring Identity-Based Fundraising in Higher Education'. *The Journal of Higher Education*. 89(3): 283.

Dunn, E.W., Ashton-James, C.E., Hanson, M.D., and Aknin, L.B. (2010). 'On the Costs of Self-interested Economic Behavior: How Does Stinginess Get Under the Skin?' *Journal of Health Psychology*. 15(4): 627–633.

Dweck, C.S. (2017). *Mindset: Changing the Way You Think to Fulfil Your Potential*. London: Robinson.

EAB (2015). 'The New Rules of Engagement: Five Strategies for Building the Next Generation of Alumni Leaders and Volunteers'. *EAB* blog. 14 October [accessed 08/11/18 https://www.eab.com/research-and-insights/advancement-forum/infographics/new-rules-of-engagement]

Eikenberry, A.M. and Breeze, B. (2018). 'Growing Philanthropy through Giving Circles: Collective Giving and the Logic of Charity'. *Social Policy & Society*. 17(3): 349–364.

Ellison, J. (2015). 'Happy Graduation, Now What? From Citizen Students to Citizen Alums'. *Change: The Magazine of Higher Learning*. January/February: 81–83.

Erickson, R. (2018). 'Alumni: Why Former Workers Can Be Long-term Assets'. LinkedIn blog. 5 August [accessed 13/08/18 https://www.linkedin.com/pulse/alumni-why-former-workers-can-long-term-assets-robin-erickson-phd/]

Favreau, A. (2016). *Stuff Every Graduate Should Know: A Handbook for the Real World*. Philadelphia: Quirk Books.

Fearn, H. (2018). 'Take Your PhD to Industry'. Sparrho Medium blog [accessed 19/02/2021 https://medium.com/sparrho/take-your-phd-to-industry-d9f657beaede]

Ferrazzi, K. (2014). *Never Eat Alone* (2nd ed.). London: Portfolio Penguin.

Field, J. (2009). *Social Capital* (2nd ed.). London: Routledge.

Finn, J. (2018). 'The Rise of the Experience Industry on Campus'. *University Affairs*. 13 March [accessed 19/02/2021 https://www.universityaffairs.ca/opinion/in-my-opinion/rise-experience-industry-campus/]

Finney, S. and Pyke, J. (2008). 'Content Relevance in Case-Study Teaching: The Alumni Connection and Its Effect on Student Motivation'. *Journal of Education for Business*. 83(5): 251–258.

Floating Doctors website [accessed 19/02/2021 https://floatingdoctors.com/]

Florida, R. (2002). *The Rise of the Creative Class*. New York: Basic Books.

Forsythe, R. (2020). LinkedIn post. 4 July [19/02/2021 https://www.linkedin.com/posts/rupertforsythe_pivot-graduation-virtualceremonies-activity-6685225708945457152-dDbe]

Freedman, J.O. (2002). 'An Honor, to a Degree'. *The Chronicle of Higher Education*. 48(37): B10.

Freeland Fisher, J. (2018). *Who You Know: Unlocking Innovations that Expand Students' Networks*. San Francisco: Jossey-Bass, p 71.

Friedman, Z. (2019). 'Is College Worth It?' *Forbes*. 13 June [accessed 19/02/2021 https://www.forbes.com/sites/zackfriedman/2019/06/13/is-college-worth-it/?sh=203b6b8e778d]

Frumkin, P. (2008). *Strategic Giving: The Art and Science of Philanthropy*. Chicago, IL: University of Chicago Press.

Furco, A. and Holland, B. (2004). 'Institutionalizing Service-Learning in Higher Education: Issues and Strategies for Chief Academic Officers'. In: Langseth, M. and Plater, W.M. (eds) *Public Work and the Academy – An Academic Administrators Guide to Civic Engagement and Service-Learning*. Boston, Anker Publishing, p 27.

Fusch, D. (2010). 'The Student-Alumni Transition: Encouraging Meaningful Giving'. *Academic Impressions Higher Ed Blog*. November/December [accessed 19/02/2021 https://www.academicimpressions.com/blog/the-student-alumni-transition-encouraging-meaningful-giving/]

Fuster, E., Padilla-Meléndez, A., Lockett, R., and del-Águila-Obra, A.R. (2019). 'The Emerging Role of University Spin-off Companies in Developing Regional Entrepreneurial University Ecosystems: The Case of Andalusia'. *Technological Forecasting and Social Change.* 141(April): 219–231.

Gaffney, M. (2012). *Flourishing.* London: Penguin.

Gallo, M.L. (2012). 'Beyond Philanthropy: Recognising the Value of Alumni to Benefit Higher Education Institutions'. *Tertiary Education and Management.* 18(1): 41–55.

Gallo, M.L. (2017). 'How Are Graduates and Alumni Featured in University Strategic Plans? Lessons from Ireland'. In: *Perspectives: Policy and Practice in Higher Education.* 22(3): 92–97.

Gallo, M.L. (2018). TEDx Ballybofey [video] 'We Are All Connected by One Word: Alumni'. [accessed 21/02/2021 https://www.youtube.com/watch? v=ppr6ptfM4_s]

Gallo, M.L. (2019). *Global Alumni Networks and Ireland: Learning from International Practice.* Dublin: KITE white paper [accessed 19/02/2021 https://www.keepintoucheducation.com/resources]

Gallo, M.L. (2021). 'Confessions of an Alumni Romantic'. Linked In Pulse blog post. 11 February [accessed 13/02/2021 https://www.linkedin.com/pulse/confessions-alumni-romantic-maria-l-gallo-edd/? trackingId=lnmaZZ9KSfK7ES%2BaoxTJtA% 3D% 3D]

Gieseke, C. (2018). 'Wellbeing: Not Just Jogging and Broccoli'. *VISIONS: Iowa State University Alumni Magazine.* Fall [accessed 03/03/19 https://www.isualum.org/s/565/17/interior.aspx? sid=565&gid=1&pgid=3503&cid=5247&ecid=5247&crid= 0&calpgid=3130&calcid=4805]

Goldseker, S. and Moody, M. (2021). *Generation Impact: How Next Gen Donors Are Revolutionizing Giving* (Revised ed.). Hoboken NJ: John Wiley & Sons.

Goldstein, D. (2014). 'Are You a Philanthropist?' TEDx SantaCatalina School [video] 14 October [accessed 19/02/2021 https://www.youtube.com/watch? v=1y9EugKh_50]

Granovetter, M.S. (1973). 'The Strength of Weak Ties'. *American Journal of Sociology.* 78(6): 1360–1380.

Granovetter, M.S. (1974). *Getting a Job: A Study of Contacts and Careers*. Cambridge, MA: Harvard University Press.

Greater Rochester Enterprise (2017). 'Major Employers in the Greater Rochester, New York Region – 2017'. Greater Rochester Enterprise webpage [accessed 11/02/2021 https://www.rochesterbiz.com/Portals/0/Major% 20employers% 20in% 20the% 20Greater% 20Rochester% 20NY% 20Region% 20-% 202017_1. pdf]

Gudbergsdottir, E. (2019). ' "Living Lives with Passion" – Group of Institute Alumni Gather in Monterey'. Middlebury Institute of International Studies website, 9 January [accessed 19/02/2021 https://www.middlebury.edu/institute/international-environmental-policy-news/living-lives-passion-group-institute-alumni-gather-monterey]

Guzman, K. (2019). 'Alumni Startup Helps Students Tame College Debt'. *Yale School of Management Alumni Magazine*. 16 January [accessed 19/02/2021 https://som.yale.edu/news/2019/01/alumni-startup-helps-students-tame-college-debt]

Haranahan, K. (2015). 'Disintermediation and Alumni Engagement: A Definition'. Switchboard blog. 1 September [accessed 17/02/2021 https://switchboardhq.com/blog/disintermediation-a-definition]

Harari, Y.N. (2019). *21 Lessons for the 21st Century*. London: Jonathan Cape.

Hempel, J. (2016). 'Inside Peter Thiel's Genius Factory'. *Wired*. 7 December [accessed 03/01/19 https://www.wired.com/2016/12/inside-peter-thiels-genius-factory/]

Henderson, W. (1982). *Under Whose Shade: A Story of a Pioneer in the Swan River Valley of Manitoba*. Nepean, ON: Henderson & Associates.

Higher Ed Live Podcast (2018). 'What Will Alumni Relations Look Like in 2027?' [accessed 16/02/2021 https://www.podbean.com/site/EpisodeDownload/PB7306A1W3YTB]

Hoey, J.K. (2017). *Build Your Dream Network*. New York: TarcherPerigee Penguin, p 49.

Hollands, F.M. and Tirthali, D. (2014). 'Why Do Institutions Offer MOOCs?' *Journal of Asynchronous Learning Networks*. 18(3): 5 [accessed 19/02/2021 https://www.learntechlib.org/p/154185/]

Hooley, T. and Grant, K. (2017). *Graduate Career Handbook: Life after Graduation, Maximise Your Employability, Get a Graduate Job.* Bath: Trotman.

Horowitz, J. (2018). 'Digital vs. In-Person Alumni Engagement: The Disparity'. *Evertrue* blog. 19 July [accessed 19/02/2021 https://www.evertrue.com/2018/07/19/digital-vs-in-person-alumni-engagement-the-disparity/].

Huie, J. (2018). *Purpose: Find Your Truth and Embrace Your Calling.* London: Hay House.

Ingham, D. (2016). 'An Answer from Research to the Teaching Excellence Framework – Student Engagement and Graduate Engagement to Evidence Legacy'. *Student Engagement in Higher Education Journal.* 1(1): 1–22.

InHive Global website [accessed 19/02/2021 www.inhiveglobal.org/]

InHive Global website – Partners – Pakistan Youth Changes Advocates webpage [accessed 19/02/2021 http://www.inhiveglobal.org/project/pakistan-youth-changes-advocates-pyca/]

Institute of Technology, Sligo (2019). [accessed 19/02/2021 https://www.itsligo.ie/courses/meng-connected-autonomous-vehicles/]

Johns Hopkins University webpage – Alumni College [accessed 19/02/2021 https://alumni.jhu.edu/alumnicollege]

Johns Hopkins University webpage – Alumni College 2014 [accessed 19/02/2021 https://alumni.jhu.edu/alumnicollege/2014/napa]

The Johnson Center (2013). *Next Gen Donors Executive Summary Report.* Johnson Center [accessed 19/02/2021 https://www.michiganfoundations.org/sites/default/files/resources/next-gen-donors-Executive-Summary.pdf]

Jones, C. (2017). 'Microvolunteering: What Is It and Why Should You Do It?' *The Guardian.* 13 April. Online International edition [accessed 19/02/2021 https://www.theguardian.com/voluntary-sector-network/2017/apr/13/microvolunteering-what-is-it-and-why-should-you-do-it]

Joshi, L. (2015). 'NUI Galway Embarks on a Mindful Adventure'. *The Irish Times*. 20 October [accessed 19/02/2021 https://www.irishtimes.com/news/education/nui-galway-embarks-on-a-mindful-adventure-1.2393166]

Kapelke-Dale, R. (2014). 'The Odd Couple'. *Brown Alumni Magazine*. [accessed 19/02/2021 https://www.brownalumnimagazine.com/articles/2014–09–03/the-odd-couple]

Kearns, D. (2018). 'University Honours Father Tony Coote for His "outstanding service to all"'. *University College Dublin News*. 10 December [accessed 19/02/2021 http://www.ucd.ie/newsandopinion/news/2018/december/10/universityhonoursfathertonycooteforhisoutstandingservicetoall]

Kennedy, J. and Rego, N. (2018). 'How the UNB Alumni Office Re-connected with 6500+ Alumni'. University of New Brunswick blog. 6 September [accessed 09/04/2020 https://blogs.unb.ca/marketing/2018/09/how-the-unb-alumni-office-re-connected-with-6500+-alumni.php]

Kent State University website [accessed 16/02/2021 https://www.kent.edu/alumni/event/dog-days-summer]

Kent State University website [accessed 19/02/2021 https://www.kent.edu/alumni/alumni-day-service]

Kivunja, C. (2015). 'Teaching Students to Learn and to Work Well with 21st Century Skills: Unpacking the Career and Life Skills Domain of the New Learning Paradigm'. *International Journal of Higher Education*. 4(1): 1–11.

Kizilcec, R.F., Reich, J., Yeomans, M., Dann, C., Brunskill, E., Lopez, G., Turkay, S., Williams, J.J., and Tingley, D. (2020). 'Scaling Up Behavioral Science Interventions in Online Education'. *PNAS Proceedings of the National Academy of Sciences of the United States of America*. 117(27): 14900–14905.

Kohler, T. (2016). 'Corporate Accelerators: Building Bridges between Corporations and Startups'. *Business Horizons*. 59(3): May/June, 347–357.

Krumboltz, J.D. (1998). 'Serendipity Is Not Serendipitous'. *Journal of Counseling Psychology*. 45(4): 390–392.

Laursen, S.L., Thiry, H., and Liston, C.S. (2012). 'The Impact of a University-Based School Science Outreach Program on Graduate Student Participants. Career Paths and Professional Socialization'. *Journal of Higher Education Outreach and Engagement.* 16(2): 47–77.

Leiber, R. (2021). *The Price You Pay for College.* New York: Harper. Kindle edition.

Lemay, K. (2009). *The Generosity Plan.* New York: Atria, Simon & Schuster.

Leslie, I. (2015). *Curious: The Desire to Know and Why Your Future Depends on It.* London: Quercus.

LifeBook website [accessed 19/02/2021 https://www.lifebookuk.com/]

Loewenstein, G. (1994). 'The Psychology of Curiosity: A Review and Reinterpretation'. *Psychological Bulletin.* 116: 75–98.

London, J. (2016). 'Join the MIT Book Club'. Slice of MIT blog [accessed 19/02/2021 https://alum.mit.edu/slice/join-mit-alumni-book-club]

Longwood University (2020). 'The Hiring Manager's Story'. [accessed 04/02/2021 http://www.longwood.edu/alumni/articles/2020/the-hiring-managers-story/]

Lorsch, J. and Tierney, T. (2002). *Aligning the Stars: How to Succeed When Professionals Drive Results.* Boston: Harvard Business School Press, p 202.

Lowry, K. (2018). 'Giving Tuesday Is Coming to UVic on Nov. 27'. The University of Victoria website. 1 November [accessed 19/02/2021 https://www.uvic.ca/news/topics/2018+giving-tuesday+news]

Lyn, K. (2018). 'UofT Music Puts Out First Ever Holiday Playlist'. 29 November [accessed 19/02/2021 https://www.utoronto.ca/news/u-t-music-puts-out-its-first-ever-holiday-playlist]

Mandery, E. (2014). 'Why I'm Skipping My Harvard Reunion (A Call to Action)'. *The Huffington Post.* 6 July [accessed 19/02/2021 https://www.huffpost.com/entry/why-im-skipping-my-harvar_b_5246982]

Mandery, E. (2020). 'We're about to Have the Longest Summer Vacation Ever. That's Going to Be a Problem'. *Politico*. 17 May [accessed 19/02/2021 https://www.politico.com/news/magazine/2020/05/17/long-summer-students-coronavirus-259201]

McDearmon, J.T. (2013). 'Hail to Thee, Our Alma Mater: Alumni Role Identity and the Relationship to Institutional Support Behaviors'. *Research in Higher Education*. 54(3): 283–302.

McGarry, P. (2019). 'Fr Tony Coote Was "the Ultimate Connector", Funeral Hears'. 2 September, *Irish Times*. [accessed 03/09/19 https://www.irishtimes.com/news/social-affairs/religion-and-beliefs/fr-tony-coote-was-the-ultimate-connector-funeral-hears-1.4005540]

McGuire, P. (2018). 'The Misunderstood Art of Networking'. *Irish Times*. 8 May [accessed 19/02/2021 https://www.irishtimes.com/news/education/the-misunderstood-art-of-networking-1.3479288]

McLuhan, M. (1970). *Counterblast*. London: Pitman Press.

McLuhan, M. (2005). *Understanding Media*. London: Routledge.

McPherson, M., Smith-Lovin, L., and Cook, J.M. (2001). 'Birds of a Feather: Homophily in Social Networks'. *Annual Review of Sociology*. 27: 415–444.

Merriam-Webster Dictionary Online website. [accessed 19/02/2021 https://www.merriam-webster.com/dictionary/alumnus]

Merriman, D. (2010). 'The College Is a Philanthropy. Yes a Philanthropy'. *The Chronicle of Education*. 31 October [accessed 13/10/18, https://www.chronicle.com/article/The-College-as-a-Philanthropy/125176]

Mitchell, J. and Belkin, D. (2017). 'Americans Losing Faith in College Degrees, Poll Finds'. *Wall Street Journal*. 7 September [accessed 19/02/2021 https://www.wsj.com/articles/americans-losing-faith-in-college-degrees-poll-finds-1504776601].

Mitchell, K.E., Levin, A.S., and Krumboltz, J.D. (1999). 'Planned Happenstance: Constructing Unexpected Career Opportunities'. *Journal of Counselling and Development*. 77(Spring): 116.

Monmouth University website (2021) Bruce Springsteen Archives & Center for American Music [accessed 18/02/2021 https://springsteenarchives.org/]

Morgan, J. (2017). 'Are Graduates Good Value for Money?' *Times Higher Education*. 12 October [accessed 19/02/2021 https://www.timeshighereducation.com/features/are-graduates-good-value-money]

Morgan, M. (2013). 'The Student Experience Practitioner Model'. In: Morgan, M. (ed.) *Supporting Student Diversity in Higher Education: A Practical Guide*. London: Routledge, p 51.

Mount St Vincent University Women's Wall of Honour website [accessed 19/02/2021 http://www.womenswallofhonour.ca/en/home/honourawoman.aspx]

Murphy, K.A., Blustein, D.L., Bohlig, A.J., and Platt, M.G. (2010). 'The College-to-Career Transition: An Exploration of Emerging Adulthood'. *Journal of Counseling & Development*. 88(2): 174–181.

Myran, G., Baker III, G.A., Simone, B., and Zeiss, T. (2003). *Leadership Strategies for Community College Executives*. Washington: American Association of Community Colleges.

NACE (2020). *Career Services Benchmark Survey Report 2019–20*. Bethlehem, PA: NACE [accessed 29/01/2021 https://www.naceweb.org/store/2020/nace-career-services-benchmark-report/]

Naisbitt, J. (2001). *High Tech, High Touch*. London: Nicholas Brealey Publishing.

National Centre for Universities and Business (2020). *State of the Relationship 2020*. London: NCUB, p 9 [accessed 19/02/2021 https://www.ncub.co.uk/index.php?

National Centre for Universities and Business (2021). *Showcasing Collaboration: Partnerships for the Planet: Highlighting University and Business Partnerships Formed to Address the Climate Crisis*. London: NCUB. [accessed 19/02/2021 https://www.ncub.co.uk/index.php? option=com_docman&view=download&alias=484–5044-partnerships-for-the-planet-v9-new&category_slug=reports&Itemid=2728]

National Co-ordinating Centre for Public Engagement website 'About the Manifesto'. [accessed 19/02/2021 https://www.publicengagement.ac.uk/support-engagement/strategy-and-planning/manifesto-public-engagement/about-manifesto]

National University of Ireland, Galway website – Mindful Way webpage [accessed 19/02/2021 http://www.nuigalway.ie/mindfulway/]

Neghabat-Wolthoff, N. (2021). 'Q&A with UTM Alumnus Teo Salgado, Founder of VerveSmith Ltd and 2020 Recipient of the UofT Arbor Award for Exceptional Volunteer Service'. UTM University of Toronto website [accessed 15/02/2021 www.utm.utoronto.ca/alumni/news/qa-utm-alumnus-teo-salgado-founder-vervesmith-ltd-and-2020-recipient-u-t-arbor-award]

Newton, D. (2020). 'The "Depressing" and "Disheartening" News about MOOCs'. *Forbes*. 21 June [accessed 19/02/2021 https://www.forbes.com/sites/dereknewton/2020/06/21/the-depressing-and-disheartening-news-about-moocs/?sh=5ba1037976ed]

Nietzel, M.T. (2019). 'Alumni Networks and the Job Market: Help or Hindrance?' *Forbes Online*. 16 January [accessed 19/02/2021 https://www.forbes.com/sites/michaeltnietzel/2019/01/16/alumni-networks-and-the-job-market-help-or-hindrance/#3f7302dfba03]

Nilsson, P. (2017). 'Lessons the Alumni Have Learnt'. *The Financial Times* [accessed 19/02/2021 https://www.ft.com/content/44a80fe0-8690-11e7-8bb1-5ba57d47eff7]

NL Alumni Network website [19/02/2021 https://www.nlalumni.nl/article/alumni-sharing-session-pre-departure-briefing-jakarta-2018/17/08/2018/344]

Nokes, A. (2018). *From Cohorts to Communities: A Guide to Working with Programme Alumni*. London: Future First Global (now InHive Global) [accessed 19/02/2021 http://www.inhiveglobal.org/project/inhive-from-cohorts-to-communities/]

Novick, N. (2019). 'Testing the Limits: An Introvert Experiments with Life as an Extrovert'. *Brown Alumni Magazine* [accessed 04/01/2021 https://www\w.brownalumnimagazine.com/articles/2019–11–05/testing-the-limits]

OECD (2018). *Preparing Our Youth for an Inclusive and Sustainable World: The OECD PISA Global Competence Framework* [accessed 11/03/2020 https://www.oecd.org/education/Global-competency-for-an-inclusive-world.pdf]

OECD (2019). *Benchmarking Higher Education System Performance: Higher Education and the Wider Social and Economic Context.* Paris: OECD Publishing [accessed 19/02/2021 http://www.oecd.org/education/benchmarking-higher-education-system-performance-be5514d7-en.htm]

Old Dominion University – Alumni webpage – 'Yappy Hour Social' [accessed 06/02/2021 https://www.odualumni.org/s/1672/bp20/interior.aspx? sid=1672&gid=2&pgid=2390&cid=4339&ecid=4339&crid=0&calpgid=388&calcid=1182]

Olivier, A. (2016). 'McGill University Casual Support Staff Kick off 5-day Strike'. *Global News* website. [23/02/19 https://globalnews.ca/news/3033641/mcgill-university-casual-support-staff-kick-off-5-day-strike/]

Onukwuba, H.O. (2019). *Alumni Leadership and University Excellence in Africa: The Case of Lagos Business School.* Cham: Palgrave, Kindle Edition, location 625.

Pace University Professional Book Club webpage [accessed 19/02/2021 https://www.pbc.guru/pace/]

Pan, J. and Kapelke-Dale, R. (2014). *Graduates in Wonderland: The International Misadventures of Two (Almost) Adults.* New York: Gotham Books.

Passini, R. (1981). 'Wayfinding: A Conceptual Framework'. *Urban Ecology.* 5(1980/81): 17–31.

Pausch, R. (2008). *The Last Lecture: Lessons in Living.* London: Hodder & Stoughton.

Peak, C. (2013). 'Alumni Business Proudly Put Acadia Front and Centre'. Acadia University website [accessed 24/06/2020 https://www2. acadiau.ca/alumni-friends/alumni/news/alumni-news-reader/alumni-business-owners-proudly-put-acadia-front-and-centre.html]

PennPAC website. Current Client webpage [accessed 19/02/2021 https://pennpac.org/our-impact/current-clients2/]; Our Impact webpage [accessed 19/02/2021 https://pennpac.org/our-impact/]

PennPAC – ImPACt Events webpage [accessed 19/02/2021 https://pennpac.org/our-impact/impact-events/]

Perry, A. and Spencer, C. (2018). 'College Didn't Prepare Me for This: The Realities of the Student Debt Crisis and the Effect It Is Having on College Graduates'. *The William & Mary Educational Review*. 6(1): 8–15.

Pettigrew, T. (2012). 'Why You'll Never Be an Alumni'. *Maclean's*. 26 April [accessed 19/02/2021, https://www.macleans.ca/education/uniandcollege/why-youll-never-be-an-alumni/]

Porter, J. (2017). 'Why You Should Make Time for Self-Reflection (Even If You Hate Doing It)'. *Harvard Business Review*. 21 March 2017 [accessed 19/02/2021 https://hbr.org/2017/03/why-you-should-make-time-for-self-reflection-even-if-you-hate-doing-it]

Post, S. and Neimark, J. (2007). *Why Good Things Happen to Good People*. New York: Broadway Books.

Poulin, M.J., Brown, S.L., Dillard, A.J., and Smith, D.M. (2013). 'Giving to Others and the Association between Stress and Mortality'. *American Journal of Public Health*. 103(9): 1649–1655.

Precedent (2009). *Alumdergraduates: Aligning the Alumni and Student Experience Online*. London: Precedent.

Prichard, M. (2019). 'Building a Valuable Network: How to Keep in Touch with Professional Contacts'. Mac's List blog [accessed 19/02/2021 https://www.macslist.org/networking/building-a-valuable-network-how-to-keep-in-touch-with-professional-contacts]

Putnam, R.D. (2000). *Bowling Alone: The Collapse and Revival of American Community*. New York: Simon & Schuster.

Rancourt, D.W. (2019). 'Wayfinding and Research as Key Work-Integrated Learning Strategies'. *University Affairs*. 16 August [accessed 29/02/2020 https://www.universityaffairs.ca/career-advice/career-advice-article/wayfinding-and-research-as-key-work-integrated-learning-strategies/]

Ranson, S. (1993). 'Markets or Democracy for Education'. *British Journal of Educational Studies*. 41(4): 333–352.

Reich, R. (2018). *Just Giving: Why Philanthropy Is Failing Democracy and How it Can Do Better*. Princeton, NJ: Princeton University Press.

Reisz, M. (2011). 'Ionic, Isn't it?' *Times Higher Education.* 20(October): 40–44.

Rhodes College website – Alumni Spotlights [accessed 19/02/2021 https://www.rhodes.edu/alumni-development/alumni-relations/alumni-spotlights]

Rincón, S. (2018). 'It's a Small World: How a Global Alumni Association Is Benefitting International Alumni and Students – in the Netherlands and Abroad'. *CASE Currents.* July/August: 32–37 [accessed 19/02/2021 https://www.case.org/currents/its-a-small-world]

Robinson, K. (2009). *The Element: How Finding Your Passion Changes Everything.* London: Penguin Books.

Royal College of Surgeons of Ireland 'In Conversation with ... the Floating Doctors'. [accessed 19/02/2021 http://www.rcsi.ie/index.jsp? n=2264&p=2259&a=11296]

Royal College of Surgeons of Ireland website [accessed 19/02/2021 https://www.rcsi.com/impact/details/2019/02/rcsi-alumni-providing-healthcare-to-the-worlds-most-isolated-communities]

Royal College of Surgeons of Ireland webpage – Student Life – Boston Marathon webpage [accessed 14/09/2020 https://www.rcsi.com/dublin/student-life/life-on-campus/student-events/boston-marathon]

Royal College of Surgeons of Ireland YouTube channel [video] 'In Conversation with ... the Floating Doctors'. [accessed 19/02/2021 https://www.youtube.com/watch? v=F1hzk2ve2y4]

Ruppell Shell, E. (2018). 'College May Not Be Worth It Anymore'. *New York Times.* 16 May 2018 [accessed 19/02/2021, https://www.nytimes.com/2018/05/16/opinion/college-useful-cost-jobs.html]

Sanchez, G.J. (2018). 'Curating Career Success for First-Generation College Alumni'. *Diversity & Democracy.* Spring 21(2) [accessed 19/02/2021 https://www.aacu.org/diversitydemocracy/2018/spring/sanchez]

Sani, S. (2018). 'Essence of Alumni Association – By Senator Shehu Sani'. *Daily NewsTimes Nigeria.* 11 November [accessed 19/02/2021 https://dailynewstimesco.wordpress.com/2018/11/11/essence-of-alumni-association-by-senator-shehu-sani/]

Schön, D.A. (1983). *The Reflective Practitioner: How Professionals Think in Action*. New York: Basic Books.

Schön, D.A. (1987). *Educating the Reflective Practitioner: Toward a New Design on Teaching and Learning in the Professions*. San Francisco: Jossey-Bass.

Schuster, E. (2018). 'Special Issue: Democracy's Graduates: Reimagining Alumnihood'. *Diversity & Democracy*. Spring, 21(2) [accessed 19/02/2021 https://www.aacu.org/diversitydemocracy/2018/spring]

Schwartzman, R. (1995). 'Are Students Customers? The Metaphoric Mismatch between Management and Education. *Education*. 116: 423–432.

Segran, E. (2020). *The Rocket Years: How Your Twenties Launch the Rest of Your Life*. New York: Harper, Kindle Edition.

Selingo, J.J. (2013). *College (Un)bound: The Future of Higher Education and What It Means for Students*. New York: Houghton Mifflin Harcourt Publishing.

Selingo, J.J. (2016). *There Is Life after College: What Parents and Students Should Know about Navigating School to Prepare for the Jobs of Tomorrow*. New York: William Morrow.

Seuss, Dr (1990). *Oh, The Places You'll Go!* New York: Harper Collins.

Shaindlin, A. (2012). 'Will the Internet Obsolete Alumni Associations?' *Huffington Post* blog. 23 May [accessed 19/02/2021 https://www.huffingtonpost.com/andrew-shaindlin/alumni-associations-facebook_b_1375765. html]

Shaindlin, A. (2018). *Alumni Community Whitepaper: Engaging Alumni Outside Academia: Emerging Practices in Foundations, Fellowships and Other Nonprofit Organizations*. Grenzebach, Glier & Associates and the Rockefeller Foundation [accessed 11/03/2020 https://www.grenzebachglier.com/wp-content/uploads/2018/07/GGA-Alumni-Community-Whitepaper-Shaindlin-UPLOAD.pdf]

Silver, B.R. and Roksa, J. (2017). 'Navigating Uncertainty and Responsibility: Understanding Inequality in the Senior-Year Transition'. *Journal of Student Affairs Research and Practice*. 54(3): 248–260.

Singh, M. (2014). 'Higher Education and the Public Good: Precarious Potential?' In: Munck R., McIlrath L., Hall B., and Tandon R. (eds) *Higher Education and Community-Based Research*. New York: Palgrave Macmillan, p 203.

Skinner, N.A. (2019). 'The Rise and Professionalization of the American Fundraising Model in Higher Education'. *Philanthropy & Education*. 3(1): 23–46.

Skotnicki, S. (2018). 'A Clean Break: Why Our Society's Obsession with Cleanliness Has Become Too Much of a Good Thing'. *The Globe & Mail*. 25 May [accessed 19/02/2021 https://www.theglobeandmail.com/opinion/article-a-clean-break-why-our-societys-obsession-with-cleanliness-has-become/?page=all&utm_source=Facebook&utm_medium=Alumni-Facebook&utm_campaign=Alumni-FB-status-post]

Stage Clip website [accessed 19/02/2021 https://stageclip.com/]

Staton, B. (2020). 'Universities to Cut Thousands of Academics on Short Contracts'. *Financial Times*. 20th July [accessed 19/02/2021 https://www.ft.com/content/67f89a9e-ac30–47d0–83e7-eba4d1284847]

Stern, C. (2014). 'Consulting for a Cause: Alumni Offers Pro Bono Services'. *The Daily Pennsylvanian*. 13 May [accessed 19/02/2021 https://www.thedp.com/article/2014/05/penn-pac-alum-consulting]

Strada-Gallup (2019). *2018 Strada-Gallup Alumni Survey Mentoring College Students to Success*. Indianapolis: Strada-Gallup [accessed 19/02/2021 https://news.gallup.com/reports/244031/2018-strada-gallup-alumni-survey-mentoring-students.aspx]

Swingle, J. and Willsea, M. (2018). 'Breaking away from the "Sea of Sameness" in Higher Ed'. WP Campus blog. 18 July [accessed 16/02/2021 https://www.wpcampus.org/blog/2018/07/breaking-away-from-the-sea-of-sameness-in-higher-ed/]

Talmage, C.A., Mark, R., Slowey, M., and Knopf, R.C. (2016). 'Age Friendly Universities and Engagement with Older Adults: Moving from Principles to Practice'. *International Journal of Lifelong Education*. 35(5): 537–554.

Tansey, L. and Gallo, M.L. (2015). 'Connecting Students on Bikes with Education: Student-led Voluntary Higher Education Bicycle Social Movements as Sites for Informal Environmental and Philanthropic Education'. ERNOP European Research Network on Philanthropy Conference, Paris, July 2015.

Thiel Fellowship website [accessed 02/01/2019 https://thielfellowship.org/]

Tight, M. (2013). 'Students: Customers, Clients or Pawns?' *Higher Education Policy*. 26: 291–307.

Times Higher Education – THE Student (2020). 'Top Universities in the World for Global Impact'. *Times Higher Education – THE Student*. 22 April [accessed 07/02/2021 https://www.timeshighereducation.com/student/best-universities/top-universities-world-global-impact]

Trinity College Dublin – Trinity Centre for People with Intellectual Disability [accessed 19/02/2021 https://www.tcd.ie/tcpid/about/]

Tromble, W.W. (1998). *The Function of the Alumni Office*. In: Tromble, W.W. *Excellence in Advancement: Applications for Higher Education and Nonprofit Organizations*. Gaithersburg, MD: Aspen Publishers.

Twigg, K. (2021). *The Career Stories Method: 11 Steps to Find Your Ideal Career – and Discover Your Awesome Self in the Process*. Vancouver: Page Two Books, p 138. Kindle Edition.

UC Davis website – 'One Aggie Network: Alumni Wine and Beer Program'. webpage [accessed 21/02/2021 https://alumni.ucdavis.edu/alumni-wine-beer-program]

UC Davis website – 'Sip, Sip Hooray! UC Davis Alumni Wine Program' [accessed 21/02/2021 https://ucdavis.imodules.com/s/1768/rd18/index.aspx?sid=1768&gid=2&pgid=2254&content_id=1385]

UNESCO (2014). 'CERN and UNESCO: 60 Years of Science for Peace'. United Nations Educational, Scientific and Cultural Organization website [accessed 13/02/2021 http://www.unesco.org/new/en/unesco/partners-donors/single-view/news/cern_and_unesco_60_years_of_science_for_peace/]

UniverCity website [accessed 19/02/2021 http://univercity.ca/about-us/]

Universidad de los Andes website (2019). 'What Is Pa'lante Caribe?' 9 October [accessed 19/02/2021 https://uniandes.edu.co/en/news/desarrollo-regional/what-is-palante-caribe]

University of Cambridge (2017). 'Physical Activity, Even in Small Amounts, Benefits Both Physical and Psychological Well-Being'. University of Cambridge Research webpage. [accessed 19/02/2021 https://www.cam.ac.uk/research/news/physical-activity-even-in-small-amounts-benefits-both-physical-and-psychological-well-being]

University College Dublin website – Alumni – Woodland Walkies webpage [accessed 19/02/2021 https://alumni.ucd.ie/woodland-walkies-2017/]

University College Dublin website – Walk While You Can webpage [accessed 19/02/2021 http://www.ucd.ie/ucdinthecommunity/newsevents/newsevents/upcomingevents/walkwhileyoucan/]

University of Edinburgh website [accessed 19/02/2021 https://www.ed.ac.uk/local/projects/cabaret-of-dangerous-ideas]

University of Greenwich Portraits website [accessed 14/09/18 https://alumni.gre.ac.uk/greenwich-portraits/]

University of Heidelberg website [accessed 12/03/19 https://www.uni-heidelberg.de/university/family-friendly/]

University of Maryland Libraries Digital Collections website – The Jim Henson Works [accessed 19/02/2021 https://digital.lib.umd.edu/henson/about]

University of Melbourne – MOOCs page [accessed 19/02/2021 https://about.unimelb.edu.au/teaching-and-learning/innovation-initiatives/digital-and-online-innovation/moocs].

University of Melbourne (2016). 'University Passes MOOC Milestone'. University of Melbourne Newsroom website. 16 May [accessed 19/02/2021 http://newsroom.melbourne.edu/news/university-passes-mooc-milestone]

University of New South Wales Business School website [accessed 19/02/2021 https://www.business.unsw.edu.au/alumni/alum-from-day-one]

University of Notre Dame website – Science of Generosity – What Is Generosity? webpage [accessed 19/02/2021 https://generosityresearch.nd.edu/more-about-the-initiative/what-is-generosity/]

Universities of Sanctuary website [accessed 19/02/2021 https://ireland.cityofsanctuary.org/universities-and-colleges-of-sanctuary]

University of Sheffield Alumni website – Alumni Authors webpage [accessed 19/02/2021 https://www.sheffield.ac.uk/alumni/our_alumni/authors]

University of Sheffield Alumni website – Alumni – Lifebook webpage [accessed 19/02/21 https://www.sheffield.ac.uk/alumni/news_archive/2013/life-book-story]

University of Sheffield (2018). 'The Professional Birdwatcher'. *Your University: The Magazine for Alumni and Friends*. Sheffield: Development, Alumni Relations & Events, The University of Sheffield, pp 16–18.

University of Toronto website – Entrepreneurs webpage [accessed 19/02/2021http://entrepreneurs.utoronto.ca/]

University of Waterloo (2018). *Welcome to the Club Young Alumni Handbook 2018*. Waterloo: UofW.

University of Waterloo – Facebook post (2014): Chris Hadfield honorary degree speech quotation. 10 June [accessed 19/02/2021 https://www.facebook.com/university.waterloo/photos/honorary-doctorate-chris-hadfield-speaks-on-june-10th-at-the-spring-2014-convoca/10152436036470758/]

University of Wisconsin-Madison website – Grandparents University webpage [accessed 19/02/2021 https://www.uwalumni.com/resources-services/alumni-learning/grandparents-university/]

Valburn, M. (2018). 'New Era for Women as Donors'. Inside Higher Ed website, 11 May [accessed 19/02/2021 https://www.insidehighered.com/news/2018/05/11/colleges-are-turning-women-philanthropists-source-new-money-fund-raising-campaigns]

Vallerand, R.J. (2010). 'On the Passion for Life Activities: The Dualistic Model of Passion'. *Advances in Experimental Social Psychology*, 42: 99–193.

Vallerand, R.J., Blanchard, C., Mageau, G.A., Koestner, R., Ratelle, C., Leonard, M., Gagne, M., and Marsolais, J. (2003). 'Les Passions de l'Âme: On Obsessive and Harmonious Passion'. *Journal of Personality and Social Psychology*. 85(4): 756–767.

Vanderlelie, J. (2015). 'Re-visioning Alumni Relationships to Improve Graduate Employability'. *STARS* – Student Transitions, Achievement, Retention and Success Conference Proceedings, Melbourne, July [accessed 19/02/2021 http://www.unistars.org/papers/STARS2015/07G.pdf]

Vlahos, C. (2017). 'The Alumni Relations Fork in the Road'. Blog post [accessed 19/02/2021 https://www.linkedin.com/pulse/alumni-relations-fork-road-christopher-vlahos/]

Wagner, L. (2007). 'Achieving Success in a Fundraising Programme'. In: Conraths, B. and Trusso, B. *Managing the University Community: Exploring Good Practice*. Brussels: European Universities Association, pp 99–100.

Walker, N. (2018). 'Featured Fellow: Meric Gertle'. *Canadian Geographic* website. 16 February [accessed 26/02/18 https://www.canadiangeographic.ca/article/featured-fellow-meric-gertler]

Weerts, D.J. and Ronca, J.M. (2008). 'Characteristics of Alumni Donors Who Volunteer at Their Alma Mater'. *Research in Higher Education*. 49(3): 274–292.

Weinstein, S. (2009). *The Complete Guide to Fundraising* (3rd ed.). New Jersey: John Wiley & Sons.

Whittemore, S. (2013). 'Alumni: Includes our Enhance Alumni Engagement Checklist'. Relationship Management: JISC Online Publication [accessed 12/10/18 https://www.jisc.ac.uk/guides/relationship-management/alumni]

Willsea, M. (2018). 'Breaking away from the "Sea of Sameness" in Higher Ed'. WP Campus blog. 18 July [Accessed 16/02/2021 https://www.wpcampus.org/blog/2018/07/breaking-away-from-the-sea-of-sameness-in-higher-ed/]

Wolk, J. (2020). 'What is "Alumnx"? One of Higher Ed's Newest Social Justice Terms, Explained'. *Campus Reform* [accessed 15/02/2021 https://www.campusreform.org/article? id=15934]

Woolcock, M. (2001). 'The Place of Social Capital in Understanding Social and Economic Outcomes'. *Isuma: Canadian Journal of Policy Research*. 2(1): 11–17.

Wright, K. (2001). 'Generosity vs. Altruism: Philanthropy and Charity in the United States and United Kingdom'. *Voluntas* 12(4): 399–416.

York University (2015). 'TASTE Program Students, Grads for Mentorship Lunch'. *yFiles*. 9 September [accessed 25/02/2020 https://yfile.news.yorku.ca/2015/09/09/taste-program-pairs-students-grads-for-mentorship-lunch/].

Zawadzki, M.J., Smyth, J.M., and Costigan, H.J. (2015). 'Real-Time Associations Between Engaging in Leisure and Daily Health and Well-Being'. *Annals of Behavioral Medicine*. 49(4): 605–615.

Zhang, C., Wu, F., and Henke, J.W. (2015). 'Leveraging Boundary Spanning Capabilities to Encourage Supplier Investment: A Comparative Study'. *Industrial Marketing Management*. 49: 84–94.

Zhong, B. (2017). 'This Group of Penn Alumni Is Helping New American Residents Jumpstart Their Careers'. 9 February [accessed 19/02/2021 https://www.thedp.com/article/2017/02/penn-pac-immigrant-training]

About the author

Maria L. Gallo is Founder of KITE – Keep in Touch Education, a social enterprise that offers research services to explore the transformative potential of alumni and diaspora connection. She also established the Alumni Way Academy to offer innovative education and thought leadership on alumni potential. An internationally renowned alumni scholar, Maria has over 20 years' experience in leadership roles in higher education management, as a scholar and alumni relations professional, including at the University of Toronto, University College Dublin, and at St Angela's – National University of Ireland, Galway. Maria received her doctorate from the University of Sheffield and is currently a visiting research fellow with the Centre for Social Innovation at the Trinity Business School – Trinity College Dublin. Her TEDx talk 'We Are All Connected by one Word: Alumni' is one of only a handful of alumni-related TED talks available. She is a passionate speaker on the power of alumni connection with professional associations and organizations worldwide. Alongside an extensive academic publication record, in 2013, the Council for Advancement and Support of Education (CASE) awarded Maria the HS Warwick Distinguished Research Publication Award in alumni relations for her academic research in the field. She remains active in many of her alma maters in all forms in Canada, Ireland, and the UK. Maria lives in County Donegal, Ireland with her husband Morgan Ferriter and their two children.

For more information on the Alumni Way and the Alumni Way Academy, visit https://www.thealumniway.com/

The Alumni Way Workbook is also available. To access your free copy of the workbook visit https://www.thealumniway.com/

Index

References to figures appear in *italic* type; references to endnotes show both the page number and the note number (231n3).

21 Lessons for the 21st Century (Harari) 67

A

Acadia University 93
#AddSprinklesUVic campaign 155
Adenuga, J. 122
advancement
  professionals 1, 5, 54, 98, 158
  treasure side of 158, 159
  university advancement work 45, 82, 158
advertising, inclusive 91
affinity
  credit card 47, 91
  diaspora 49–50
  groups *see* career communities
  partnerships 91
  travel programmes 125
  for university 50
Age Friendly University 108
Aikins, K. 76
Albom, M. 128
Aligning the Stars (Lorsch and Tierney) 60
alma mater 4, 13, 15, 16, 32, 36, 49, 50, 60, 105–106, 131–134, 188
alumni as lifelong shareholders in 21, 36
alumni relationship with 25, 26, 53
celebrating talents with 146–149
engaging in passions 179
personal connection with 141
potential for connection to weak ties 57
providing learning opportunities 110

role in process of life discovery 14
sharing good news with 84, 86
support for business 90
ties in 165
see also universities
'Alum from Day One' strategy 31, 59–60
building Alumni Way 62
checklist 61–62
key messages 60–61
alum in absentia 21
alumna 13
alumnae 13
alumni 13–14, 70
affinity travel programmes 125
ambassador programmes 145
association 60, 92, 123, 129, 143, 144, 152, 180
community 12, 16, 51
connection 1–2, 16, 24, 127–129, 176, 180
directory 48
diversity in 15, 71, 91, 122, 142, 176
grinch 38, 53
identity 17–19, 56, 120, 175, 185
International Environmental Policy (IEP) 129
leadership 11, 143, 181
mentorship programme 15, 74
premium 16
relations 2, 14, 45–46, 72, 82, 145, 152, 171
reunions ix, x, 2, 15, 47, 72, 80, 95, 129, 143, 183, 187
revolution 5
role in higher education landscape 19

volunteers 140, 142–143, 145, 148, 170
alumni–alma mater relationship 19, 21, 89
alumni–alumni mentorship 181
alumni call to action
  building Alumni Way 186
  checklist 186
  fixed mindset 186
  generating momentum for Alumni Way health check 187–188
  growth mindset 185
alumni capital 4, 5, 14, 15, 26, 33, 46–47, 83, 97, 105–106, 175, 177, 186, 188
  bonding and bridging 15–16
  claiming alumni identity 17–19
  key categories 16
  leverage for business 89–90
  'university is a city' concept 90–95
  linking capital 16
  mining 71–75
  nourishment of wellness through 109–117
  opening to growth mindset 23–24
  reclaiming university investment 19–23
  ties and 139, 161
  visual representation 17
alumni citizen(ship) 68, 70–71, 122, 137, 139, 181, 185
  advance ourselves as 45–46
  alumni services wish list creation 46–49
  global alumni passport recognition 49–53
  updating alumni record 53–57
  engagement 36–39
  giving time as 142–146
Alumni Fridays 73–74
alumni hypernetwork 69–71
  building by assembling career stories 75–80
  learning about earning on campus 80–84
  mining alumni capital 71–73
  sharing good news 84–88
alumni-ness 176, 180
alumni network 1–2, 50, 56, 72–73, 181–182
  corporate 180, 182

diversity in 15, 71, 91, 122, 142, 176
followers on social media 71
inclusiveness 70
InHive model in 180–181
NL Alumni Network 52
scholarship programme 53
Alumni Networks Less Helpful Than Advertised 72
alumni opportunities 25–26, 32, 47
  hyperawareness of 60
alumni potential 1, 2, 3, 7, 33, 60
alumni relations 2, 14, 45–46, 72, 82, 145, 152, 171
alumni-self flourishing 119–120
  following heart to guide passion 120–125
  leading with soul 126–129
alumni-university relationship 2–3, 157, 180
Alumni Way 1–2, 3, 12, 21, 24, 27, 49, 62, 185, 189
  connecting with alumni 16
  growth mindset 23–24
  inclusivity 176–178
  promotion 175–176
  shared experiences 178–184
  traits 2–7
  transformational 176–178
  universality 176–178
Alumni Wine Program 112
alumnus 13
alumnx 191n6
American University of Rome (AUR) 41
Aristotle 106, 138
Arizona State University (ASU) 164–165
Arnstein, S. 38
artificial intelligence 110
Association of Fundraising Professionals (AFP) 213n23
Association for Healthcare Philanthropy (AHP) 213n23
Astrof, J.E. 148
Atwood, M. 32
Avni, R. 97–99
Azim Premji University (APU) 42

B

Bathmaker, A.A. 20
Bauer College of Business 93
#bauerloveshouston campaign 93

Berg, M. 78
Big Onion Walking
    Tours 125, 208n20
Bike Kitchen (non-profit
    community bike shop) 122
Birkhead, T. 109
Black British Business Awards
    (BBBA) 163–164
Block, P. 147
Bonovich-Marvich, M. 42
book clubs 112
boundary spanning 163–164, 167
Bourdieu, P. 69–70
Bowling Alone (Putnam) 15
Boylan, K. 89, 94, 181
Bradley, R. 89
Brandeis University 97, 128
Breeze, B. 164
Brentas, O. 50
Bright Club 111
Brown, B. 110–111
Brown, P. 69
Brown University 46, 84
Build Your Dream Network
    (Hoey) 163
Burgess, K. 115
Burkus, D. 71, 182

C

Cabaret of Dangerous Ideas 120
Campbell University 51
Campus Insights 91
Canadian Council for Advancement
    of Education (CCAE) 82
career communities 73, 74
career services 14, 47, 66, 73, 78,
    82, 85, 86, 88, 100, 145, 158
career stories of alumni
    assembling 75–80
    sharing 87
Career Stories Method, The
    (Twigg) 75
Carnegie Mellon University 128
CASE (Council for Advancement
    and Support of Education) 54
Catherwood, R. 76
CERN (European Organization for
    Nuclear Research) 182
CEU 32
Chandak, S. 42
Chronicle of Higher Education,
    The 139
city-building organization 36

city-citizenship metaphor 38
City University of New York
    (CUNY) 187
Clark, A. 83
Clark, D. 56
class notes of alumni 56
Clelland, T. 42
Cohen, R. 143, 195n6
Colgate University 73
community
    alumni 12, 13, 16, 47, 49, 51, 56
    cohesive 127
    college 32
    diversity in an alumni 15, 71, 91,
        122, 142, 176
    engagement initiatives 142
    feeling 41
    inclusive 2, 16
    outreach programmes in
        universities 123, 124
    supportive 38
connection-ready students and
    activated alumni 77
Conroy, P. 180
Coote, T. 161–163
Cornell Alumni Leadership
    Conference 72
Cornell University 72
corporate alumni networks 180,
    182–183
Covey, S. 109, 176
COVID-19 pandemic 67, 81, 92
    family-friendly programming in
        universities during 123
    impact on higher
        education 19–20
Cripton, J. 70
Cross, S. 111
curiosity 2, 4–5, 66, 67, 179
    alumni capital and 97–99
    alumni hypernetwork 69–71
    building by assembling career
        stories 75–80
    learning about earning on
        campus 80–84
    mining alumni capital 71–75
    sharing good news 84–88
    building Alumni Way 100–101
    checklist 100
    employability 66–67
    framework for global
        competence 68
    game analogy 67

key messages 98–99
leverage alumni capital for
    business 89–90
    'university is a city'
        concept 90–95
    New Learning Paradigm 67
    planned happenstance 65–66
    see also generosity;
        passion; reflection
*Curious: The Desire to Know and
    Why Our Future Depends on It*
    (Leslie) 66
curriculum 67, 107
    development 124, 146–147
    refinement 146–147
customer relationship management
    systems (CRMs) 54

D

Da Vinci Engineering Enrichment
    Programme (DEEP) 124
Dalhousie University 121
degree-to-career coupling 4
Dewey, J. 18, 66
disengaged alumni with fixed
    mindset 26, 61, 99, 133, 171
disintermediation 46
Dobson, G. 164
'doer' identity of alumni 14
Dog Days of Summer 115
donation to universities 156–157,
    158
Donor Bill of Rights 159,
    159, 213n23
donor identity of alumni 14
dormant ties 56, 71
Drezner, N. 156
Dublin City University 108
Dweck, C. 23, 40, 56, 66, 131, 185
dynamic alumni with growth
    mindset 26, 61, 99, 133, 171

E

'education-as-degree' linear
    thinking 18
education voyeurism 112
Eikenberry, A. 164
*Element: How Finding Your Passion
    Changes Everything, The*
    (Robinson) 106
elitism 70
Ellison, J. 144
employability 66–67, 131

Engaging Alumni initiative 145
Erickson, R. 183
ERNOP (European Research
    Network on Philanthropy
    Conference) 207n9
Estrada Prada, L. 41
European Space Agency 41
Eusebe, M. 163–164

F

Facebook 46, 178
family-friendly programming in
    universities 123
Family Friendly University
    certification 108
Favreau, A. 14
Ferrazzi, K. 107, 141
Firecloud 365 89, 91–92, 94, 181
Fisher, J.F. 166
fixed mindset 23, 185, 186
    disengaged alumni with 26, 61,
        99, 133, 171
Floating Doctors 123, 207n12
Florida, R. 36
Flourishing (Gaffney) 120
focused investment 22
Forsythe, R. 92, 128
foundation investment 21–22
Friend of a Friend (Burkus) 71
friend-raising 157–158, 213n21
fundraising
    campaigns 152, 157
    to universities 45, 54, 82,
        157–161, 165

G

Gaffney, M. 120
game analogy 67, 69
General Data Protection Regulation
    (GDPR) 55
*Generation Impact: How Next Gen
    Donors are Revolutionizing
    Giving* (Goldseker and
    Moody) 170
generosity 2, 5–7, 137–138, 179
    building Alumni Way 172
    checklist 172
    key messages 170–171
    recognizing as
        philanthropists 139–144
    celebrating talents with alma
        mater 146–147
    volunteering 142–146

as service 169–170
understanding power of
    giving 151–153
  connecting generously with
    ties 161–163
  power of treasure and
    ties 153–157
  see also curiosity;
    passion; reflection
Georgetown University 31
Gertler, M. 36
gift
  financial 155
  graduation 12, 14
  planning 157, 158
  transformational 163
  to universities 156–157
  to university visitors 121
giving, power of 151–153
  connecting generously with
    ties 161–167
  power of treasure and ties 153–161
global alumni networks 52, 184
global alumni passport
    recognition 49–53
Global Goals micro-reflection 126
global village 38
GOLDs (Graduates of the Last
    Decade) 56
Goldseker, S. 170
Goldstein, D. 139
good news of alumni,
    sharing 84–88
Google 46
Gourley, T. 72
graduate employability 131
*Graduates in Wonderland: The
    International Misadventures of
    Two (Almost) Adults* (Pan) 84
graduation *3*, 11–12, 18, 142
  advice to graduates 14
  feelings after 12–14
  feelings of uncertainty 32
Grandparents University
    (GPU) 123
Granovetter, M. 56, 71
Greenwich Snapshots series 87
growth mindset 83, 84, 107,
    110, 185
  dynamic alumni with 26, 61, 99,
    133, 171
  opening to 23–24
  reflection and 40–41, 43

H

Hadfield, C. 169, 215n1
Harari, Y.N. 67
Harvard 187
Harvard Alumni for Mental Health
    (HAMH) 127
Harvard Business Review 40
Harvard Student Agencies 90–91
Heidelberg University in
    Germany 108
Henson, J. 121
High-Energy Network 182
'High Tech, High Touch', 71
higher education 131
  funding for 151
  Pa'lante Caribe campaign for 154
  phases of investment 21–22
  role of alumni in 19
  as tool for social mobility 155
hiking clubs for alumni 115
Hoey, J.K. 79, 163
homophily 70
Horowitz, J. 47
hourglass of university
    relationship 2–6, *3*
How to Be a Happy Academic (Clark
    and Sousa) 83
Huie, J. 119, 163–164
humanity, love of 141
hyperawareness of alumni
    opportunities 60

I

identity groups 73, 74
ImPACt events 148
inclusive civic spaces 144–145
informational interview 75, 77–80,
    83–84, 98, 129
InHive model 180–181
Instagram 143, 178
Institute of Technology Sligo 94
interdependence 71, 177
intra-university networks 83
Iowa State University 116
Irish Times, The 55

J

James, C. 93
Jay John College of Criminal
    Justice, City University of
    New York 187
JME *see* Adenuga, J.

Johns Hopkins University's Alumni College 125
Jones, M. 38
Joshi, L. 127
Just Giving (Reich) 153

K

Kapelke-Dale, R. 84, 85
'keep in touch' call 31–33
Kent State University 115, 144
Khoo, R. 41
Kivunja, C. 67, 197n5
Krumboltz, J. 65

L

La Brot, B. 123
learning about earning on university campus 80–84
legacy funding 137
Leslie, I. 66
Letterkenny Institute of Technology 89
life identities 18–19, 60–62
LifeBook 91
lifelong learning 110–112, 177
lifelong shareholders in alma mater 21
LinkedIn 46, 51, 73, 75, 78, 178
LocalizED 97
Longwood University 76
Lorsch, J. 60

M

MacBride, S. 81–82
Mandery, E. 187
Manifesto for Public Engagement 111
Massachusetts Institute of Technology (MIT) Alumni Book Club 112
Massive Open Online Course (MOOC) 111–112, 114
McCormick, R. 123
McDearmon, J.T. 106
McGill University 32
McLuhan, M. 38
mentorship 76, 180
  alumni–alumni 181
  alumni mentorship programme 15, 48, 74, 76
  diaspora 97
  structured 59
Merriam-Webster Dictionary Online 191n5

Merriman, D. 139–140
micro-mentorship opportunities 76
Middlebury Institute of International Studies 31
Mindful Way conference 127
Mindset: Changing the Way You Think to Fulfil Your Potential (Dweck) 23
mining alumni capital 71–75
'mission critical' decision 20
Moëd, R. 91
Monash University 41
Monmouth University 121
Moody, M. 170
Morgan, M. 33
Morrow, J. 31–32, 51
Mount St Vincent University (MSVU) 156

N

National University of Ireland, Galway 127
Netherlands (NL) Alumni Network 52
'network-minded' reputation 163
networking 75–76, 99, 137, 163, 166
  alumni 72, 144
  career-focused networking mixers 48
  industry-focused networking events 59
  mining 71
  opportunities 72
  relational 97
  social networking sites 178
Never Eat Alone (Ferrazzi) 107
New Learning Paradigm 67
NL Alumni Network-The Netherlands (NLAn-NL) 52
North Carolina-based Campbell University 51
nourishment of wellness 109
  lifelong learning 110–112
  nurturing our body 114–117
NUS 32

O

Oh, The Places You'll Go! (Seuss) 12
Old Dominion University 115
online community 52, 57
  alumni 74, 78
  University of Toronto 70

Onukwuba, H. 146
opportunity trap 69
Organization for Economic
    Cooperation and Development
    (OECD) study 12
Oxford University 32

P

Pace University 112
Pa'lante Caribe campaign 154–155
Pan, J. 84, 85
passion 2, 5, 106, 131–132
  building Alumni Way 134
  checklist 134
  immersing in 105–108
  key messages 132–133
  nourishment of wellness through
    alumni capital 109
    lifelong learning 110–114
    nurturing our body 114–117
  watching alumni-self
    flourishing 119–120
  following heart to guide
    passion 120–123
  leading with soul 126–129
  see also curiosity;
    generosity; reflection
Pausch, R. 128
Peak, C. 202n11
PennPAC 148
people, flows of 16, 26, 43, 106,
    113–114, 177, 184
personal alignment 59–60
Pettigrew, T. 13
philanthropic culture 165
'philanthropic mirroring' 156
philanthropy 139–142, 154–155,
    159–161, 159, 164
  celebrating talents with alma
    mater 146–149
  volunteering 142–146
planned happenstance 65–66
Plato 106
PleaseTalk (national
    movement) 162
Porter, J. 40
Post, S. 137
Prichard, M. 72
Principles of Practice for Alumni
    Relations Professionals at
    Educational Institutions,
    The 54
public engagement 111

Purpose (Huie) 119
Putnam, R. 15

R

reflection 2, 4, 40, 59, 179
  advance ourselves as 45–46
  alumni services wish list
    creation 46–49
  global alumni passport
    recognition 49–53
  updating alumni record 53–57
  'Alum from Day One' strategy 31,
    59–60
  building Alumni Way 62
  checklist 61–62
  key messages 60–61
  'keep in touch' call 31–33
  recognizing as city 35–36, 37
  engaging alumni
    citizenship 36–39
  reflecting on university
    story 40–43
  see also curiosity;
    generosity; reflection
reflection-on-action concept 40
Reich, R. 153
relational memories 141
Rentfrow, J. 116
resilience 67, 75, 87, 131
resources, flows of 16, 26, 43, 106,
    166, 177, 184
Rhodes College 42
Rincón, S. 52
Rise of the Creative Class, The
    (Florida) 36
Robinson, Sir K. 106, 119
Roselli, G. 93
Royal College of Surgeons in
    Ireland (RCSI) 123

S

Salgado, T. 41, 93
Sanchez, G. 86
Sani, S. 129
savvy alumni 1, 19, 152, 166, 175
Schön, D. 40
'sea of sameness', 32
Seeber, B. 78
Segran, E. 132
Selingo, J. 75
serendipity 65, 79, 98, 153
Seuss, Dr 12
Shaindlin, A. 46, 180

Shakiba, N. 124–125
shared experiences connecting
    alumni 6, 50, 70, 163,
    175, 178
    alumni community 180
    alumni-ness 180
    alumni networks 181–184
    generosity 179
    InHive model 180–181
    self-reflection 179
    social networking sites 178–179
Sheahan, M. 113
Simon Fraser University (SFU) 35
Singh, M. 131
Slack 73
Slow Professor, The (Berg and
    Seeber) 78
social capital
    bonding and bridging
        components 15
    see also alumni capital
social media 46, 47
    activities of alumni 54
    alumni class notes, with 56
    alumni networks 16, 71
    campaign for UNB 55
    communications platforms 73,
        78, 166
Solent University 113
solicitation 54, 160
Sorry I'm Late, I Didn't Want to
    Come: One Introvert's Year of
    Saying Yes (Pan) 85
soul of alma mater 126–131
Sousa, B. 83
Southwestern College 139
Spatz, R. (Women Wall of
    Honour) 156
StageClip 128
STEAM (science, technology,
    engineering, arts, and
    mathematics activities) 184
STEM (science, technology,
    engineering, mathematics)
    outreach programmes 124
stewardship 121, 147, 154, 158, 160
strategic, lifelong investment in
    education 22
student life 2, 3, 31, 43, 82,
    140, 145
Stuff Every Graduate Should Know:
    A Handbook for the Real World
    (Favreau) 14

Summer (financial management
    app) 91–92
Sustainable Development Goals
    (SDGs) see United Nations
    Sustainable Development
    Goals (SDGs)

T

talents with alma mater,
    celebrating 146–149
TASTE (Take a Student to
    Eat) 76
The Rocket Years: How Your Twenties
    Launch the Rest of Your Life
    (Segran) 132
There Is Life after College
    (Selingo) 75
Thiel, P. 177
Thiel Fellowship (2011) 177–178
three 'Ts' (technology, talent, and
    tolerance) 36
Tierney, T. 60
ties
    connecting generously
        with 161–167
    dormant 56, 71
    power of 153–161
    see also alumni capital
Tight, M. 20
Times Higher Education Impact
    Rankings 108, 144
traits of Alumni Way
    curiosity see curiosity
    generosity see generosity
    passion see passion
    reflection see reflection
treasure and ties, power of 153–161
Trinity Centre for People with
    Intellectual Disability at Trinity
    College Dublin 204n12
Trinity College Dublin 107–108,
    162
Tuesdays with Morrie (Albom) 128
Twain, M. 177
Twigg, K. 75, 87
Twitter 178
Tzedakah see philanthropy

U

UC Davis 112
UCD Volunteers Overseas 162
UCL 32

Under New Management
  (Burkus) 182
Unilever 94
United Nations Sustainable
  Development Goals
  (SDGs) 108, 123, 126, 144
UniverCity 35
Universidad de los Andes 154
Universidad del Norte 154
Universidad Pontificia
  Bolivariana 154
Universidad Tecnológica de
  Bolívar 154
universities 35
  administration 83
  advancement work 158
  alumni education 31
  arts and 121
  community 113, 114, 122,
    125, 146
  designing events 110
  freedom of speech and expression
    in 122
  institutional passion 107–108
  New Learning Paradigm 67
  programming and
    initiatives 47–48
  recognizing as city 35–36, 37
    engaging alumni
      citizenship 36–39
    reflecting on university
      story 40–43
  university investment,
    reclaiming 19–23
  see also alma mater
Universities of Sanctuary 107
University College Dublin
  (UCD) 55, 162
university–community
  relationship 36
  see also community
'university is a city' concept 90–95
University of Auckland 108
University of Birmingham 128
University of British Columbia 122
University of Cambridge 116
University of Canterbury in
  Christchurch 107
University of Edinburgh 50, 120
University of Greenwich 87
University of Groningen 112
University of Houston 93
University of Limerick 55

University of Malta 110
University of Maryland
  Libraries 121
University of Melbourne 111–112
University of New Brunswick
  (UNB) 55
University of New South Wales
  Business School 59
University of Pennsylvania 148
University of Rochester 81
University of Sheffield 85
University of Southern
  California 86
University of Suffolk 115
University of Toronto 115,
  141, 163
University of Victoria x, 79, 155
University of Warwick 112
University of Waterloo 169
University of Waterloo Handbook
  for New Graduates 56
University of
  Wisconsin-Madison 123

V

Valburn, M. 165
Vallerand, R. 105, 106
Vanderlelie, J. 145
VerveSmith independent education
  consultants 41, 93
volunteer(ing) 142, 145–146
  alumni ambassador
    programmes 145
  alumni donors 165
  as alumni leaders 143
  organizing class reunion 143–144
  recognition programmes 142
  sustained involvement of
    alumni 144
  in university operations 142

W

Walk While You Can
  (Coote) 161–162
Wayman, R. 113
weak ties 56–57, 71, 74
WeChat 73
'Welcome to the City' initiative 51
WhatsApp 73
*Who You Know: Unlocking
  Innovations That Expand
  Students' Networks* (Fisher) 166

Why Good Things Happen to Good People (Post) 137

Y

Yale School of Management 92
Yale University 32

Yappy Hour Social 115
Yeh, C. 129
York University 76